H A M M O N D

EXPLORER Atlas OF THE WORLD

Contents

Interpreting Maps

Designed to enhance your knowledge and enjoyment of the atlas, these pages explain map principles, scales, symbology and how to locate information quickly.

Geographic Comparisons

These eight pages contain flags and important facts about each independent country, plus dimensions of the earth's major mountains, longest rivers and largest lakes and islands.

Maps of the World

New maps, derived from a computer database, accurately present political detail while proprietary map projections show the most distortion-free views of the continents.

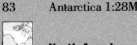

Index

A 6,000-entry A to Z index lists major places and geographic features in the atlas, complete with page numbers and easy-to-use alpha-numeric references.

Library of Congress
Cataloging-in-
Publication Data

Hammond Incorporated.
Explorer atlas of the world.
p. cm.
At head of title: Hammond
Includes index.
ISBN 0-8437-1186-8
1. Atlases. I. Title.
II: Title: Hammond explorer atlas of the world.
G1021. H2457 1994 <G&M>
912--dc20 94-7293
CIP
MAP

Map Projections

Simply stated, the mapmaker's challenge is to project the earth's curved surface onto a flat plane. To achieve this elusive goal, cartographers have developed map projections — equations which govern this conversion of geographic data.

This section explores some of the most widely used projections. It also introduces a new projection, the Hammond Optimal Conformal.

General Principles and Terms

The earth rotates around its axis once a day. Its end points are the North and South poles; the line circling the earth midway between the poles is the equator. The arc from the equator to either pole is divided into 90 degrees of latitude. The equator represents 0° latitude. Circles of equal latitude, called parallels, are traditionally shown at every fifth or tenth degree.

The equator is divided into 360 degrees. Lines circling the globe from pole to pole through the degree points on the equator are called meridians, or great circles. All meridians are equal in length, but by international agreement the meridian passing through the Greenwich Observatory near London has been chosen as the prime meridian or 0° longitude. The distance in degrees from the prime meridian to any point east or west is its longitude.

While meridians are all equal in length, parallels become shorter as they approach the poles. Whereas one degree of latitude represents approximately 69 miles (112 km.) anywhere on the globe, a degree of longitude varies from 69 miles (112 km.) at the equator to zero at the poles. Each degree of latitude and longitude is divided into 60 minutes. One minute of latitude equals one nautical mile (1.15 land miles or 1.85 km.).

How to Flatten a Sphere: The Art of Controlling Distortion

There is only one way to represent a sphere with absolute precision: on a globe. All attempts to project our planet's surface onto a plane unevenly stretch or tear the sphere as it flattens, inevitably distorting shapes, distances, area (sizes appear larger or smaller than actual size), angles or direction.

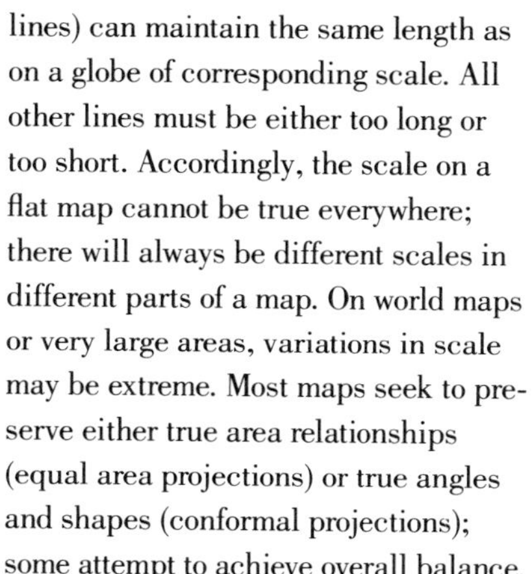

Figure 1 **Mercator Projection**

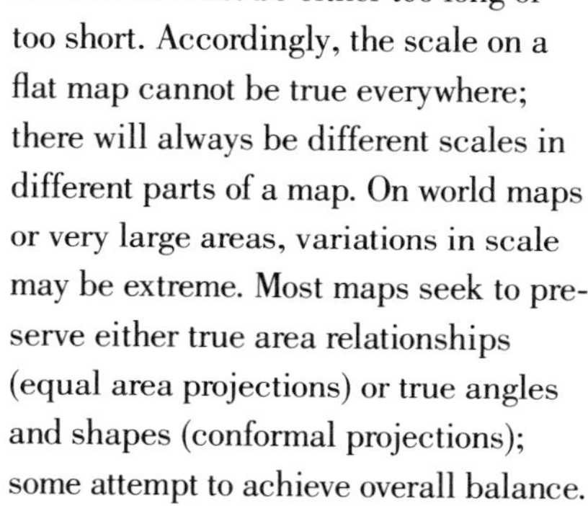

Figure 2 **Robinson Projection**

Since representing a sphere on a flat plane always creates distortion, only the parallels or the meridians (or some other set of lines) can maintain the same length as on a globe of corresponding scale. All other lines must be either too long or too short. Accordingly, the scale on a flat map cannot be true everywhere; there will always be different scales in different parts of a map. On world maps or very large areas, variations in scale may be extreme. Most maps seek to preserve either true area relationships (equal area projections) or true angles and shapes (conformal projections); some attempt to achieve overall balance.

Projections: Selected Examples

Mercator (Fig. 1): This projection is especially useful because all compass directions appear as straight lines, making it a valuable navigational tool. Moreover, every small region conforms to its shape on a globe — hence the name conformal. But because its meridians are evenly-spaced vertical lines which never converge (unlike the globe), the horizontal parallels must be drawn farther and farther apart at higher latitudes to maintain a correct relationship. Only the equator is true to scale, and the size of areas in the higher latitudes is dramatically distorted.

Robinson (Fig. 2): To create the thematic maps in Global Relationships and the two-page world map in the Maps of the World section, the Robinson projection was used. It combines elements of both conformal and equal area projections to show the whole earth with relatively true shapes and reasonably equal areas.

Conic (Fig. 3): This projection has been used frequently for air navigation charts and to create most of the national and regional maps in this atlas. (See text in margin at left).

Hammond's Optimal Conformal

As its name implies, this new conformal projection (Fig. 4) presents the optimal view of an area by reducing shifts in scale over an entire region to the minimum degree possible. While conformal maps generally preserve all small shapes, large shapes can become very distorted because of varying scales, causing considerable inaccuracy in distance measurements. The concept underlying the Optimal Conformal is that for any region on the globe, there is an ideal projection for which scale variation can be made as small as possible. Consequently, unlike other projections, the Optimal Conformal does not use one standard formula to construct a map. Each map is a unique projection — the optimal projection for that particular area.

After a cartographer defines the subject area, a sophisticated computer program evaluates the size and shape of the region, projecting the most distortion-free map possible. All of the continent maps in this atlas, except Antarctica, have been drawn using the Optimal projection.

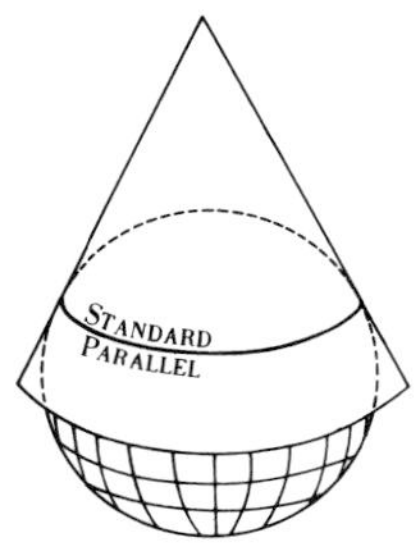

Figure 3
Conic Projection
The original idea of a conic projection is to cap the globe with a cone, and then project onto the cone from the planet's center the lines of latitude and longitude (the parallels and meridians). To produce a working map, the cone is simply cut open and laid flat. The conic projection used here is a modification of this idea. A cone can be made tangent to any standard parallel you choose. One popular version of a conic projection, the Lambert Conformal Conic, uses two standard parallels near the top and bottom of the map to further reduce errors of scale.

Figure 4
Hammond's Optimal Conformal Projection
Like all conformal maps, the Optimal projection preserves angles exactly and minimizes distortion in shapes. This projection is more successful than any previous projection at spreading curvature across the entire map, producing the most distortion-free map possible.

Using This Atlas

How to Locate Information Quickly

Our Maps of the World section is organized by continent. If you're looking for a major region of the world, consult the Contents on page two.

World Reference Guide

This concise guide lists the countries of the world alphabetically. If you're looking for the largest scale map of any country, you'll find a page and alpha-numeric reference at a glance, as well as information about each country, including its flag.

Master Index

When you're looking for a specific place or physical feature, your quickest route is the Master Index. This 6,000-entry alphabetical index lists both the page number and alpha-numeric reference for major places and features in Maps of the World.

This new atlas is created from a unique digital database, and its computer-generated maps represent a new phase in map-making technology.

How Computer-Generated Maps Are Made

To build a digital database capable of generating this world atlas, the latitude and longitude of every significant town, river, coastline, natural and political border, transportation network and peak elevation was researched and digitized. Hundreds of millions of data points describing every important geographic feature are organized into thousands of different map feature codes.

There are no maps in this unique system. Rather, it consists entirely of coded points, lines and polygons. To create a map, cartographers simply determine what specific information they wish to show, based upon considerations of scale, size, density and importance of different features.

New technology developed by mathematical physicist Mitchell Feigenbaum uses fractal geometry to describe and re-configure coastlines, borders and mountain ranges to fit a variety of map scales and projections. Dr. Feigenbaum has also created a computerized type placement program which allows thousands of map labels to be placed accurately in minutes. After these steps have been completed, the computer then draws the final map.

Each section of this atlas has been designed to be both easy and enjoyable to use. Familiarizing yourself with its organization will help you to benefit fully from its use.

World Flags and Reference Guide

This colorful section portrays each nation of the world, its flag, important geographical data, such as size, population and capital, and its location in the Maps of the World section.

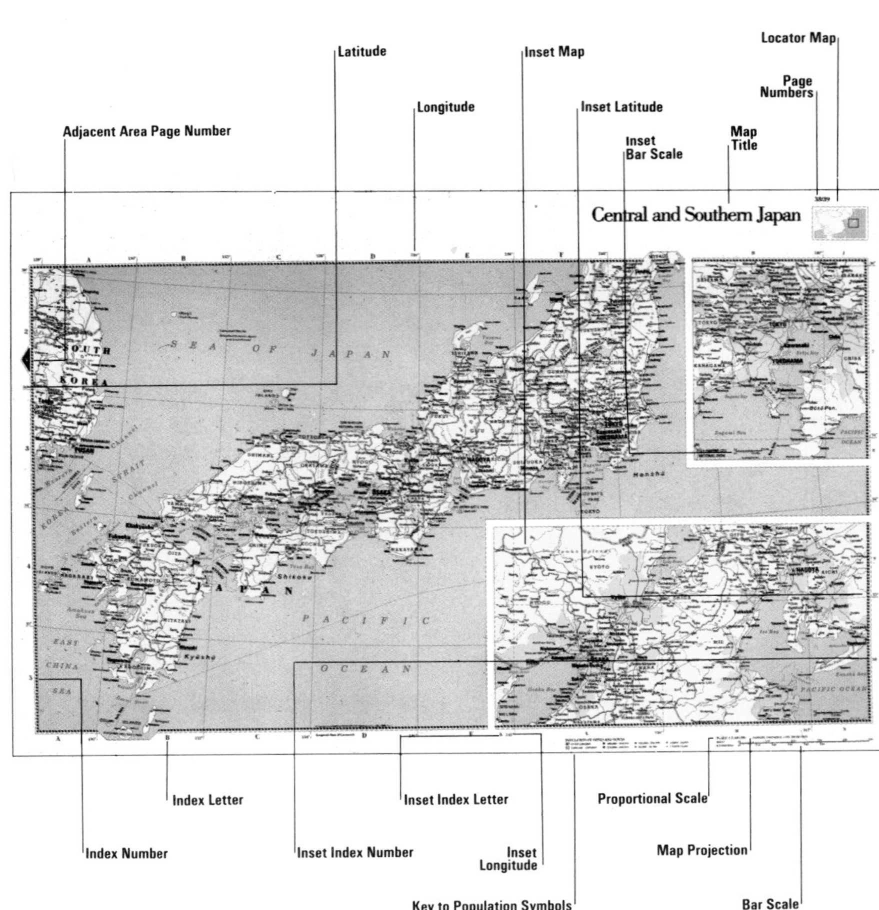

Symbols Used on Maps of the World

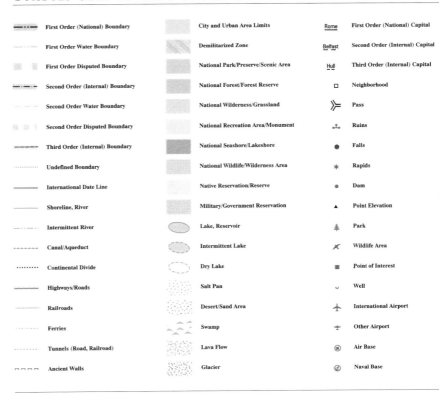

First Order (National) Boundary	City and Urban Area Limits	Rome — First Order (National) Capital
First Order Water Boundary	Demilitarized Zone	Belfast — Second Order (Internal) Capital
First Order Disputed Boundary	National Park/Preserve/Scenic Area	Hull — Third Order (Internal) Capital
Second Order (Internal) Boundary	National Forest/Forest Reserve	Neighborhood
Second Order Water Boundary	National Wilderness/Grassland	Pass
Second Order Disputed Boundary	National Recreation Area/Monument	Ruins
Third Order (Internal) Boundary	National Seashore/Lakeshore	Falls
Undefined Boundary	National Wildlife/Wilderness Area	Rapids
International Date Line	Native Reservation/Reserve	Dam
Shoreline, River	Military/Government Reservation	Point Elevation
Intermittent River	Lake, Reservoir	Park
Canal/Aqueduct	Intermittent Lake	Wildlife Area
Continental Divide	Dry Lake	Point of Interest
Highways/Roads	Salt Pan	Well
Railroads	Desert/Sand Area	International Airport
Ferries	Swamp	Other Airport
Tunnels (Road, Railroad)	Lava Flow	Air Base
Ancient Walls	Glacier	Naval Base

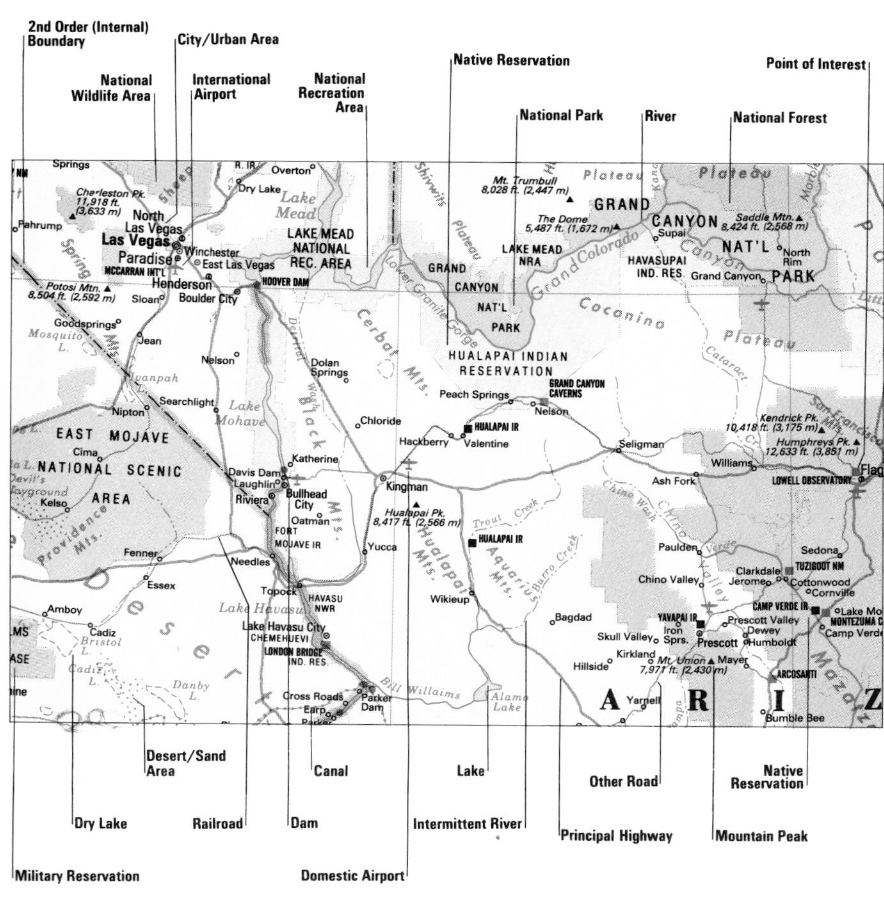

Principal Map Abbreviations

Abor. Rsv.	Aboriginal Reserve
Admin.	Administration
AFB	Air Force Base
Amm. Dep.	Ammunition Depot
Arch.	Archipelago
Arpt.	Airport
Aut.	Autonomous
B.	Bay
Bfld.	Battlefield
Bk.	Brook
Bor.	Borough
Br.	Branch
C.	Cape
Can.	Canal
Cap.	Capital
C.G.	Coast Guard
Chan.	Channel
Co.	County
Cr.	Creek
Ctr.	Center
Dep.	Depot
Depr.	Depression
Dept.	Department
Des.	Desert
Dist.	District
DMZ	Demilitarized Zone
Dpcy.	Dependency
Eng.	Engineering
Est.	Estuary
Fd.	Fiord, Fjord
Fed.	Federal
Fk.	Fork
Fld.	Field
For.	Forest
Ft.	Fort
G.	Gulf
Gov.	Governor
Govt.	Government
Gd.	Grand
Gt.	Great
Har.	Harbor
Hd.	Head
Hist.	Historic(al)
Hts.	Heights
I., Is.	Island(s)

Ind. Res.	Indian Reservation
Int'l	International
IR	Indian Reservation
Isth.	Isthmus
Jct.	Junction
L.	Lake
Lag.	Lagoon
Lakesh.	Lakeshore
Mem.	Memorial
Mil.	Military
Miss.	Missile
Mon.	Monument
Mt.	Mount
Mtn.	Mountain
Mts.	Mountains
Nat.	Natural
Nat'l	National
Nav.	Naval
NB	National Battlefield
NBP	National Battlefield Park
NBS	National Battlefield Site
NHP	National Historical Park
NHPP	National Historical Park and Preserve
NHS	National Historic Site
NL	National Lakeshore
NM	National Monument
NMEMP	National Memorial Park
NMILP	National Military Park
No.	Northern
NP	National Park
NPP	National Park and Preserve
NPRSV	National Preserve
NRA	National Recreation Area
NRSV	National Reserve
NS	National Seashore

NWR	National Wildlife Reserve
Obl.	Oblast
Occ.	Occupied
Okr.	Okrug
Par.	Parish
Passg.	Passage
Pen.	Peninsula
Pk.	Peak
Plat.	Plateau
PN	Park National
Pref.	Prefecture
Prom.	Promontory
Prov.	Province
Prsv.	Preserve
Pt.	Point
R.	River
RA	Recreation Area
Ra.	Range
Rec.	Recreation(al)
Ref.	Refuge
Reg.	Region
Rep.	Republic
Res.	Reservoir, Reservation
Rvwy.	Riverway
Sa.	Sierra
Sd.	Sound
Seash.	Seashore
So.	Southern
SP	State Park
Spr., Sprs.	Spring, Springs
St.	State
Sta.	Station
Stm.	Stream
Str.	Strait
Terr.	Territory
Tun.	Tunnel
Twp.	Township
Val.	Valley
Vill.	Village
Vol.	Volcano
Wild.	Wildlife, Wilderness
Wtr.	Water

World Statistics

World Statistics lists the dimensions of the earth's principal mountains, islands, rivers and lakes, along with other useful geographic information.

Maps of the World

These detailed regional maps are arranged by continent, and introduced by a political map of that continent. The continent maps, which utilize Hammond's new Optimal Conformal projection, are distinguished by individual colors for each country to highlight political divisions.

On the regional maps, different colors and textures highlight distinctive features such as parks, forests, deserts and urban areas. These maps also provide considerable information concerning geographic features and political divisions.

Master Index

This is an A-Z listing of names found on the political maps. It also has its own abbreviation list which, along with other Index keys, appears on page 110.

Map Scales

A map's scale is the relationship of any length on the map to an identical length on the earth's surface. A scale of 1:3,000,000 means that one inch on the map represents 3,000,000 inches (47 miles, 76 km.) on the earth's surface. Thus, a 1:1,000,000 scale is larger than 1:3,000,000, just as 1/1 is larger than 1/3.

The most densely populated areas are shown at a scale of 1:1,170,000, while selected metropolitan areas are covered at either 1:587,000 or 1:1,170,000. Other populous areas are presented at 1:3,500,000 and 1:7,000,000, allowing you to accurately compare areas and distances of similar regions. Remaining regions are scaled at 1:10,500,000. The continent maps, as well as the United States, Canada, Russia, Pacific and World have smaller scales.

Boundary Policies

This atlas observes the boundary policies of the U.S. Department of State. Boundary disputes are customarily handled with a special symbol treatment, but de facto boundaries are favored if they seem to have any degree of permanence, in the belief that boundaries should reflect current geographic and political realities. The portrayal of independent nations in the atlas follows their recognition by the United Nations and/or the United States government.

Hammond also uses accepted conventional names for certain major foreign places. Usually, space permits the inclusion of the local form in parentheses. To make the maps more readily understandable to English-speaking readers, many foreign physical features are translated into more recognizable English forms.

A Word About Names

Our source for all foreign names and physical names in the United States is the decision lists of the U.S. Board of Geographic Names, which contain hundreds of thousands of place names. If a place is not listed, the Atlas follows the name form appearing on official foreign maps or in official gazetteers of the country concerned. For rendering domestic city, town and village names, this atlas follows the forms and spelling of the U.S. Postal Service.

World Flags and Reference Guide

Afghanistan
Page/Location: 53/H2
Area: 250,775 sq. mi.
649,507 sq. km.
Population: 16,450,000
Capital: Kabul
Largest City: Kabul
Highest Point: Noshaq
Monetary Unit: afghani

Albania
Page/Location: 39/F2
Area: 11,100 sq. mi.
28,749 sq. km.
Population: 3,335,000
Capital: Tiranë
Largest City: Tiranë
Highest Point: Korab
Monetary Unit: lek

Algeria
Page/Location: 76/F2
Area: 919,591 sq. mi.
2,381,740 sq. km.
Population: 26,022,000
Capital: Algiers
Largest City: Algiers
Highest Point: Tahat
Monetary Unit: Algerian dinar

Andorra
Page/Location: 35/F1
Area: 188 sq. mi.
487 sq. km.
Population: 53,000
Capital: Andorra la Vella
Largest City: Andorra la Vella
Highest Point: Coma Pedrosa
Monetary Unit: Fr. franc, Sp. peseta

Angola
Page/Location: 82/C3
Area: 481,351 sq. mi.
1,246,700 sq. km.
Population: 8,668,000
Capital: Luanda
Largest City: Luanda
Highest Point: Morro de Môco
Monetary Unit: kwanza

Antigua and Barbuda
Page/Location: 104/F3
Area: 171 sq. mi.
443 sq. km.
Population: 64,000
Capital: St. John's
Largest City: St. John's
Highest Point: Boggy Peak
Monetary Unit: East Caribbean dollar

Argentina
Page/Location: 109/C4
Area: 1,072,070 sq. mi.
2,776,661 sq. km.
Population: 32,664,000
Capital: Buenos Aires
Largest City: Buenos Aires
Highest Point: Cerro Aconcagua
Monetary Unit: Argentine peso

Armenia
Page/Location: 45/H5
Area: 11,506 sq. mi.
29,800 sq. km.
Population: 3,283,000
Capital: Yerevan
Largest City: Yerevan
Highest Point: Alagez
Monetary Unit: Armenian ruble

Australia
Page/Location: 70
Area: 2,966,136 sq. mi.
7,682,300 sq. km.
Population: 17,288,000
Capital: Canberra
Largest City: Sydney
Highest Point: Mt. Kosciusko
Monetary Unit: Australian dollar

Austria
Page/Location: 33/L3
Area: 32,375 sq. mi.
83,851 sq. km.
Population: 7,666,000
Capital: Vienna
Largest City: Vienna
Highest Point: Grossglockner
Monetary Unit: schilling

Azerbaijan
Page/Location: 45/H4
Area: 33,436 sq. mi.
86,600 sq. km.
Population: 7,029,000
Capital: Baku
Largest City: Baku
Highest Point: Bazardyuzyu
Monetary Unit: manat

Bahamas
Page/Location: 104/B2
Area: 5,382 sq. mi.
13,939 sq. km.
Population: 252,000
Capital: Nassau
Largest City: Nassau
Highest Point: 207 ft. (63 m)
Monetary Unit: Bahamian dollar

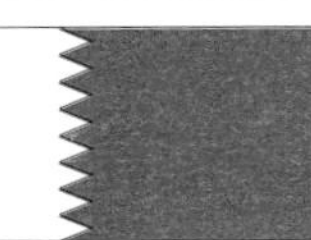

Bahrain
Page/Location: 52/F3
Area: 240 sq. mi.
622 sq. km.
Population: 537,000
Capital: Manama
Largest City: Manama
Highest Point: Jabal Dukhān
Monetary Unit: Bahraini dinar

Bangladesh
Page/Location: 60/E3
Area: 55,126 sq. mi.
142,776 sq. km.
Population: 116,601,000
Capital: Dhaka
Largest City: Dhaka
Highest Point: Keokradong
Monetary Unit: taka

Barbados
Page/Location: 104/G4
Area: 166 sq. mi.
430 sq. km.
Population: 255,000
Capital: Bridgetown
Largest City: Bridgetown
Highest Point: Mt. Hillaby
Monetary Unit: Barbadian dollar

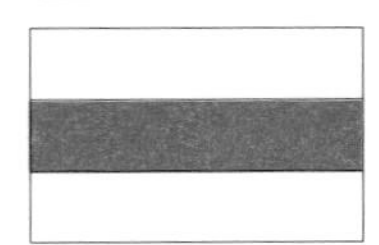

Belarus
Page/Location: 18/F3
Area: 80,154 sq. mi.
207,600 sq. km.
Population: 10,200,000
Capital: Minsk
Largest City: Minsk
Highest Point: Dzerzhinskaya
Monetary Unit: Belarusian ruble

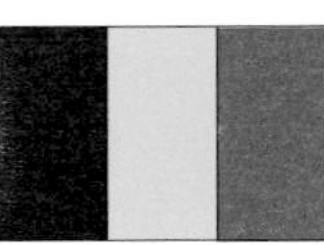

Belgium
Page/Location: 30/C2
Area: 11,781 sq. mi.
30,513 sq. km.
Population: 9,922,000
Capital: Brussels
Largest City: Brussels
Highest Point: Botrange
Monetary Unit: Belgian franc

Belize
Page/Location: 102/D2
Area: 8,867 sq. mi.
22,966 sq. km.
Population: 228,000
Capital: Belmopan
Largest City: Belize City
Highest Point: Victoria Peak
Monetary Unit: Belize dollar

Benin
Page/Location: 79/F4
Area: 43,483 sq. mi.
112,620 sq. km.
Population: 4,832,000
Capital: Porto-Novo
Largest City: Cotonou
Highest Point: Nassoukou
Monetary Unit: CFA franc

Bhutan
Page/Location: 62/E2
Area: 18,147 sq. mi.
47,000 sq. km.
Population: 1,598,000
Capital: Thimphu
Largest City: Thimphu
Highest Point: Kula Kangri
Monetary Unit: ngultrum

Bolivia
Page/Location: 106/F7
Area: 424,163 sq. mi.
1,098,582 sq. km.
Population: 7,157,000
Capital: La Paz; Sucre
Largest City: La Paz
Highest Point: Nevado Ancohuma
Monetary Unit: Bolivian peso

Bosnia and Herzegovina
Page/Location: 40/C3
Area: 19,940 sq. mi.
51,645 sq. km.
Population: 4,124,256
Capital: Sarajevo
Largest City: Sarajevo
Highest Point: Maglič
Monetary Unit: —

Botswana
Page/Location: 52/D5
Area: 224,764 sq. mi.
582,139 sq. km.
Population: 1,258,000
Capital: Gaborone
Largest City: Gaborone
Highest Point: Tsodilo Hills
Monetary Unit: pula

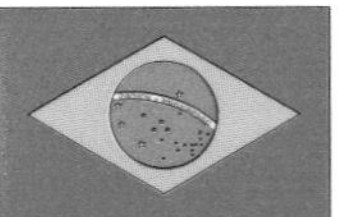

Brazil
Page/Location: 105/D3
Area: 3,284,426 sq. mi.
8,506,663 sq. km.
Population: 155,356,000
Capital: Brasília
Largest City: São Paulo
Highest Point: Pico da Neblina
Monetary Unit: cruzeiro real

Brunei
Page/Location: 66/D2
Area: 2,226 sq. mi.
5,765 sq. km.
Population: 398,000
Capital: Bandar Seri Begawan
Largest City: Bandar Seri Begawan
Highest Point: Bukit Pagon
Monetary Unit: Brunei dollar

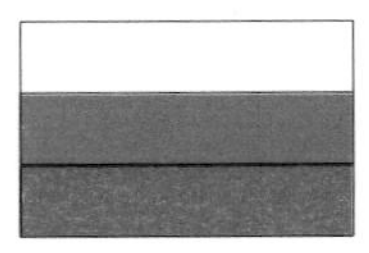

Bulgaria
Page/Location: 41/G4
Area: 42,823 sq. mi.
110,912 sq. km.
Population: 8,911,000
Capital: Sofia
Largest City: Sofia
Highest Point: Musala
Monetary Unit: lev

Burkina Faso
Page/Location: 79/E3
Area: 105,869 sq. mi.
274,200 sq. km.
Population: 9,360,000
Capital: Ouagadougou
Largest City: Ouagadougou
Highest Point: 2,405 ft. (733 m)
Monetary Unit: CFA franc

Burma
Page/Location: 63/G3
Area: 261,789 sq. mi.
678,034 sq. km.
Population: 42,112,000
Capital: Rangoon
Largest City: Rangoon
Highest Point: Hkakabo Razi
Monetary Unit: kyat

Burundi
Page/Location: 82/E1
Area: 10,747 sq. mi.
27,835 sq. km.
Population: 5,831,000
Capital: Bujumbura
Largest City: Bujumbura
Highest Point: 8,760 ft. (2,670 m)
Monetary Unit: Burundi franc

Cambodia
Page/Location: 65/D3
Area: 69,898 sq. mi.
181,036 sq. km.
Population: 7,146,000
Capital: Phnom Penh
Largest City: Phnom Penh
Highest Point: Phnum Aoral
Monetary Unit: riel

Cameroon
Page/Location: 76/H7
Area: 183,568 sq. mi.
475,441 sq. km.
Population: 11,390,000
Capital: Yaoundé
Largest City: Douala
Highest Point: Mt. Cameroon
Monetary Unit: CFA franc

Canada
Page/Location: 86
Area: 3,851,787 sq. mi.
9,976,139 sq. km.
Population: 27,296,859
Capital: Ottawa
Largest City: Toronto
Highest Point: Mt. Logan
Monetary Unit: Canadian dollar

Cape Verde
Page/Location: 74/K9
Area: 1,557 sq. mi.
4,033 sq. km.
Population: 387,000
Capital: Praia
Largest City: Praia
Highest Point: 9,282 ft. (2,829 m)
Monetary Unit: Cape Verde escudo

Central African Republic
Page/Location: 77/J6
Area: 242,000 sq. mi.
626,780 sq. km.
Population: 2,952,000
Capital: Bangui
Largest City: Bangui
Highest Point: Mt. Kayagangiri
Monetary Unit: CFA franc

Chad
Page/Location: 77/J4
Area: 495,752 sq. mi.
1,283,998 sq. km.
Population: 5,122,000
Capital: N'Djamena
Largest City: N'Djamena
Highest Point: Emi Koussi
Monetary Unit: CFA franc

Chile
Page/Location: 109/B3
Area: 292,257 sq. mi.
756,946 sq. km.
Population: 13,287,000
Capital: Santiago
Largest City: Santiago
Highest Point: Nevado Ojos del Salado
Monetary Unit: Chilean peso

China
Page/Location: 48/J6
Area: 3,691,000 sq. mi.
9,559,690 sq. km.
Population: 1,151,487,000
Capital: Beijing
Largest City: Shanghai
Highest Point: Mt. Everest
Monetary Unit: yuan

Colombia
Page/Location: 106/D3
Area: 439,513 sq. mi.
1,138,339 sq. km.
Population: 33,778,000
Capital: Bogotá
Largest City: Bogotá
Highest Point: Pico Cristóbal Colón
Monetary Unit: Colombian peso

Comoros
Page/Location: 74/G6
Area: 719 sq. mi.
1,862 sq. km.
Population: 477,000
Capital: Moroni
Largest City: Moroni
Highest Point: Karthala
Monetary Unit: Comorian franc

Congo
Page/Location: 74/D5
Area: 132,046 sq. mi.
342,000 sq. km.
Population: 2,309,000
Capital: Brazzaville
Largest City: Brazzaville
Highest Point: Lékéti Mts.
Monetary Unit: CFA franc

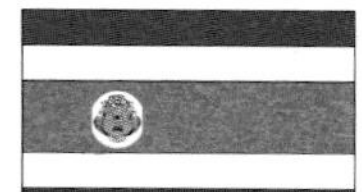

Costa Rica
Page/Location: 103/F4
Area: 19,575 sq. mi.
50,700 sq. km.
Population: 3,111,000
Capital: San José
Largest City: San José
Highest Point: Cerro Chirripó Grande
Monetary Unit: Costa Rican colón

Croatia
Page/Location: 40/C3
Area: 22,050 sq. mi.
57,110 sq. km.
Population: 4,601,469
Capital: Zagreb
Largest City: Zagreb
Highest Point: Veliki Troglav
Monetary Unit: Croatian dinar

Cuba
Page/Location: 103/F1
Area: 44,206 sq. mi.
114,494 sq. km.
Population: 10,732,000
Capital: Havana
Largest City: Havana
Highest Point: Pico Turquino
Monetary Unit: Cuban peso

Cyprus
Page/Location: 49/C2
Area: 3,473 sq. mi.
8,995 sq. km.
Population: 709,000
Capital: Nicosia
Largest City: Nicosia
Highest Point: Olympus
Monetary Unit: Cypriot pound

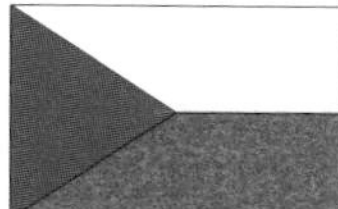

Czech Republic
Page/Location: 27/H4
Area: 30,449 sq. mi.
78,863 sq. km.
Population: 10,291,927
Capital: Prague
Largest City: Prague
Highest Point: Sněžka
Monetary Unit: Czech koruna

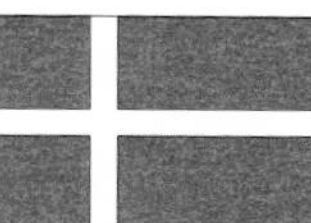

Denmark
Page/Location: 20/C5
Area: 16,629 sq. mi.
43,069 sq. km.
Population: 5,133,000
Capital: Copenhagen
Largest City: Copenhagen
Highest Point: Yding Skovhøj
Monetary Unit: Danish krone

Djibouti
Page/Location: 77/P5
Area: 8,880 sq. mi.
23,000 sq. km.
Population: 346,000
Capital: Djibouti
Largest City: Djibouti
Highest Point: Moussa Ali
Monetary Unit: Djibouti franc

Dominica
Page/Location: 104/F4
Area: 290 sq. mi.
751 sq. km.
Population: 86,000
Capital: Roseau
Largest City: Roseau
Highest Point: Morne Diablotin
Monetary Unit: Dominican dollar

Dominican Republic
Page/Location: 104/D3
Area: 18,704 sq. mi.
48,443 sq. km.
Population: 7,385,000
Capital: Santo Domingo
Largest City: Santo Domingo
Highest Point: Pico Duarte
Monetary Unit: Dominican peso

Ecuador
Page/Location: 106/C4
Area: 109,483 sq. mi.
283,561 sq. km.
Population: 10,752,000
Capital: Quito
Largest City: Guayaquil
Highest Point: Chimborazo
Monetary Unit: sucre

Egypt
Page/Location: 77/L2
Area: 386,659 sq. mi.
1,001,447 sq. km.
Population: 54,452,000
Capital: Cairo
Largest City: Cairo
Highest Point: Mt. Catherine
Monetary Unit: Egyptian pound

El Salvador
Page/Location: 102/D3
Area: 8,260 sq. mi.
21,393 sq. km.
Population: 5,419,000
Capital: San Salvador
Largest City: San Salvador
Highest Point: Santa Ana
Monetary Unit: Salvadoran colón

Equatorial Guinea
Page/Location: 76/G7
Area: 10,831 sq. mi.
28,052 sq. km.
Population: 379,000
Capital: Malabo
Largest City: Malabo
Highest Point: Pico de Santa Isabel
Monetary Unit: CFA franc

Eritrea
Page/Location: 77/N4
Area: 36,170 sq. mi.
93,679 sq. km.
Population: 3,500,000
Capital: Asmera
Largest City: Asmera
Highest Point: Soira
Monetary Unit: birr

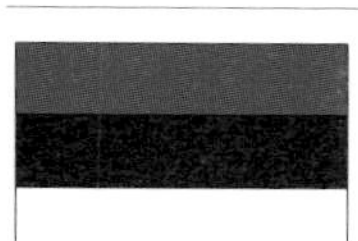

Estonia
Page/Location: 42/E4
Area: 17,413 sq. mi.
45,100 sq. km.
Population: 1,573,000
Capital: Tallinn
Largest City: Tallinn
Highest Point: Munamägi
Monetary Unit: kroon

Ethiopia
Page/Location: 77/N6
Area: 435,606 sq. mi.
1,128,220 sq. km.
Population: 51,617,000
Capital: Addis Ababa
Largest City: Addis Ababa
Highest Point: Ras Dashen Terara
Monetary Unit: birr

Fiji
Page/Location: 68/G6
Area: 7,055 sq. mi.
18,272 sq. km.
Population: 744,000
Capital: Suva
Largest City: Suva
Highest Point: Tomaniivi
Monetary Unit: Fijian dollar

Finland
Page/Location: 20/H2
Area: 130,128 sq. mi.
337,032 sq. km.
Population: 4,991,000
Capital: Helsinki
Largest City: Helsinki
Highest Point: Kahperusvaara
Monetary Unit: markka

France
Page/Location: 32/D3
Area: 210,038 sq. mi.
543,998 sq. km.
Population: 58,073,553
Capital: Paris
Largest City: Paris
Highest Point: Mont Blanc
Monetary Unit: French franc

Gabon
Page/Location: 76/H7
Area: 103,346 sq. mi.
267,666 sq. km.
Population: 1,080,000
Capital: Libreville
Largest City: Libreville
Highest Point: Mt. Iboundji
Monetary Unit: CFA franc

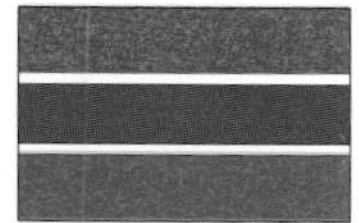

Gambia
Page/Location: 78/B3
Area: 4,127 sq. mi.
10,689 sq. km.
Population: 875,000
Capital: Banjul
Largest City: Banjul
Highest Point: 98 ft. (30 m)
Monetary Unit: dalasi

Georgia
Page/Location: 45/G4
Area: 26,911 sq. mi.
69,700 sq. km.
Population: 5,449,000
Capital: Tbilisi
Largest City: Tbilisi
Highest Point: Kazbek
Monetary Unit: lari

Germany
Page/Location: 26/E3
Area: 137,753 sq. mi.
356,780 sq. km.
Population: 79,548,000
Capital: Berlin
Largest City: Berlin
Highest Point: Zugspitze
Monetary Unit: Deutsche mark

Ghana
Page/Location: 79/E4
Area: 92,099 sq. mi.
238,536 sq. km.
Population: 15,617,000
Capital: Accra
Largest City: Accra
Highest Point: Afadjoto
Monetary Unit: cedi

Greece
Page/Location: 39/G3
Area: 50,944 sq. mi.
131,945 sq. km.
Population: 10,043,000
Capital: Athens
Largest City: Athens
Highest Point: Mt. Olympus
Monetary Unit: drachma

Grenada
Page/Location: 104/F5
Area: 133 sq. mi.
344 sq. km.
Population: 84,000
Capital: St. George's
Largest City: St. George's
Highest Point: Mt. St. Catherine
Monetary Unit: East Caribbean dollar

World Flags and Reference Guide

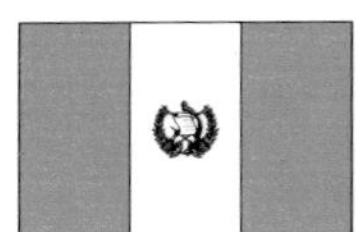

Guatemala
Page/Location: 102/D3
Area: 42,042 sq. mi.
108,889 sq. km.
Population: 9,266,000
Capital: Guatemala
Largest City: Guatemala
Highest Point: Tajumulco
Monetary Unit: quetzal

Guinea
Page/Location: 78/C4
Area: 94,925 sq. mi.
245,856 sq. km.
Population: 7,456,000
Capital: Conakry
Largest City: Conakry
Highest Point: Mt. Nimba
Monetary Unit: Guinea franc

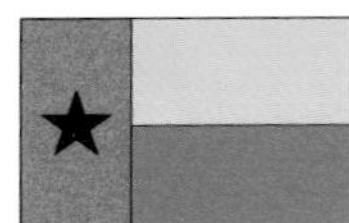

Guinea-Bissau
Page/Location: 78/B3
Area: 13,948 sq. mi.
36,125 sq. km.
Population: 943,000
Capital: Bissau
Largest City: Bissau
Highest Point: 689 ft. (210 m)
Monetary Unit: Guinea-Bissau peso

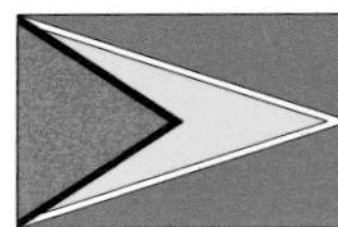

Guyana
Page/Location: 106/G2
Area: 83,000 sq. mi.
214,970 sq. km.
Population: 1,024,000
Capital: Georgetown
Largest City: Georgetown
Highest Point: Mt. Roraima
Monetary Unit: Guyana dollar

Haiti
Page/Location: 103/H2
Area: 10,694 sq. mi.
27,697 sq. km.
Population: 6,287,000
Capital: Port-au-Prince
Largest City: Port-au-Prince
Highest Point: Pic la Selle
Monetary Unit: gourde

Honduras
Page/Location 102/E3
Area: 43,277 sq. mi.
112,087 sq. km.
Population: 4,949,000
Capital: Tegucigalpa
Largest City: Tegucigalpa
Highest Point: Cerro de las Minas
Monetary Unit: lempira

Hungary
Page/Location: 40/D2
Area: 35,919 sq. mi.
93,030 sq. km.
Population: 10,558,000
Capital: Budapest
Largest City: Budapest
Highest Point: Kékes
Monetary Unit: forint

Iceland
Page/Location: 20/N7
Area: 39,768 sq. mi.
103,000 sq. km.
Population: 260,000
Capital: Reykjavík
Largest City: Reykjavík
Highest Point: Hvannadalshnúkur
Monetary Unit: króna

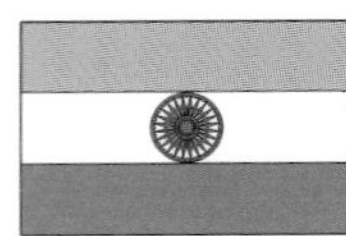

India
Page/Location: 62/C3
Area: 1,269,339 sq. mi.
3,287,588 sq. km.
Population: 869,515,000
Capital: New Delhi
Largest City: Calcutta
Highest Point: Nanda Devi
Monetary Unit: Indian rupee

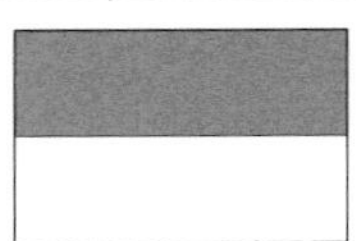

Indonesia
Page/Location: 67/E4
Area: 788,430 sq. mi.
2, 042,034 sq. km.
Population: 19,560,000
Capital: Jakarta
Largest City: Jakarta
Highest Point: Puncak Jaya
Monetary Unit: rupiah

Iran
Page/Location: 51/H3
Area: 636,293 sq. mi.
1,648,000 sq. km.
Population: 59,051,000
Capital: Tehran
Largest City: Tehran
Highest Point: Qolleh-ye Damāvand
Monetary Unit: Iranian rial

Iraq
Page/Location: 50/E3
Area: 172,476 sq. mi.
446,713 sq. km.
Population: 19,525,000
Capital: Baghdad
Largest City: Baghdad
Highest Point: Haji Ibrahim
Monetary Unit: Iraqi dinar

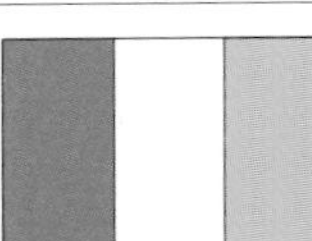

Ireland
Page/Location: 21/A4
Area: 27,136 sq. mi.
70,282 sq. km.
Population: 3,489,000
Capital: Dublin
Largest City: Dublin
Highest Point: Carrantuohill
Monetary Unit: Irish pound

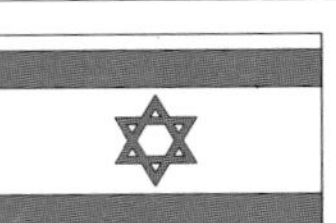

Israel
Page/Location: 49/D3
Area: 7,847 sq. mi.
20,324 sq. km.
Population: 4,558,000
Capital: Jerusalem
Largest City: Tel Aviv-Yafo
Highest Point: Har Meron
Monetary Unit: shekel

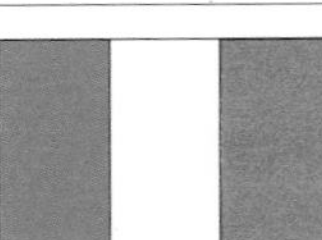

Italy
Page/Location: 18/E4
Area; 116,303 sq. mi.
301,225 sq. km.
Population: 57,772,000
Capital: Rome
Largest City: Rome
Highest Point: Monte Rosa
Monetary Unit: Italian lira

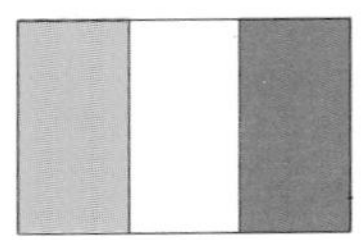

Ivory Coast
Page/Location: 78/D5
Area: 124,504 sq. mi.
322,465 sq. km.
Population: 12,978,000
Capital: Yamoussoukro
Largest City: Abidjan
Highest Point: Mt. Nimba
Monetary Unit: CFA franc

Jamaica
Page/Location: 103/G2
Area: 4,411 sq. mi.
11,424 sq. km.
Population: 2,489,000
Capital: Kingston
Largest City: Kingston
Highest Point: Blue Mountain Pk.
Monetary Unit: Jamaican dollar

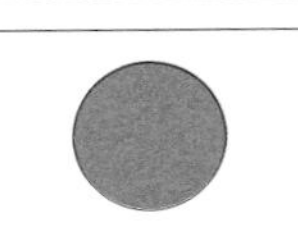

Japan
Page/Location: 55/M4
Area: 145,730 sq. mi.
377,441 sq. km.
Population: 124,017,000
Capital: Tokyo
Largest City: Tokyo
Highest Point: Fujiyama
Monetary Unit: yen

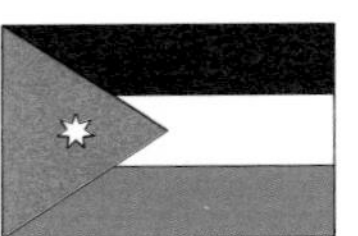

Jordan
Page/Location: 49/E4
Area: 35,000 sq. mi.
90,650 sq. km.
Population: 3,413,000
Capital: Amman
Largest City: Amman
Highest Point: Jabal Ramm
Monetary Unit: Jordanian dinar

Kazakhstan
Page/Location: 46/G5
Area: 1,048,300 sq. mi.
2,715,100 sq. km.
Population: 16,538,000
Capital: Alma-Ata
Largest City: Alma-Ata
Highest Point: Khan-Tengri
Monetary Unit: Kazakhstani ruble

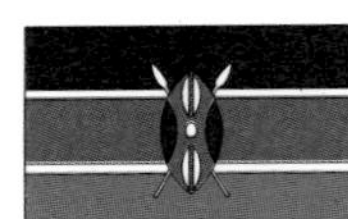

Kenya
Page/Location: 77/M7
Area: 224,960 sq. mi.
582,646 sq. km.
Population: 25,242,000
Capital: Nairobi
Largest City: Nairobi
Highest Point: Mt. Kenya
Monetary Unit: Kenya shilling

Kiribati
Page/Location: 69/H5
Area: 291 sq. mi.
754 sq. km.
Population: 71,000
Capital: Bairiki
Largest City: —
Highest Point: Banaba Island
Monetary Unit: Australian dollar

Korea, North
Page/Location: 58/D2
Area: 46,540 sq. mi.
120,539 sq. km.
Population: 21,815,000
Capital: P'yŏngyang
Largest City: P'yŏngyang
Highest Point: Paektu-san
Monetary Unit: North Korean won

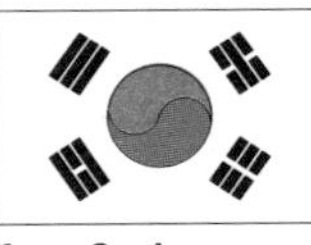

Korea, South
Page/Location: 58/D4
Area: 38,175 sq. mi.
98,873 sq. km.
Population: 43,134,000
Capital: Seoul
Largest City: Seoul
Highest Point: Halla-san
Monetary Unit: South Korean won

Kuwait
Page/Location: 51/F4
Area: 6,532 sq. mi.
16,918 sq. km.
Population: 2,204,000
Capital: Al Kuwait
Largest City: Al Kuwait
Highest Point: 951 ft. (290 m)
Monetary Unit: Kuwaiti dinar

Kyrgyzstan
Page/Location: 46/H5
Area: 76,641 sq. mi.
198,500 sq. km.
Population: 4,291,000
Capital: Bishkek
Largest City: Bishkek
Highest Point: Pik Pobedy
Monetary Unit: som

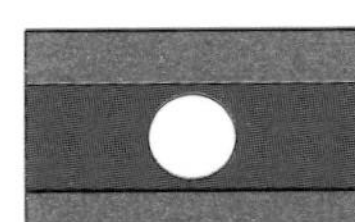

Laos
Page/Location: 65/C2
Area: 91,428 sq. mi.
236,800 sq. km.
Population: 4,113,000
Capital: Vientiane
Largest City: Vientiane
Highest Point: Phou Bia
Monetary Unit: kip

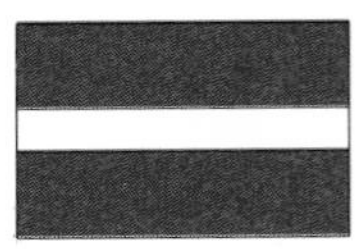

Latvia
Page/Location: 42/E4
Area: 24,595 sq. mi.
63,700 sq. km.
Population: 2,681,000
Capital: Riga
Largest City: Riga
Highest Point: Gaizina Kalns
Monetary Unit: lats

Lebanon
Page/Location: 49/D3
Area: 4,015 sq. mi.
10,399 sq. km.
Population: 3,385,000
Capital: Beirut
Largest City: Beirut
Highest Point: Qurnat as Sawdā
Monetary Unit: Lebanese pound

Lesotho
Page/Location: 80/E3
Area: 11,720 sq. mi.
30,355 sq. km.
Population: 1,801,000
Capital: Maseru
Largest City: Maseru
Highest Point: Thabana-Ntlenyana
Monetary Unit: loti

Liberia
Page/Location: 78/C4
Area: 43,000 sq. mi.
111,370 sq. km.
Population: 2,730,000
Capital: Monrovia
Largest City: Monrovia
Highest Point: Mt. Wuteve
Monetary Unit: Liberian dollar

Libya
Page/Location: 77/J2
Area: 679,358 sq. mi.
1,759,537 sq. km.
Population: 4,353,000
Capital: Tripoli
Largest City: Tripoli
Highest Point: Picco Bette
Monetary Unit: Libyan dinar

Liechtenstein
Page/Location: 37/F3
Area: 61 sq. mi.
158 sq. km.
Population: 28,000
Capital: Vaduz
Largest City: Vaduz
Highest Point: Grauspitz
Monetary Unit: Swiss franc

Lithuania
Page/Location: 42/D5
Area: 25,174 sq. mi.
65,200 sq. km.
Population: 3,690,000
Capital: Vilnius
Largest City: Vilnius
Highest Point: Nevaišių
Monetary Unit: litas

Luxembourg
Page/Location: 31/F4
Area: 999 sq. mi.
2,587 sq. km.
Population: 388,000
Capital: Luxembourg
Largest City: Luxembourg
Highest Point: Ardennes Plateau
Monetary Unit: Luxembourg franc

Macedonia
Page/Location: 39/G2
Area: 9,889 sq. mi.
25,612 sq. km.
Population: 1,909,136
Capital: Skopje
Largest City: Skopje
Highest Point: Korab
Monetary Unit: denar

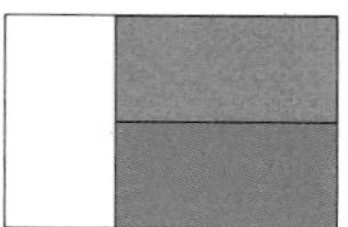

Madagascar
Page/Location: 81/H8
Area: 226,657 sq. mi.
587,041 sq. km.
Population: 12,185,000
Capital: Antananarivo
Largest City: Antananarivo
Highest Point: Maromokotro
Monetary Unit: Malagasy franc

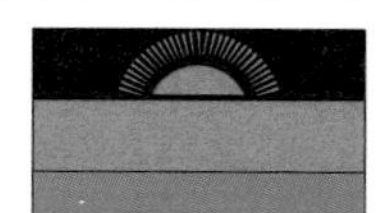

Malawi
Page/Location: 82/F3
Area: 45,747 sq. mi.
118, 485 sq. km.
Population: 9,438,000
Capital: Lilongwe
Largest City: Blantyre
Highest Point: Mulanje Mts.
Monetary Unit: Malawi kwacha

Malaysia
Page/Location: 67/C2
Area: 128,308 sq. mi.
332,318 sq. km.
Population: 17,982,000
Capital: Kuala Lumpur
Largest City: Kuala Lumpur
Highest Point: Gunung Kinabalu
Monetary Unit: ringgit

Maldives
Page/Location: 48/G9
Area: 115 sq. mi.
298 sq. km.
Population: 226,000
Capital: Male
Largest City: Male
Highest Point: 20 ft. (6 m)
Monetary Unit: rufiyaa

Mali
Page/Location: 76/E4
Area: 464,873 sq. mi.
1,204,021 sq. km.
Population: 8,339,000
Capital: Bamako
Largest City: Bamako
Highest Point: Hombori Tondo
Monetary Unit: CFA franc

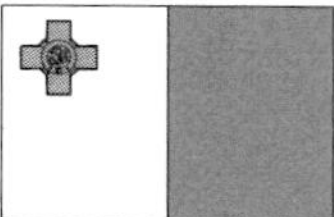

Malta
Page/Location: 38/D5
Area: 122 sq. mi.
316 sq. km.
Population: 356,000
Capital: Valletta
Largest City: Sliema
Highest Point: 830 ft. (253 m)
Monetary Unit: Maltese lira

Marshall Islands
Page/Location: 68/G3
Area: 70 sq. mi.
181 sq. km.
Population: 48,000
Capital: Majuro
Largest City: —
Highest Point: 20 ft. (6 m)
Monetary Unit: U.S. dollar

Mauritania
Page/Location: 76/C4
Area: 419,229 sq. mi.
1,085, 803 sq. km.
Population: 1,996,000
Capital: Nouakchott
Largest City: Nouakchott
Highest Point: Kediet Ijill
Monetary Unit: ouguiya

Mauritius
Page/Location: 81/S15
Area: 790 sq. mi.
2,046 sq. km.
Population: 1,081,000
Capital: Port Louis
Largest City: Port Louis
Highest Point: 2,713 ft. (827 m)
Monetary Unit: Mauritian rupee

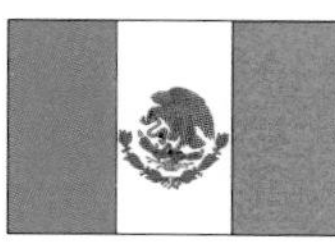

Mexico
Page/Location: 84/G7
Area: 761,601 sq. mi.
1,972,546 sq. km.
Population: 90,007,000
Capital: Mexico City
Largest City: Mexico City
Highest Point: Citlaltépetl
Monetary Unit: Mexican peso

Micronesia
Page/Location: 68/D4
Area: 271 sq. mi.
702 sq. km.
Population: 108,000
Capital: Kolonia
Largest City: —
Highest Point: —
Monetary Unit: U.S. dollar

Moldova
Page/Location: 41/J2
Area: 13,012 sq. mi.
33,700 sq. km.
Population: 4,341,000
Capital: Chişinău
Largest City: Chişinău
Highest Point: 1,408 ft. (429 m)
Monetary Unit: leu

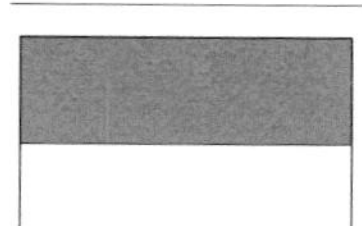

Monaco
Page/Location: 33/G5
Area: 368 acres
149 hectares
Population: 30,000
Capital: Monaco
Largest City: —
Highest Point: —
Monetary Unit: French franc

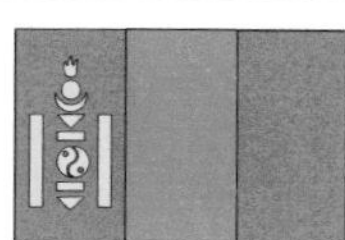

Mongolia
Page/Location: 54/D2
Area: 606,163 sq. mi.
1,569, 962 sq. km.
Population: 2,247,000
Capital: Ulaanbaatar
Largest City: Ulaanbaatar
Highest Point: Tavan Bogd Uul
Monetary Unit: tughrik

Morocco
Page/Location: 76/C1
Area: 172,414 sq. mi.
446,550 sq. km.
Population: 26,182,000
Capital: Rabat
Largest City: Casablanca
Highest Point: Jebel Toubkal
Monetary Unit: Moroccan dirham

Mozambique
Page/Location: 82/G4
Area: 303,769 sq. mi.
786,762 sq. km.
Population: 15,113,000
Capital: Maputo
Largest City: Maputo
Highest Point: Monte Binga
Monetary Unit: metical

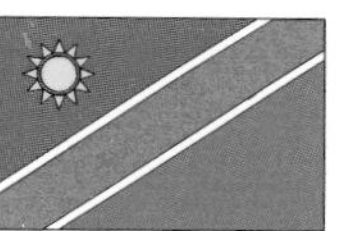

Namibia
Page/Location: 82/C5
Area: 317,827 sq. mi.
823,172 sq. km.
Population: 1,521,000
Capital: Windhoek
Largest City: Windhoek
Highest Point: Brandberg
Monetary Unit: rand

Nauru
Page/Location: 68/F5
Area: 7.7 sq. mi.
20 sq. km.
Population: 9,000
Capital: Yaren (district)
Largest City: —
Highest Point: 230 ft. (70 m)
Monetary Unit: Australian dollar

Nepal
Page/Location: 62/D2
Area: 54,663 sq. mi.
141,577 sq. km.
Population: 19,612,000
Capital: Kathmandu
Largest City: Kathmandu
Highest Point: Mt. Everest
Monetary Unit: Nepalese rupee

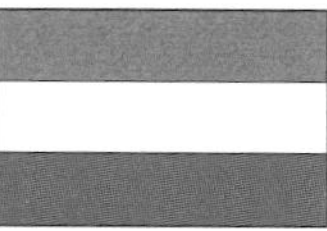

Netherlands
Page/Location: 28/B5
Area: 15,892 sq. mi.
41,160 sq. km.
Population: 15,022,000
Capital: The Hague; Amsterdam
Largest City: Amsterdam
Highest Point: Vaalserberg
Monetary Unit: Netherlands guilder

New Zealand
Page/Location: 71/Q10
Area: 103,736 sq. mi.
268,676 sq. km.
Population: 3,309,000
Capital: Wellington
Largest City: Auckland
Highest Point: Mt. Cook
Monetary Unit: New Zealand dollar

Nicaragua
Page/Location: 103/E3
Area: 45,698 sq. mi.
118,358 sq. km.
Population: 3,752,000
Capital: Managua
Largest City: Managua
Highest Point: Pico Mogotón
Monetary Unit: córdoba

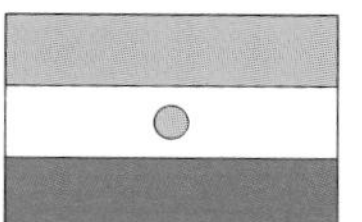

Niger
Page/Location: 76/G4
Area: 489,189 sq. mi.
1,267,000 sq. km.
Population: 8,154,000
Capital: Niamey
Largest City: Niamey
Highest Point: Bagzane
Monetary Unit: CFA franc

Nigeria
Page/Location: 76/G6
Area: 357,000 sq. mi.
924,630 sq. km.
Population: 122,471,000
Capital: Abuja
Largest City: Lagos
Highest Point: Dimlang
Monetary Unit: naira

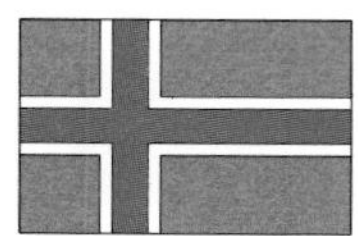

Norway
Page/Location: 20/C3
Area: 125,053 sq. mi.
323,887 sq. km.
Population: 4,273,000
Capital: Oslo
Largest City: Oslo
Highest Point: Glittertjnden
Monetary Unit: Norwegian krone

Oman
Page/Location: 53/G4
Area: 120,000 sq. mi.
310,800 sq. km.
Population: 1,534,000
Capital: Muscat
Largest City: Muscat
Highest Point: Jabal ash Shām
Monetary Unit: Omani rial

Pakistan
Page/Location: 53/H3
Area: 310,403 sq. mi.
803,944 sq. km.
Population: 117,490,000
Capital: Islamabad
Largest City: Karachi
Highest Point: K2 (Godwin Austen)
Monetary Unit: Pakistani rupee

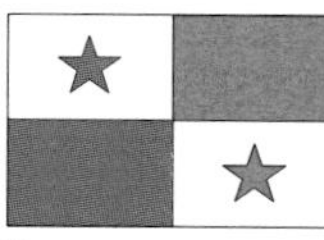

Panama
Page/Location: 103/F4
Area: 29,761 sq. mi.
77,082 sq. km.
Population: 2,476,000
Capital: Panamá
Largest City: Panamá
Highest Point: Barú
Monetary Unit: balboa

Papua New Guinea
Page/Location: 68/D5
Area: 183,540 sq. mi.
475,369 sq. km.
Population: 3,913,000
Capital: Port Moresby
Largest City: Port Moresby
Highest Point: Mt. Wilhelm
Monetary Unit: kina

Paraguay
Page/Location: 105/D5
Area: 157,047 sq. mi.
406,752 sq. km.
Population: 4,799,000
Capital: Asunción
Largest City: Asunción
Highest Point: Sierra de Amambay
Monetary Unit: guaraní

World Flags and Reference Guide

Peru
Page/Location: 106/C5
Area: 496,222 sq. mi.
1,285,215 sq. km.
Population: 22,362,000
Capital: Lima
Largest City: Lima
Highest Point: Nevado Huascarán
Monetary Unit: nuevo sol

Philippines
Page/Location: 48/M8
Area: 115,707 sq. mi.
299,681 sq. km.
Population: 65,759,000
Capital: Manila
Largest City: Manila
Highest Point: Mt. Apo
Monetary Unit: Philippine peso

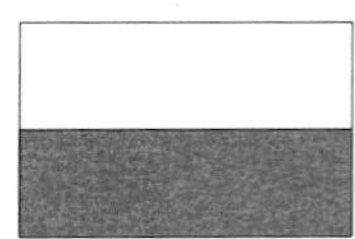

Poland
Page/Location: 27/K2
Area: 120,725 sq. mi.
312,678 sq. km.
Population: 37,800,000
Capital: Warsaw
Largest City: Warsaw
Highest Point: Rysy
Monetary Unit: zloty

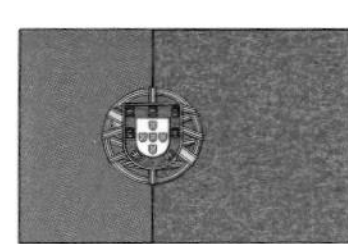

Portugal
Page/Location: 34/A3
Area: 35,549 sq. mi.
92,072 sq. km.
Population: 10,388,000
Capital: Lisbon
Largest City: Lisbon
Highest Point: Serra da Estrela
Monetary Unit: Portuguese escudo

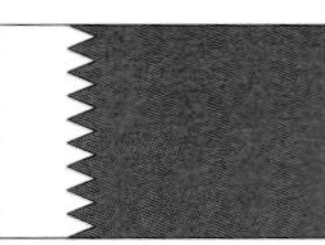

Qatar
Page/Location: 52/F3
Area: 4,247 sq. mi.
11,000 sq. km.
Population: 518,000
Capital: Doha
Largest City: Doha
Highest Point: Dukhān Heights
Monetary Unit: Qatari riyal

Romania
Page/Location: 41/F3
Area: 91,699 sq. mi.
237,500 sq. km.
Population: 23,397,000
Capital: Bucharest
Largest City: Bucharest
Highest Point: Moldoveanul
Monetary Unit: leu

Russia
Page/Location: 46/H3
Area: 6,592,812 sq. mi.
17,075,400 sq. km.
Population: 147,386,000
Capital: Moscow
Largest City: Moscow
Highest Point: El'brus
Monetary Unit: Russian ruble

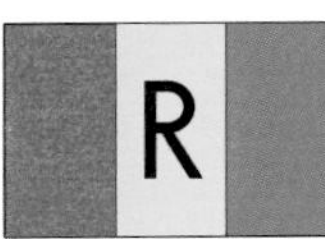

Rwanda
Page/Location: 82/E1
Area: 10,169 sq. mi.
26,337 sq. km.
Population: 7,903,000
Capital: Kigali
Largest City: Kigali
Highest Point: Karisimbi
Monetary Unit: Rwanda franc

Saint Kitts and Nevis
Page/Location: 104/F3
Area: 104 sq. mi.
269 sq. km.
Population: 40,000
Capital: Basseterre
Largest City: Basseterre
Highest Point: Mt. Misery
Monetary Unit: East Caribbean dollar

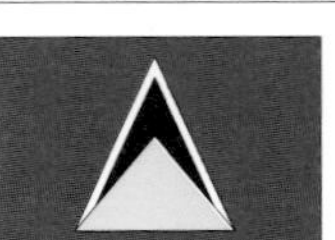

Saint Lucia
Page/Location: 104/F4
Area: 238 sq. mi.
616 sq. km.
Population: 153,000
Capital: Castries
Largest City: Castries
Highest Point: Mt. Gimie
Monetary Unit: East Caribbean dollar

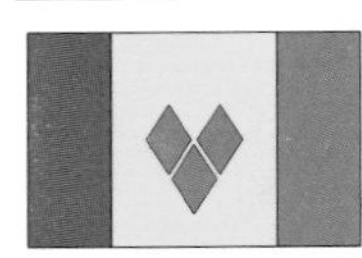

Saint Vincent and the Grenadines
Page/Location: 104/F4
Area: 150 sq. mi.
388 sq. km.
Population: 114,000
Capital: Kingstown
Largest City: Kingstown
Highest Point: Soufrière
Monetary Unit: East Caribbean dollar

San Marino
Page/Location: 33/K5
Area: 23.4 sq. mi.
60.6 sq. km.
Population: 23,000
Capital: San Marino
Largest City: San Marino
Highest Point: Monte Titano
Monetary Unit: Italian lira

São Tomé and Príncipe
Page/Location: 76/G7
Area: 372 sq. mi.
963 sq. km.
Population: 128,000
Capital: São Tomé
Largest City: São Tomé
Highest Point: Pico de São Tomé
Monetary Unit: dobra

Saudi Arabia
Page/Location: 104/F3
Area: 829,995 sq. mi.
2,149,687 sq. km.
Population: 17,870,000
Capital: Riyadh
Largest City: Riyadh
Highest Point: Jabal Sawdā'
Monetary Unit: Saudi riyal

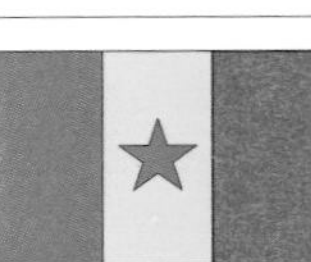

Senegal
Page/Location: 78/B3
Area: 75,954 sq. mi.
196,720 sq. km.
Population: 7,953,000
Capital: Dakar
Largest City: Dakar
Highest Point: Fouta Djallon
Monetary Unit: CFA franc

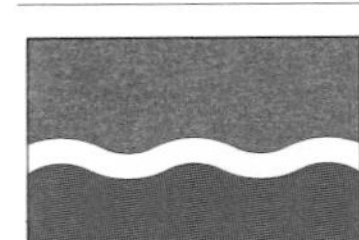

Seychelles
Page/Location: 74/H5
Area: 145 sq. mi.
375 sq. km.
Population: 69,000
Capital: Victoria
Largest City: Victoria
Highest Point: Morne Seychellois
Monetary Unit: Seychellois rupee

Sierra Leone
Page/Location: 78/B4
Area: 27,925 sq. mi.
72,325 sq. km.
Population: 4,275,000
Capital: Freetown
Largest City: Freetown
Highest Point: Loma Mansa
Monetary Unit: leone

Singapore
Page/Location: 66/B3
Area: 226 sq. mi.
585 sq. km.
Population: 2,756,000
Capital: Singapore
Largest City: Singapore
Highest Point: Bukit Timah
Monetary Unit: Singapore dollar

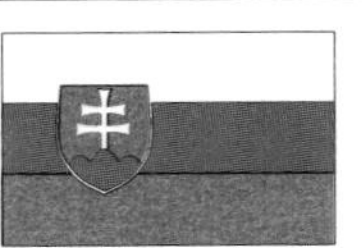

Slovakia
Page/Location: 27/K4
Area: 18,924 sq. mi.
49,013 sq. km.
Population: 4,991,168
Capital: Bratislava
Largest City: Bratislava
Highest Point: Gerlachovský Štít
Monetary Unit: Slovak koruna

Slovenia
Page/Location: 40/B3
Area: 7,898 sq. mi.
20,456 sq. km.
Population: 1,891,864
Capital: Ljubljana
Largest City: Ljubljana
Highest Point: Triglav
Monetary Unit: tolar

Solomon Islands
Page/Location: 68/E6
Area: 11,500 sq. mi.
29,785 sq. km.
Population: 347,000
Capital: Honiara
Largest City: Honiara
Highest Point: Mt. Makarakomburu
Monetary Unit: Solomon Islands dollar

Somalia
Page/Location: 77/Q6
Area: 246,200 sq. mi.
637,658 sq. km.
Population: 6,709,000
Capital: Mogadishu
Largest City: Mogadishu
Highest Point: Shimber Berris
Monetary Unit: Somali shilling

South Africa
Page/Location: 80/C3
Area: 455,318 sq. mi.
1,179,274 sq. km.
Population: 40,601,000
Capital: Cape Town; Pretoria
Largest City: Johannesburg
Highest Point: Injasuti
Monetary Unit: rand

Spain
Page/Location: 34/C2
Area: 194,881 sq. mi.
504,742 sq. km.
Population: 39,385,000
Capital: Madrid
Largest City: Madrid
Highest Point: Pico de Teide
Monetary Unit: peseta

Sri Lanka
Page/Location: 62/D6
Area: 25,332 sq. mi.
65,610 sq. km.
Population: 17,424,000
Capital: Colombo
Largest City: Colombo
Highest Point: Pidurutalagala
Monetary Unit: Sri Lanka rupee

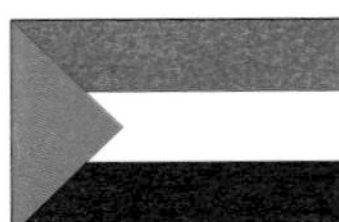

Sudan
Page/Location: 77/L5
Area: 967,494 sq. mi.
2,505,809 sq. km.
Population: 27,220,000
Capital: Khartoum
Largest City: Omdurman
Highest Point: Jabal Marrah
Monetary Unit: Sudanese pound

Suriname
Page/Location: 107/G3
Area: 55,144 sq. mi.
142,823 sq. km.
Population: 402,000
Capital: Paramaribo
Largest City: Paramaribo
Highest Point: Juliana Top
Monetary Unit: Suriname guilder

Swaziland
Page/Location: 81/E2
Area: 6,705 sq. mi.
17,366 sq. km.
Population: 859,000
Capital: Mbabane
Largest City: Mbabane
Highest Point: Emlembe
Monetary Unit: lilangeni

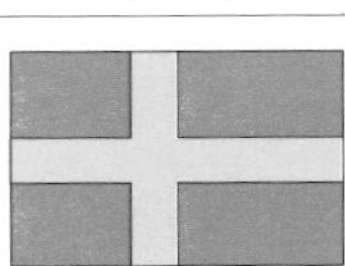

Sweden
Page/Location: 20/E3
Area: 173,665 sq. mi.
449,792 sq. km.
Population: 8,564,000
Capital: Stockholm
Largest City: Stockholm
Highest Point: Kebnekaise
Monetary Unit: krona

Switzerland
Page/Location: 36/D4
Area: 15,943 sq. mi.
41,292 sq. km.
Population: 6,784,000
Capital: Bern
Largest City: Zürich
Highest Point: Dufourspitze
Monetary Unit: Swiss franc

Syria
Page/Location: 50/D3
Area: 71,498 sq. mi.
185,180 sq. km.
Population: 12,966,000
Capital: Damascus
Largest City: Damascus
Highest Point: Jabal ash Shaykh
Monetary Unit: Syrian pound

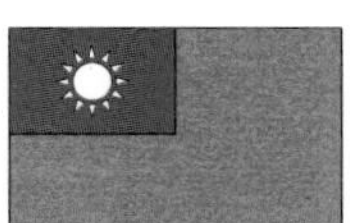

Taiwan
Page/Location: 61/J3
Area: 13,971 sq. mi.
36,185 sq. km.
Population: 16,609,961
Capital: Taipei
Largest City: Taipei
Highest Point: Yü Shan
Monetary Unit: new Taiwan dollar

Tajikistan
Page/Location: 46/H6
Area: 55,251 sq. mi.
143,100 sq. km.
Population: 5,112,000
Capital: Dushanbe
Largest City: Dushanbe
Highest Point: Communism Peak
Monetary Unit: Tajik ruble

Tanzania
Page/Location: 82/F2
Area: 363,708 sq. mi.
942,003 sq. km.
Population: 26,869,000
Capital: Dar es Salaam
Largest City: Dar es Salaam
Highest Point: Kilimanjaro
Monetary Unit: Tanzanian shilling

Thailand
Page/Location: 65/C3
Area: 198,455 sq. mi.
513,998 sq. km.
Population: 56,814,000
Capital: Bangkok
Largest City: Bangkok
Highest Point: Doi Inthanon
Monetary Unit: baht

Togo
Page/Location: 79/F4
Area: 21,622 sq. mi.
56,000 sq. km.
Population: 3,811,000
Capital: Lomé
Largest City: Lomé
Highest Point: Mt. Agou
Monetary Unit: CFA franc

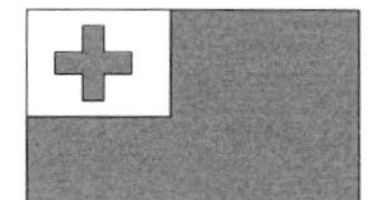

Tonga
Page/Location: 69/H7
Area: 270 sq. mi.
699 sq. km.
Population: 102,000
Capital: Nuku'alofa
Largest City: Nuku'alofa
Highest Point: Kao Island
Monetary Unit: pa'anga

Trinidad and Tobago
Page/Location: 104/F5
Area: 1,980 sq. mi.
5,128 sq. km.
Population: 1,285,000
Capital: Port-of-Spain
Largest City: Port-of-Spain
Highest Point: El Cerro del Aripo
Monetary Unit: Trin. & Tobago dollar

Tunisia
Page/Location: 76/G1
Area: 63,378 sq. mi.
164,149 sq. km.
Population: 8,276,000
Capital: Tunis
Largest City: Tunis
Highest Point: Jabal ash Sha'nabī
Monetary Unit: Tunisian dinar

Turkey
Page/Location: 50/C2
Area: 300,946 sq. mi.
779,450 sq. km.
Population: 58,581,000
Capital: Ankara
Largest City: Istanbul
Highest Point: Mt. Ararat
Monetary Unit: Turkish lira

Turkmenistan
Page/Location: 46/F6
Area: 188,455 sq. mi.
488,100 sq. km.
Population: 3,534,000
Capital: Ashkhabad
Largest City: Ashkhabad
Highest Point: Rize
Monetary Unit: manat

Tuvalu
Page/Location: 68/G5
Area: 9.78 sq. mi.
25.33 sq. km.
Population: 9,000
Capital: Fongafale
Largest City: —
Highest Point: 16 ft. (5 m)
Monetary Unit: Australian dollar

Uganda
Page/Location: 77/M7
Area: 91,076 sq. mi.
235,887 sq. km.
Population: 18,690,000
Capital: Kampala
Largest City: Kampala
Highest Point: Margherita Peak
Monetary Unit: Ugandan shilling

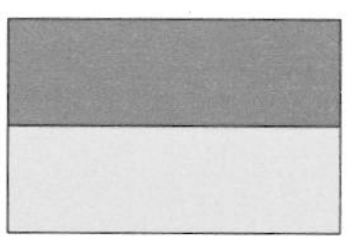

Ukraine
Page/Location: 44/D2
Area: 233,089 sq. mi.
603,700 sq. km.
Population: 51,704,000
Capital: Kiev
Largest City: Kiev
Highest Point: Goverla
Monetary Unit: grivna

United Arab Emirates
Page/Location: 52/F4
Area: 32,278 sq. mi.
83,600 sq. km.
Population: 2,390,000
Capital: Abu Dhabi
Largest City: Dubayy
Highest Point: Hajar Mts.
Monetary Unit: Emirian dirham

United Kingdom
Page/Location: 21
Area: 94,399 sq. mi.
244,493 sq. km.
Population: 57,515,000
Capital: London
Largest City: London
Highest Point: Ben Nevis
Monetary Unit: pound sterling

United States
Page/Location: 88
Area: 3,623,420 sq. mi.
9,384,658 sq. km.
Population: 252,502,000
Capital: Washington
Largest City: New York
Highest Point: Mt. McKinley
Monetary Unit: U.S. dollar

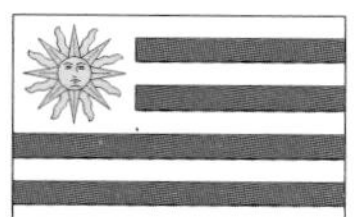

Uruguay
Page/Location: 109/E3
Area: 72,172 sq. mi.
186,925 sq. km.
Population: 3,121,000
Capital: Montevideo
Largest City: Montevideo
Highest Point: Cerro Catedral
Monetary Unit: Uruguayan peso

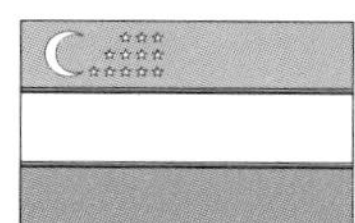

Uzbekistan
Page/Location: 46/G5
Area: 173,591 sq. mi.
449,600 sq. km.
Population: 19,906,000
Capital: Tashkent
Largest City: Tashkent
Highest Point: Khodzha-Pir'yakh
Monetary Unit: Uzbek ruble

Vanuatu
Page/Location: 68/F6
Area: 5,700 sq. mi.
14,763 sq. km.
Population: 170,000
Capital: Vila
Largest City: Vila
Highest Point: Tabwemasana
Monetary Unit: vatu

Vatican City
Page/Location: 38/C2
Area: 108.7 acres
44 hectares
Population: 1,000
Capital: —
Largest City: —
Highest Point: —
Monetary Unit: Italian lira

Venezuela
Page/Location: 106/E2
Area: 352,143 sq. mi.
912,050 sq. km.
Population: 20,189,000
Capital: Caracas
Largest City: Caracas
Highest Point: Pico Bolívar
Monetary Unit: bolívar

Vietnam
Page/Location: 65/D2
Area: 128,405 sq. mi.
332,569 sq. km.
Population: 67,568,000
Capital: Hanoi
Largest City: Ho Chi Minh City
Highest Point: Fan Si Pan
Monetary Unit: dong

Western Samoa
Page/Location: 69/H6
Area: 1,133 sq. mi.
2,934 sq. km.
Population: 190,000
Capital: Apia
Largest City: Apia
Highest Point: Mt. Silisili
Monetary Unit: tala

Yemen
Page/Location: 52/E5
Area: 188,321 sq. mi.
487,752 sq. km.
Population: 10,063,000
Capital: Sanaa
Largest City: Aden
Highest Point: Nabī Shu'ayb
Monetary Unit: Yemeni rial

Yugoslavia
Page/Location: 40/E3
Area: 38,989 sq. mi.
100,982 sq. km.
Population: 11,371,275
Capital: Belgrade
Largest City: Belgrade
Highest Point: Đaravica
Monetary Unit: Yugoslav new dinar

Zaire
Page/Location: 74/E5
Area: 905,063 sq. mi.
2,344,113 sq. km.
Population: 37,832,000
Capital: Kinshasa
Largest City: Kinshasa
Highest Point: Margherita Peak
Monetary Unit: zaire

Zambia
Page/Location: 82/E3
Area: 290,586 sq. mi.
752,618 sq. km.
Population: 8,446,000
Capital: Lusaka
Largest City: Lusaka
Highest Point: Sunzu
Monetary Unit: Zambian kwacha

Zimbabwe
Page/Location: 82/E4
Area: 150,803 sq. mi.
390,580 sq. km.
Population: 10,720,000
Capital: Harare
Largest City: Harare
Highest Point: Inyangani
Monetary Unit: Zimbabwe dollar

World Statistics

Elements of the Solar System

	Mean Distance from Sun: in Miles	in Kilometers	Period of Revolution around Sun	Period of Rotation on Axis	Equatorial Diameter in Miles	in Kilometers	Surface Gravity (Earth = 1)	Mass (Earth = 1)	Mean Density (Water = 1)	Number of Satellites
Mercury	35,990,000	57,900,000	87.97 days	59 days	3,032	4,880	0.38	0.055	5.5	0
Venus	67,240,000	108,200,000	224.70 days	243 days†	7,523	12,106	0.90	0.815	5.25	0
Earth	93,000,000	149,700,000	365.26 days	23h 56m	7,926	12,755	1.00	1.00	5.5	1
Mars	141,730,000	228,100,000	687.00 days	24h 37m	4,220	6,790	0.38	0.107	4.0	2
Jupiter	483,880,000	778,700,000	11.86 years	9h 50m	88,750	142,800	2.87	317.9	1.3	16
Saturn	887,130,000	1,427,700,000	29.46 years	10h 39m	74,580	120,020	1.32	95.2	0.7	23
Uranus	1,783,700,000	2,870,500,000	84.01 years	17h 24m†	31,600	50,900	0.93	14.6	1.3	15
Neptune	2,795,500,000	4,498,800,000	164.79 years	17h 50m	30,200	48,600	1.23	17.2	1.8	8
Pluto	3,667,900,000	5,902,800,000	247.70 years	6.39 days(?)	1,500	2,400	0.03(?)	0.01(?)	0.7(?)	1

† Retrograde motion

Dimensions of the Earth

	Area in: Sq. Miles	Sq. Kilometers
Superficial area	196,939,000	510,073,000
Land surface	57,506,000	148,941,000
Water surface	139,433,000	361,132,000
	Distance in: Miles	**Kilometers**
Equatorial circumference	24,902	40,075
Polar circumference	24,860	40,007
Equatorial diameter	7,926.4	12,756.4
Polar diameter	7,899.8	12,713.6
Equatorial radius	3,963.2	6,378.2
Polar radius	3,949.9	6,356.8
Volume of the Earth	2.6×10^{11} cubic miles	10.84×10^{11} cubic kilometers
Mass or weight	6.6×10^{21} short tons	6.0×10^{21} metric tons
Maximum distance from Sun	94,600,000 miles	152,000,000 kilometers
Minimum distance from Sun	91,300,000 miles	147,000,000 kilometers

Oceans and Major Seas

	Area in: Sq. Miles	Sq. Kms.	Greatest Depth in: Feet	Meters
Pacific Ocean	64,186,000	166,241,700	36,198	11,033
Atlantic Ocean	31,862,000	82,522,600	28,374	8,648
Indian Ocean	28,350,000	73,426,500	25,344	7,725
Arctic Ocean	5,427,000	14,056,000	17,880	5,450
Caribbean Sea	970,000	2,512,300	24,720	7,535
Mediterranean Sea	969,000	2,509,700	16,896	5,150
South China Sea	895,000	2,318,000	15,000	4,600
Bering Sea	875,000	2,266,250	15,800	4,800
Gulf of Mexico	600,000	1,554,000	12,300	3,750
Sea of Okhotsk	590,000	1,528,100	11,070	3,370
East China Sea	482,000	1,248,400	9,500	2,900
Yellow Sea	480,000	1,243,200	350	107
Sea of Japan	389,000	1,007,500	12,280	3,740
Hudson Bay	317,500	822,300	846	258
North Sea	222,000	575,000	2,200	670
Black Sea	185,000	479,150	7,365	2,245
Red Sea	169,000	437,700	7,200	2,195
Baltic Sea	163,000	422,170	1,506	459

The Continents

	Area in: Sq. Miles	Sq. Kms.	Percent of World's Land
Asia	17,128,500	44,362,815	29.5
Africa	11,707,000	30,321,130	20.2
North America	9,363,000	24,250,170	16.2
South America	6,875,000	17,806,250	11.8
Antarctica	5,500,000	14,245,000	9.5
Europe	4,057,000	10,507,630	7.0
Australia	2,966,136	7,682,300	5.1

Major Ship Canals

	Length in: Miles	Kms.	Minimum Depth in: Feet	Meters
Volga-Baltic, Russia	225	362	–	–
Baltic-White Sea, Russia	140	225	16	5
Suez, Egypt	100.76	162	42	13
Albert, Belgium	80	129	16.5	5
Moscow-Volga, Russia	80	129	18	6
Volga-Don, Russia	62	100	–	–
Göta, Sweden	54	87	10	3
Kiel (Nord-Ostsee), Germany	53.2	86	38	12
Panama Canal, Panama	50.72	82	41.6	13
Houston Ship, U.S.A.	50	81	36	11

Largest Islands

	Area in: Sq. Miles	Sq. Kms.
Greenland	840,000	2,175,600
New Guinea	305,000	789,950
Borneo	290,000	751,100
Madagascar	226,400	586,376
Baffin, Canada	195,928	507,454
Sumatra, Indonesia	164,000	424,760
Honshu, Japan	88,000	227,920
Great Britain	84,400	218,896
Victoria, Canada	83,896	217,290
Ellesmere, Canada	75,767	196,236
Celebes, Indonesia	72,986	189,034
South I., New Zealand	58,393	151,238
Java, Indonesia	48,842	126,501
North I., New Zealand	44,187	114,444
Newfoundland, Canada	42,031	108,860
Cuba	40,533	104,981
Luzon, Philippines	40,420	104,688
Iceland	39,768	103,000
Mindanao, Philippines	36,537	94,631
Ireland	31,743	82,214
Sakhalin, Russia	29,500	76,405
Hispaniola, Haiti & Dom. Rep.	29,399	76,143

	Area in: Sq. Miles	Sq. Kms.
Hokkaido, Japan	28,983	75,066
Banks, Canada	27,038	70,028
Ceylon,Sri Lanka	25,332	65,610
Tasmania, Australia	24,600	63,710
Svalbard, Norway	23,957	62,049
Devon, Canada	21,331	55,247
Novaya Zemlya (north isl.), Russia	18,600	48,200
Marajó, Brazil	17,991	46,597
Tierra del Fuego, Chile & Argentina	17,900	46,360
Alexander, Antarctica	16,700	43,250
Axel Heiberg, Canada	16,671	43,178
Melville, Canada	16,274	42,150
Southhampton, Canada	15,913	41,215
New Britain, Papua New Guinea	14,100	36,519
Taiwan, China	13,836	35,835
Kyushu, Japan	13,770	35,664
Hainan, China	13,127	33,999
Prince of Wales, Canada	12,872	33,338
Spitsbergen, Norway	12,355	31,999
Vancouver, Canada	12,079	31,285
Timor, Indonesia	11,527	29,855
Sicily, Italy	9,926	25,708

	Area in: Sq. Miles	Sq. Kms.
Somerset, Canada	9,570	24,786
Sardinia, Italy	9,301	24,090
Shikoku, Japan	6,860	17,767
New Caledonia, France	6,530	16,913
Nordaustlandet, Norway	6,409	16,599
Samar, Philippines	5,050	13,080
Negros, Philippines	4,906	12,707
Palawan, Philippines	4,550	11,785
Panay, Philippines	4,446	11,515
Jamaica	4,232	10,961
Hawaii, United States	4,038	10,458
Viti Levu, Fiji	4,010	10,386
Cape Breton, Canada	3,981	10,311
Mindoro, Philippines	3,759	9,736
Kodiak, Alaska, U.S.A.	3,670	9,505
Cyprus	3,572	9,251
Puerto Rico, U.S.A.	3,435	8,897
Corsica, France	3,352	8,682
New Ireland, Papua New Guinea	3,340	8,651
Crete, Greece	3,218	8,335
Anticosti, Canada	3,066	7,941
Wrangel, Russia	2,819	7,301

Principal Mountains

	Height in : Feet	Meters
Everest, Nepal-China	29,028	8,848
K2 (Godwin Austen), Pakistan-China	28,250	8,611
Makalu, Nepal-China	27,789	8,470
Dhaulagiri, Nepal	26,810	8,172
Nanga Parbat, Pakistan	26,660	8,126
Annapurna, Nepal	26,504	8,078
Rakaposhi, Pakistan	25,550	7,788
Kongur Shan, China	25,325	7,719
Tirich Mir, Pakistan	25,230	7,690
Gongga Shan, China	24,790	7,556
Communism Peak, Tajikistan	24,590	7,495
Pobedy Peak, Kyrgyzstan	24,406	7,439
Chomo Lhari, Bhutan-China	23,997	7,314
Muztag, China	23,891	7,282
Cerro Aconcagua, Argentina	22,831	6,959
Ojos del Salado, Chile-Argentina	22,572	6,880
Bonete, Chile-Argentina	22,546	6,872
Tupungato, Chile-Argentina	22,310	6,800
Pissis, Argentina	22,241	6,779
Mercedario, Argentina	22,211	6,770
Huascarán, Peru	22,205	6,768
Llullaillaco, Chile-Argentina	22,057	6,723
Nevada Ancohuma, Bolivia	21,489	6,550
Chimborazo, Ecuador	20,561	6,267
McKinley, Alaska	20,320	6,194
Logan, Yukon, Canada	19,524	5,951
Cotopaxi, Ecuador	19,347	5,897
Kilimanjaro, Tanzania	19,340	5,895
El Misti, Peru	19,101	5,822
Pico Cristóbal Colón, Colombia	18,947	5,775
Huila, Colombia	18,865	5,750
Citlaltépetl (Orizaba), Mexico	18,701	5,700
Damavand, Iran	18,606	5,671
El'brus, Russia	18,510	5,642
St. Elias, Alaska, U.S.A.-Yukon, Canada	18,008	5,489
Dykh-tau, Russia	17,070	5,203
Batian (Kenya), Kenya	17,058	5,199
Ararat, Turkey	16,946	5,165
Vinson Massif, Antarctica	16,864	5,140
Margherita (Ruwenzori), Africa	16,795	5,119
Kazbek, Georgia-Russia	16,558	5,047
Puncak Jaya, Indonesia	16,503	5,030
Blanc, France	15,771	4,807
Klyuchevskaya Sopka, Russia	15,584	4,750
Fairweather, Br. Col., Canada	15,300	4,663
Dufourspitze (Mte. Rosa), Italy-Switzerland	15,203	4,634
Ras Dashen, Ethiopia	15,157	4620
Matterhorn, Switzerland	14,691	4,478
Whitney, California, U.S.A.	14,494	4,418
Elbert, Colorado, U.S.A.	14,433	4,399
Rainier, Washington, U.S.A.	14,410	4,392
Shasta, California, U.S.A.	14,162	4,317
Pikes Peak, Colorado, U.S.A.	14,110	4,301
Finsteraarhorn, Switzerland	14,022	4, 274
Mauna Kea, Hawaii, U.S.A.	13,796	4,205
Mauna Loa, Hawaii, U.S.A.	13,677	4,169
Jungfrau, Switzerland	13,642	4,158
Grossglockner, Austria	12,457	3,797
Fujiyama, Japan	12,389	3,776
Cook, New Zealand	12,349	3,764
Etna, Italy	10,902	3,323
Kosciusko, Australia	7,310	2,228
Mitchell, North Carolina, U.S.A.	6,684	2,037

Longest Rivers

	Length in: Miles	Kms.
Nile, Africa	4,145	6,671
Amazon, S. America	3,915	6,300
Chang Jiang (Yangtze), China	3,900	6,276
Mississippi-Missouri-Red Rock, U.S.A.	3,741	6,019
Ob'-Irtysh-Black Irtysh, Russia-Kazakhstan	3,362	5,411
Yenisey-Angara, Russia	3,100	4,989
Huang He (Yellow), China	2,877	4,630
Amur-Shilka-Onon, Asia	2,744	4,416
Lena, Russia	2,734	4,400
Congo (Zaire), Africa	2,718	4,374
Mackenzie-Peace-Finlay,Canada	2,635	4,241
Mekong, Asia	2,610	4,200
Missouri-Red Rock, U.S.A.	2,564	4,125
Niger, Africa	2,548	4,101
Paraná-La Plata, S. America	2,450	3,943
Mississippi, U.S.A.	2,348	3,778
Murray-Darling, Australia	2,310	3,718
Volga, Russia	2,194	3,531
Madeira, S. America	2,013	3,240
Purus, S. America	1,995	3,211
Yukon, Alaska-Canada	1,979	3,185
St. Lawrence, Canada-U.S.A.	1,900	3,058
Rio Grande, Mexico-U.S.A.	1,885	3,034
Syrdar'ya-Naryn, Asia	1,859	2,992
São Francisco, Brazil	1,811	2,914
Indus, Asia	1,800	2,897
Danube, Europe	1,775	2,857
Salween, Asia	1,770	2,849
Brahmaputra, Asia	1,700	2,736
Euphrates, Asia	1,700	2,736
Tocantins, Brazil	1,677	2,699
Xi (Si), China	1,650	2,601
Amudar'ya, Asia	1,616	2,601
Nelson-Saskatchewan, Canada	1,600	2,575
Orinoco, S. America	1,600	2,575
Zambezi, Africa	1,600	2,575
Paraguay, S. America	1,584	2,549
Kolyma, Russia	1,562	2,514
Ganges, Asia	1,550	2,494
Ural, Russia-Kazakhstan	1,509	2,428
Japurá, S. America	1,500	2,414
Arkansas, U.S.A.	1,450	2,334
Colorado, U.S.A.-Mexico	1.450	2,334
Negro, S. America	1,400	2,253
Dnieper, Russia-Belarus-Ukraine	1,368	2,202
Orange, Africa	1,350	2,173
Irrawaddy, Burma	1,325	2,132
Brazos, U.S.A.	1,309	2,107
Ohio-Allegheny, U.S.A.	1,306	2,102
Kama, Russia	1,252	2,031
Don, Russia	1,222	1,967
Red, U.S.A.	1,222	1,966
Columbia, U.S.A.-Canada	1,214	1,953
Saskatchewan, Canada	1,205	1,939
Peace-Finlay, Canada	1,195	1,923
Tigris, Asia	1,181	1,901
Darling, Australia	1,160	1,867
Angara, Russia	1,135	1,827
Sungari, Asia	1,130	1,819
Pechora, Russia	1,124	1,809
Snake, U.S.A.	1,038	1,670
Churchill, Canada	1,000	1,609
Pilcomayo, S. America	1,000	1,609
Uruguay, S. America	994	1.600
Platte-N. Platte, U.S.A.	990	1,593
Ohio, U.S.A.	981	1,578
Magdalena, Colombia	956	1,538
Pecos, U.S.A.	926	1,490
Oka, Russia	918	1,477
Canadian, U.S.A.	906	1,458
Colorado, Texas, U.S.A.	894	1,439
Dniester, Ukraine-Moldova	876	1,410
Fraser, Canada	850	1,369
Rhine, Europe	820	1,319
Northern Dvina, Russia	809	1,302

Principal Natural Lakes

	Area in: Sq. Miles	Sq. Kms.	Max. Depth in: Feet	Meters
Caspian Sea, Asia	143,243	370,999	3,264	995
Lake Superior, U.S.A.-Canada	31,820	82,414	1,329	405
Lake Victoria, Africa	26,724	69,215	270	82
Lake Huron, U.S.A.-Canada	23,010	59,596	748	228
Lake Michigan, U.S.A.	22,400	58,016	923	281
Aral Sea, Kazakhstan-Uzbekistan	15,830	41,000	213	65
Lake Tanganyika, Africa	12,650	32,764	4,700	1,433
Lake Baykal, Russia	12,162	31,500	5,316	1,620
Great Bear Lake, Canada	12,096	31,328	1,356	413
Lake Nyasa (Malawi), Africa	11,555	29,928	2,320	707
Great Slave Lake, Canada	11,031	28,570	2,015	614
Lake Erie, U.S.A.-Canada	9,940	25,745	210	64
Lake Winnipeg, Canada	9,417	24,390	60	18
Lake Ontario, U.S.A.-Canada	7,540	19,529	775	244
Lake Ladoga, Russia	7,104	18,399	738	225
Lake Balkhash, Kazakhstan	7,027	18,200	87	27
Lake Maracaibo, Venezuela	5,120	13,261	100	31
Lake Chad, Africa	4,000 – 10,000	10,360 – 25,900	25	8
Lake Onega, Russia	3,710	9,609	377	115
Lake Eyre, Australia	3,500-0	9,000-0	–	–
Lake Titicaca, Peru-Bolivia	3,200	8,288	1, 000	305
Lake Nicaragua, Nicaragua	3,100	8,029	230	70
Lake Athabasca, Canada	3,064	7,936	400	122
Reindeer Lake, Canada	2,568	6,651	–	–
Lake Turkana (Rudolf), Africa	2,463	6,379	240	73
Issyk-Kul', Kyrgyzstan	2,425	6,281	2,303	702
Lake Torrens, Australia	2,230	5,776	–	–
Vänern, Sweden	2,156	5,584	328	100
Nettilling Lake, Canada	2,140	5,543	–	–
Lake Winnipegosis, Canada	2,075	5,374	38	12
Lake Mobutu Sese Seko (Albert), Africa	2,075	5,374	160	49
Kariba Lake, Zambia-Zimbabwe	2,050	5,310	295	90
Lake Nipigon, Canada	1,872	4,848	540	165
Lake Mweru, Zaire-Zambia	1,800	4,662	60	18
Lake Manitoba, Canada	1,799	4,659	12	4
Lake Taymyr, Russia	1,737	4,499	85	26
Lake Khanka, China-Russia	1,700	4,403	33	10
Lake Kioga, Uganda	1,700	4,403	25	8
Lake of the Woods, U.S.A.-Canada	1,679	4,349	70	21J2

ARCTIC OCEAN
CANADA BASIN
Beaufort Sea
QUEEN ELIZABETH ISLANDS
Ellesmere I.
Devon I.
GREENLAND
Wrangel I.
Pt. Barrow
Banks I.
Victoria I.
Baffin Bay
Baffin Island
Chukchi Sea
Arctic Circle
Denmark Str.
Norwegian Sea
Iceland
Mac Kenzie
Great Bear L.
Great Slave L.
Yukon
Mt. McKinley
Rocky Mountains
Peace
Hudson Bay
LABRADOR BASIN
IRMINGER BASIN
ICELAND BASIN
Great Britain
Bering Sea
Gulf of Alaska
ALEUTIAN BASIN
ALEUTIAN ISLANDS
ALEUTIAN TRENCH
NORTH AMERICA
Great Plains
CHARLIE-GIBBS FRACTURE ZONE
Ireland
Great Lakes
Newfoundland
C. Race
Appalachian Mts.
MENDOCINO FRACTURE ZONE
C. Mendocino
Missouri
Ohio
Colorado
Mississippi
C. Hatteras
ATLANTIC
MID-ATLANTIC RIDGE
Rio Grande
HAWAIIAN ISLANDS
HAWAIIAN RIDGE
MOLOKAI FRACTURE ZONE
Lower California
Tropic of Cancer
Gulf of Mexico
Cuba
WEST INDIES
−28,232 ft. (−8605 m)
Caribbean Sea
C. Verde
CLIPPERTON FRACTURE ZONE
CENTRAL PACIFIC BASIN
PACIFIC
GUATEMALA BASIN
Orinoco
Equator
Negro
Amazon
Madeira
Andes
PERU-CHILE TRENCH
ROMANCHE FRACTURE ZONE
C. de São Roque
EAST PACIFIC RISE
PERU BASIN
SOUTH AMERICA
São Francisco
BRAZIL BASIN
OCEAN
TONGA TRENCH
Tropic of Capricorn
NAZCA RIDGE
−26,457 ft. (−8064 m)
Paraná
CHILE BASIN
Cerro Aconcagua
KERMADEC TRENCH
SOUTHWEST PACIFIC BASIN
Mountains
ARGENTINE BASIN
Falkland Is.
Tierra del Fuego
−27,313 ft. (−8325 m)
C. Horn
SOUTH SANDWICH TRENCH
Drake Passage
PACIFIC-ANTARCTIC RIDGE
AMUNDSEN ABYSSAL PLAIN
Antarctic Circle
Antarctic Peninsula
WEDDELL ABYSSAL PLAIN
Bellingshausen Sea
Weddell Sea
Ross Sea
ANTARCTICA

World

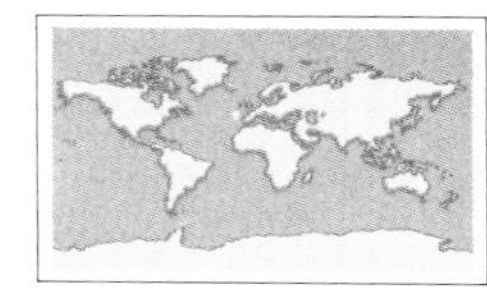

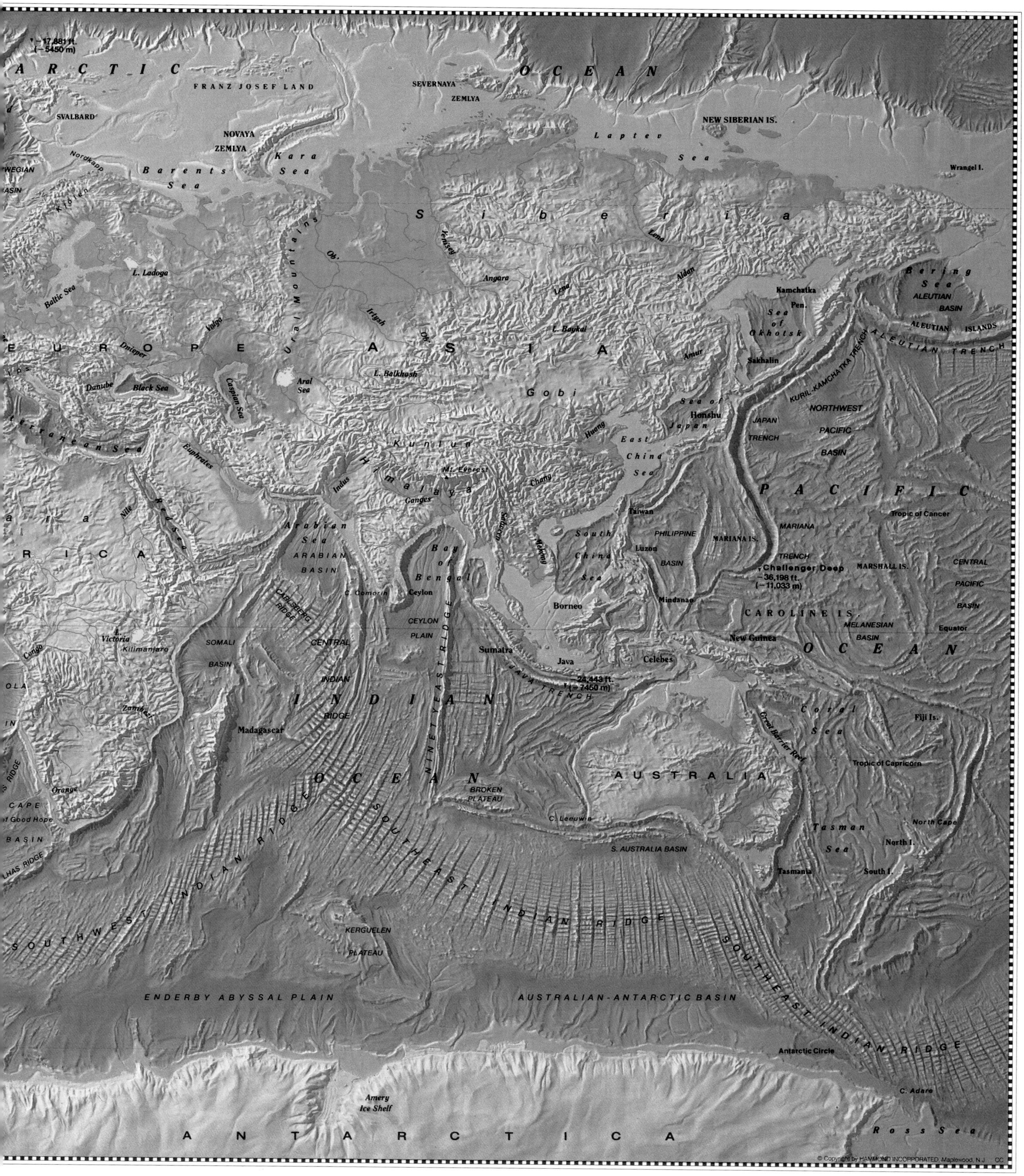

−17,881 ft. (−5450 m)
ARCTIC
OCEAN
FRANZ JOSEF LAND
SEVERNAYA ZEMLYA
SVALBARD
NEW SIBERIAN IS.
NOVAYA ZEMLYA
Laptev Sea
Kara Sea
Barents Sea
Nordkapp
Wrangel I.
Kjølen
Siberia
Ural Mountains
Ob'
Yenisey
Lena
Aldan
Bering Sea
ALEUTIAN BASIN
Kamchatka Pen.
L. Ladoga
Angara
Baltic Sea
Irtysh
Lena
Sea of Okhotsk
ALEUTIAN ISLANDS
ALEUTIAN TRENCH
Volga
L. Baykal
EUROPE
ASIA
Dnieper
Amur
Sakhalin
KURIL-KAMCHATKA TRENCH
Aral Sea
L. Balkhash
Danube
Black Sea
Caspian Sea
Gobi
Sea of Japan
Honshu
NORTHWEST PACIFIC BASIN
JAPAN TRENCH
Mediterranean Sea
Euphrates
Kunlun
Huang
East China Sea
Himalaya
Mt. Everest
Indus
Chang
PACIFIC
Nile
Red Sea
Ganges
Arabian Sea
Tropic of Cancer
Salween
Taiwan
Mekong
MARIANA
South China Sea
PHILIPPINE BASIN
MARIANA IS.
Luzon
ARABIAN BASIN
Bay of Bengal
TRENCH
Challenger Deep −36,198 ft. (−11,033 m)
MARSHALL IS.
CENTRAL PACIFIC BASIN
AFRICA
C. Comorin
Ceylon
CARLSBERG RIDGE
Borneo
Mindanao
CAROLINE IS.
CEYLON PLAIN
MELANESIAN BASIN
Equator
L. Victoria
Kilimanjaro
SOMALI BASIN
CENTRAL INDIAN RIDGE
Sumatra
New Guinea
OCEAN
Congo
Java
Celebes
NINETYEAST RIDGE
JAVA TRENCH
−24,443 ft. (−7450 m)
INDIAN
Zambezi
Coral Sea
Great Barrier Reef
Fiji Is.
Madagascar
OCEAN
AUSTRALIA
Tropic of Capricorn
Orange
BROKEN PLATEAU
CAPE of Good Hope BASIN
C. Leeuwin
North Cape
Tasman Sea
North I.
AGULHAS RIDGE
S. AUSTRALIA BASIN
Tasmania
South I.
SOUTHWEST INDIAN RIDGE
SOUTHEAST INDIAN RIDGE
KERGUELEN PLATEAU
ENDERBY ABYSSAL PLAIN
AUSTRALIAN-ANTARCTIC BASIN
SOUTHEAST INDIAN RIDGE
Antarctic Circle
Amery Ice Shelf
C. Adare
Ross Sea
ANTARCTICA

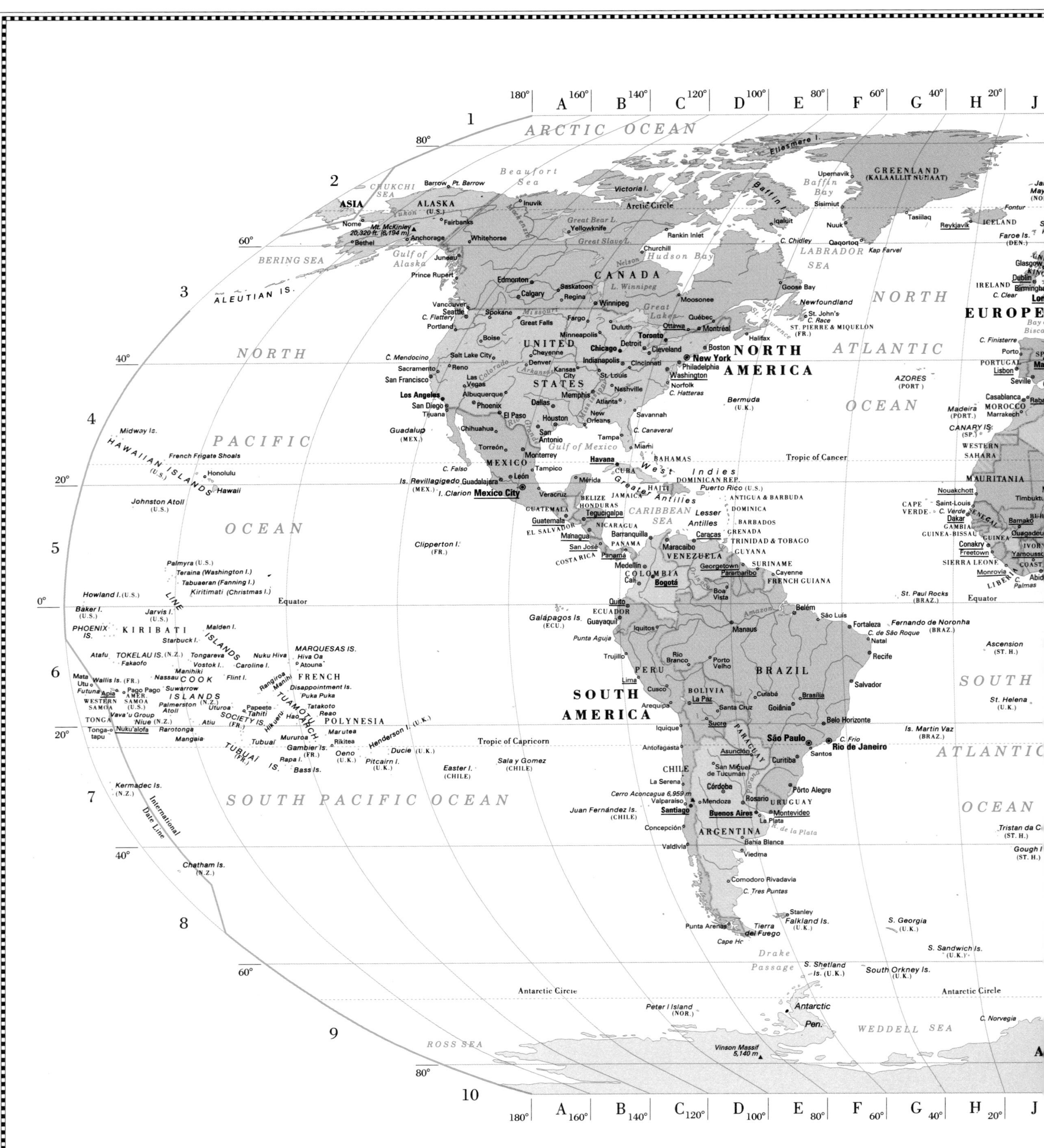

180°
A 160°
B 140°
C 120°
D 100°
E 80°
F 60°
G 40°
H 20°
J
1
2
3
4
5
6
7
8
9
10
80°
60°
40°
20°
0°
ARCTIC OCEAN
Ellesmere I.
Beaufort Sea
CHUKCHI SEA
ASIA
Barrow
Pt. Barrow
ALASKA (U.S.)
Inuvik
Victoria I.
Arctic Circle
GREENLAND (KALAALLIT NUNAAT)
Upernavik
Baffin Bay
Baffin I.
Sisimiut
Nome
Mt. McKinley 20,320 ft. (6,194 m)
Fairbanks
Great Bear L.
Yellowknife
Iqaluit
Nuuk
Tasiilaq
Reykjavik
ICELAND
Bethel
Anchorage
Whitehorse
Great Slave L.
Rankin Inlet
C. Chidley
Qaqortoq
Kap Farvel
Faroe Is. (DEN.)
BERING SEA
Gulf of Alaska
Juneau
Churchill
Hudson Bay
LABRADOR SEA
Prince Rupert
Edmonton
Saskatoon
CANADA
L. Winnipeg
Goose Bay
NORTH
IRELAND
C. Clear
Dublin
ALEUTIAN IS.
Calgary
Regina
Moosonee
Newfoundland
Vancouver
Seattle
C. Flattery
Portland
Spokane
Great Falls
Winnipeg
Great Lakes
Québec
Montréal
Ottawa
St. John's
C. Race
ST. PIERRE & MIQUELON (FR.)
EUROPE
Fargo
Duluth
Toronto
Halifax
C. Finisterre
Porto
Minneapolis
Boise
UNITED STATES
Detroit
Boston
NORTH AMERICA
ATLANTIC
NORTH
C. Mendocino
Cheyenne
Salt Lake City
Chicago
Cleveland
New York
Philadelphia
Washington
PORTUGAL
Lisbon
Sacramento
Reno
Denver
Indianapolis
Cincinnati
San Francisco
Las Vegas
Kansas City
St. Louis
Norfolk
C. Hatteras
AZORES (PORT.)
Seville
Nashville
Los Angeles
San Diego
Tijuana
Albuquerque
Phoenix
Memphis
Atlanta
Bermuda (U.K.)
OCEAN
Casablanca
Madeira (PORT.)
MOROCCO
Marrakech
Dallas
El Paso
Houston
New Orleans
Savannah
Midway Is.
PACIFIC
Guadalupe (MEX.)
Chihuahua
San Antonio
C. Canaveral
CANARY IS. (SP.)
HAWAIIAN ISLANDS (U.S.)
Torreón
Monterrey
Gulf of Mexico
Tampa
Miami
WESTERN SAHARA
French Frigate Shoals
Honolulu
Hawaii
MEXICO
C. Falso
Havana
BAHAMAS
Tropic of Cancer
Tampico
CUBA
West Indies
Is. Revillagigedo (MEX.)
Guadalajara
León
Mérida
Greater Antilles
HAITI
DOMINICAN REP.
Puerto Rico (U.S.)
MAURITANIA
Johnston Atoll (U.S.)
I. Clarion
Mexico City
Veracruz
BELIZE
JAMAICA
ANTIGUA & BARBUDA
Nouakchott
HONDURAS
Tegucigalpa
GUATEMALA
Guatemala
EL SALVADOR
CARIBBEAN SEA
Lesser Antilles
DOMINICA
BARBADOS
CAPE VERDE
Saint-Louis
C. Verde
Dakar
GAMBIA
GUINEA-BISSAU
OCEAN
NICARAGUA
Managua
Barranquilla
Caracas
GRENADA
TRINIDAD & TOBAGO
Clipperton I. (FR.)
San José
COSTA RICA
PANAMA
Panamá
Maracaibo
VENEZUELA
GUYANA
Georgetown
Paramaribo
SURINAME
Cayenne
FRENCH GUIANA
SIERRA LEONE
Monrovia
LIBERIA
C. Palmas
Palmyra (U.S.)
Teraina (Washington I.)
Tabuaeran (Fanning I.)
Kiritimati (Christmas I.)
Medellín
Cali
COLOMBIA
Bogotá
Boa Vista
Howland I. (U.S.)
LINE
Equator
Quito
ECUADOR
Guayaquil
Amazon
Belém
São Luís
St. Paul Rocks (BRAZ.)
Equator
Baker I. (U.S.)
Jarvis I. (U.S.)
PHOENIX IS.
KIRIBATI
Malden I.
Galápagos Is. (ECU.)
Iquitos
Manaus
Fortaleza
Fernando de Noronha (BRAZ.)
C. de São Roque
Natal
Starbuck I.
ISLANDS
Punta Aguja
Ascension (ST. H.)
Atafu
TOKELAU IS. (N.Z.)
Fakaofo
Tongareva
Vostok I.
Caroline I.
Nuku Hiva
MARQUESAS IS.
Hiva Oa
Atuona
Trujillo
Rio Branco
Porto Velho
Recife
Manihiki
Nassau
COOK
Flint I.
Rangiroa
Manihi
FRENCH
PERU
BRAZIL
Wallis Is. (FR.)
Futuna
Apia
Pago Pago
AMER. SAMOA (U.S.)
WESTERN SAMOA
Suwarrow
ISLANDS
Palmerston
Uturoa
Papeete
Tahiti
Disappointment Is.
Puka Puka
Lima
Cusco
BOLIVIA
La Paz
Cuiabá
Brasília
Salvador
SOUTH
Vava'u Group
TONGA
Niue (N.Z.)
Atiu
SOCIETY IS. (FR.)
Hikueru
TUAMOTU
Tatakoto
Reao
Hao
POLYNESIA
SOUTH AMERICA
Arequipa
Santa Cruz
Goiânia
St. Helena (U.K.)
Tonga-tapu
Nuku'alofa
Rarotonga
Mangaia
Tubuai
Mururoa
Marutea
Rikitea
Henderson I. (U.K.)
Iquique
Sucre
PARAGUAY
Belo Horizonte
São Paulo
Rio de Janeiro
C. Frio
Santos
Is. Martin Vaz (BRAZ.)
Tropic of Capricorn
Antofagasta
Asunción
TUBUAI IS. (FR.)
Gambier Is. (FR.)
Rapa I.
Bass Is.
Oeno (U.K.)
Ducie (U.K.)
Pitcairn I. (U.K.)
Easter I. (CHILE)
Sala y Gomez (CHILE)
CHILE
San Miguel de Tucumán
Curitiba
ATLANTIC
La Serena
Córdoba
Pôrto Alegre
Kermadec Is. (N.Z.)
SOUTH PACIFIC OCEAN
Cerro Aconcagua 6,959 m
Valparaíso
Mendoza
Rosario
URUGUAY
Santiago
Buenos Aires
Montevideo
La Plata
Juan Fernández Is. (CHILE)
R. de la Plata
OCEAN
International Date Line
Concepción
ARGENTINA
Tristan da C (ST. H.)
Valdivia
Bahía Blanca
Gough I (ST. H.)
Chatham Is. (N.Z.)
Viedma
Comodoro Rivadavia
C. Tres Puntas
Stanley
Falkland Is. (U.K.)
S. Georgia (U.K.)
Punta Arenas
Tierra del Fuego
Cape Ho
S. Sandwich Is. (U.K.)
Drake Passage
S. Shetland Is. (U.K.)
South Orkney Is. (U.K.)
Antarctic Circle
Peter I Island (NOR.)
Antarctic Pen.
C. Norvegia
WEDDELL SEA
ROSS SEA
Vinson Massif 5,140 m

World

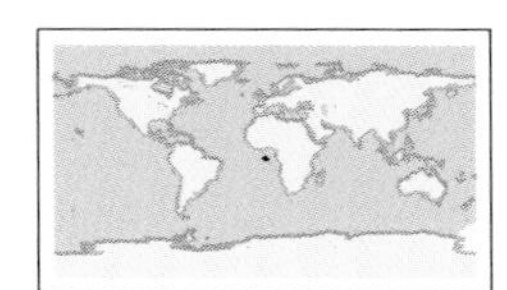

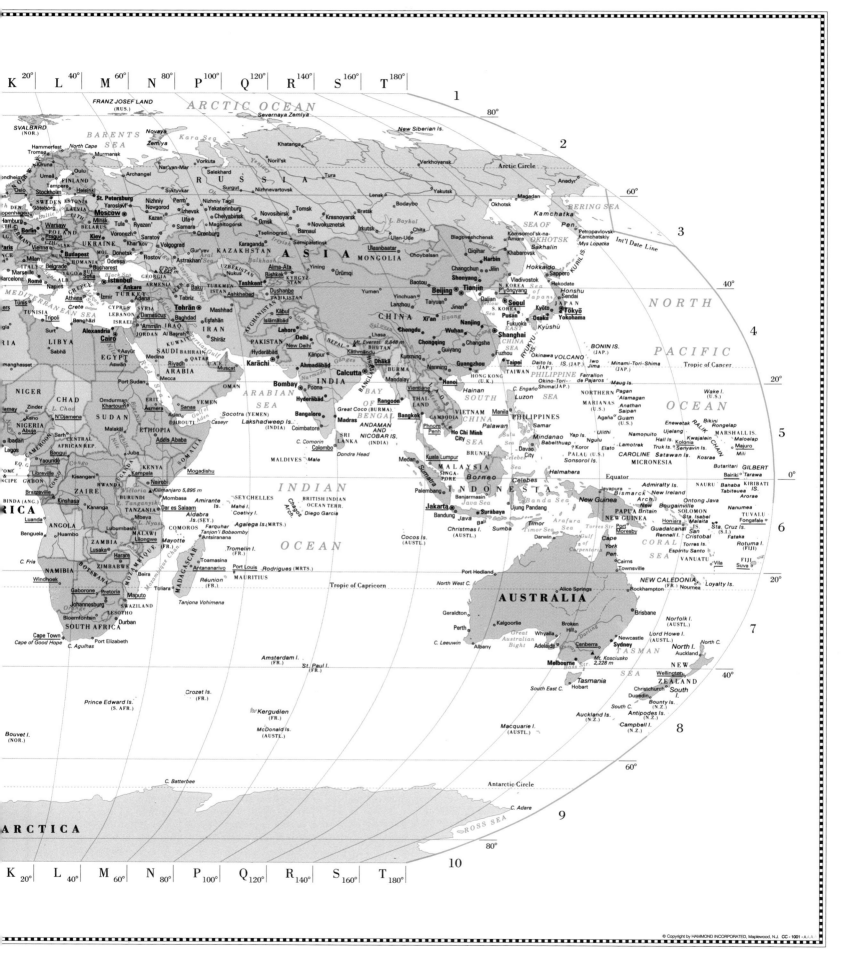

POPULATION OF CITIES AND TOWNS

- ◉ OVER 5,000,000
- ● 2,000,000 - 4,999,999
- ◎ 500,000 - 1,999,999
- ○ UNDER 500,000

SCALE 1:81,700,000 ROBINSON PROJECTION STANDARD PARALLELS 38°N AND 38°S

MILES 0 1000 2000 3000 4000

KILOMETERS 0 1000 2000 3000 4000

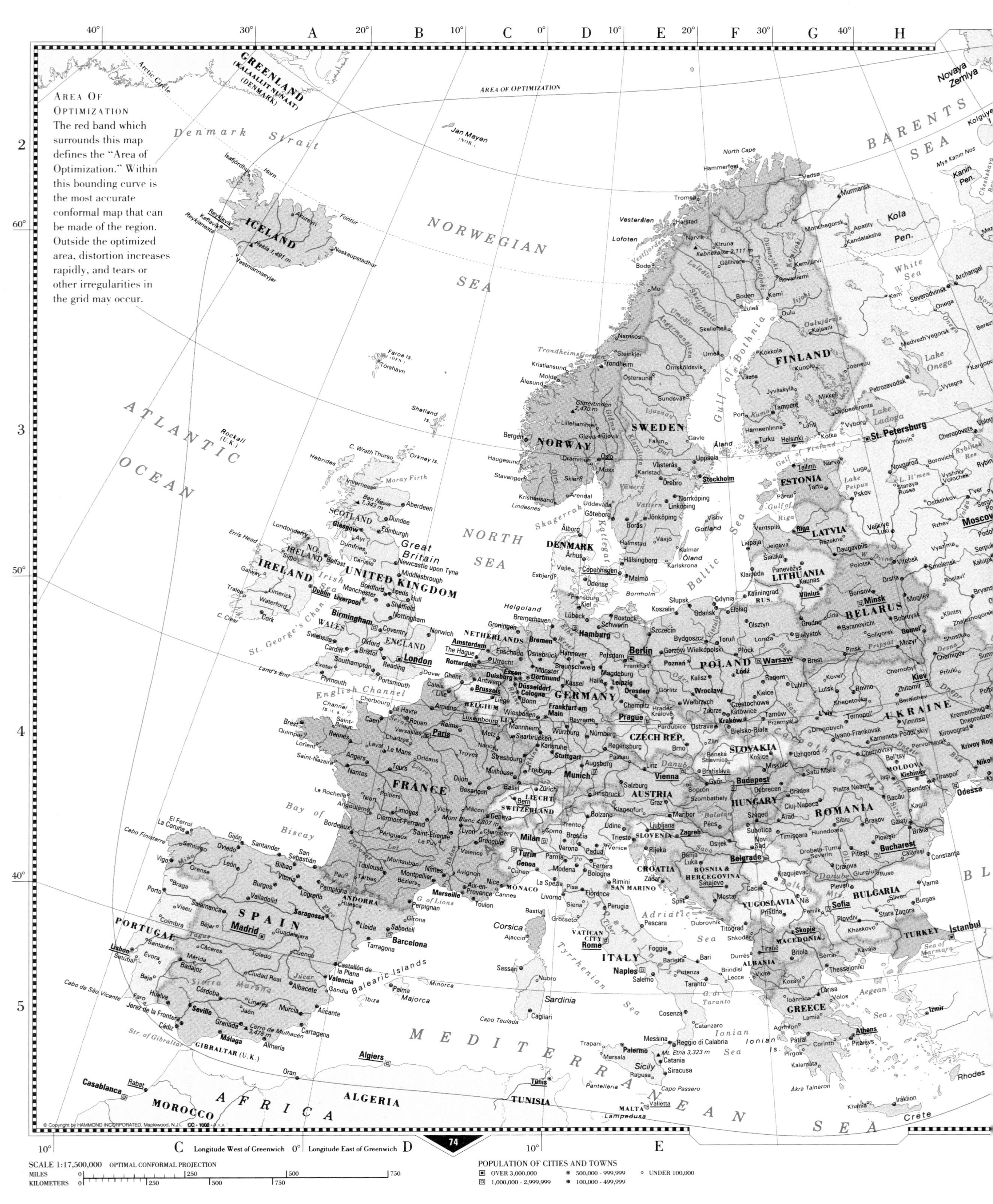

AREA OF OPTIMIZATION
The red band which surrounds this map defines the "Area of Optimization." Within this bounding curve is the most accurate conformal map that can be made of the region. Outside the optimized area, distortion increases rapidly, and tears or other irregularities in the grid may occur.
AREA OF OPTIMIZATION
GREENLAND (KALAALLIT NUNAAT) (DENMARK)
Arctic Circle
Denmark Strait
ICELAND
Reykjavík
Akureyri
Hekla 1,491 m
Jan Mayen (NOR.)
NORWEGIAN SEA
BARENTS SEA
Novaya Zemlya
North Cape
Kola Pen.
White Sea
Faroe Is. (DEN.)
Tórshavn
Shetland Is.
Rockall (U.K.)
ATLANTIC OCEAN
NORWAY
SWEDEN
FINLAND
Gulf of Bothnia
Oslo
Stockholm
Helsinki
St. Petersburg
Tallinn
ESTONIA
Riga
LATVIA
Vilnius
LITHUANIA
Minsk
BELARUS
Moscow
NORTH SEA
Baltic Sea
Skagerrak
Kattegat
DENMARK
Copenhagen
Orkney Is.
Hebrides
Great Britain
SCOTLAND
Edinburgh
Glasgow
NO. IRELAND
Belfast
IRELAND
Dublin
UNITED KINGDOM
WALES
ENGLAND
London
Irish Sea
St. George's Chan.
English Channel
Channel Is. (U.K.)
NETHERLANDS
Amsterdam
The Hague
BELGIUM
Brussels
LUX.
Luxembourg
GERMANY
Berlin
Hamburg
Munich
POLAND
Warsaw
CZECH REP.
Prague
SLOVAKIA
AUSTRIA
Vienna
HUNGARY
Budapest
UKRAINE
Kiev
MOLDOVA
Kishinev
ROMANIA
Bucharest
FRANCE
Paris
SWITZERLAND
Bern
LIECHT.
Mont Blanc 4,807 m
Bay of Biscay
SPAIN
Madrid
PORTUGAL
Lisbon
ANDORRA
MONACO
ITALY
Rome
VATICAN CITY
SAN MARINO
SLOVENIA
Ljubljana
CROATIA
Zagreb
BOSNIA & HERCEGOVINA
Sarajevo
YUGOSLAVIA
Belgrade
MACEDONIA
Skopje
ALBANIA
Tiranë
BULGARIA
Sofia
GREECE
Athens
TURKEY
Istanbul
Sea of Marmara
Aegean Sea
Ionian Sea
Adriatic Sea
Tyrrhenian Sea
Corsica
Sardinia
Sicily
Balearic Islands
MALTA
Valletta
Crete
Rhodes
MEDITERRANEAN SEA
Str. of Gibraltar
GIBRALTAR (U.K.)
MOROCCO
Rabat
Casablanca
ALGERIA
Algiers
TUNISIA
Tunis
AFRICA
© Copyright by HAMMOND INCORPORATED, Maplewood, N.J.
Longitude West of Greenwich 0° Longitude East of Greenwich
SCALE 1:17,500,000 OPTIMAL CONFORMAL PROJECTION
MILES 0 250 500 750
KILOMETERS 0 250 500 750
POPULATION OF CITIES AND TOWNS
OVER 3,000,000
1,000,000 - 2,999,999
500,000 - 999,999
100,000 - 499,999
UNDER 100,000

Europe

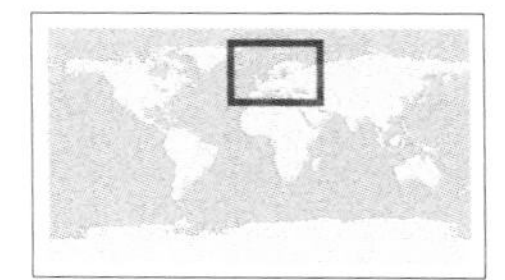

Boroughs indicated by number:

1 HAMMERSMITH & FULHAM
2 ISLINGTON
3 KENSINGTON & CHELSEA
4 CITY OF LONDON
5 SOUTHWARK
6 TOWER HAMLETS
7 WALTHAM FOREST
8 CITY OF WESTMINSTER

SCALE 1:587,000 LAMBERT CONFORMAL CONIC PROJECTION

MILES 0 10 20

KILOMETERS 0 10 20

Scandinavia and Finland, Iceland

SCALE 1:7,000,000 LAMBERT CONFORMAL CONIC PROJECTION

MILES 0 100 200 300

KILOMETERS 0 100 200 300

United Kingdom, Ireland

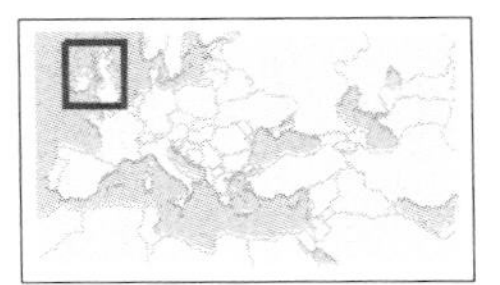

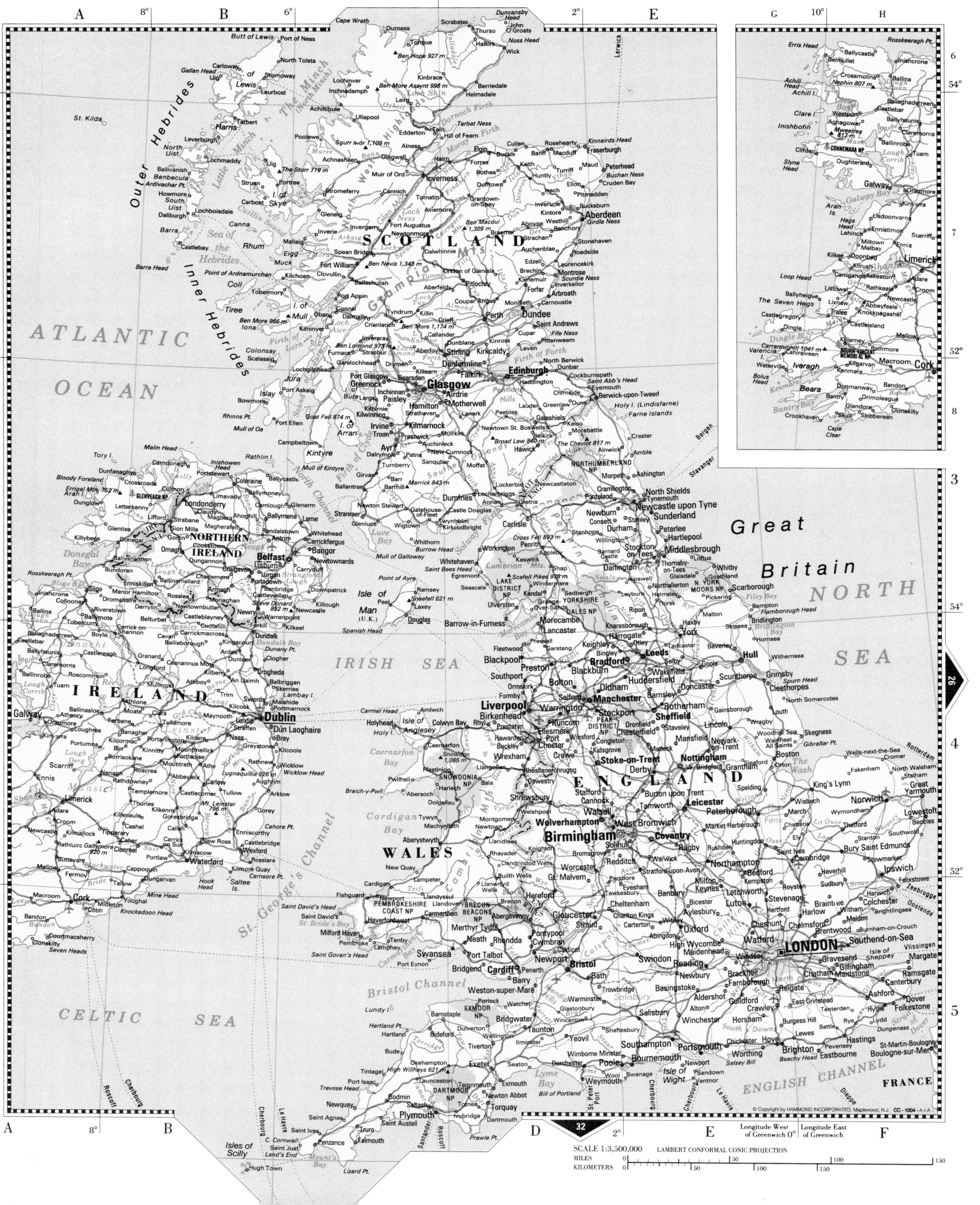

ATLANTIC OCEAN

CELTIC SEA

IRISH SEA

NORTH SEA

ENGLISH CHANNEL

SCOTLAND

NORTHERN IRELAND

IRELAND

ENGLAND

WALES

Great Britain

FRANCE

LONDON

SCALE 1:3,500,000 LAMBERT CONFORMAL CONIC PROJECTION

MILES 0 50 100

KILOMETERS 0 50 100 150

Longitude West of Greenwich 0° Longitude East of Greenwich

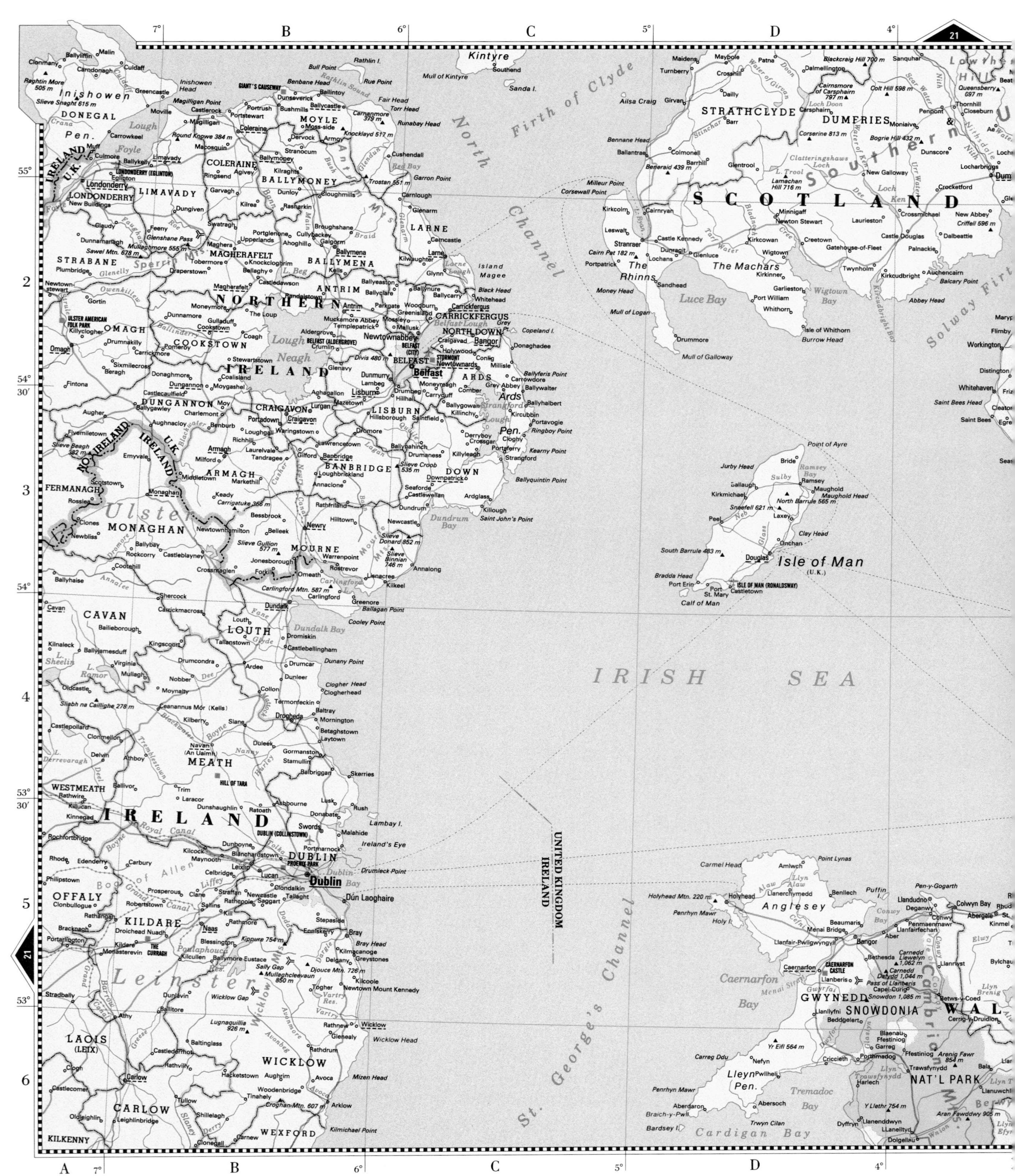

21
A
B
C
D
7°
6°
5°
4°
55°
54° 30′
54°
53° 30′
53°
2
3
4
5
6
Kintyre
Southend
Mull of Kintyre
Sanda I.
Rathlin I.
Rathlin Sound
Firth of Clyde
North Channel
Ailsa Craig
Girvan
Turnberry
Maidens
Maybole
Crosshill
Patna
Dailly
Dalmellington
Blackcraig Hill 700 m
Sanquhar
Cairnsmore of Carsphairn 797 m
Carsphairn
Colt Hill 598 m
Queensberry 697 m
Thornhill
Closeburn
Penpont
Moniaive
STRATHCLYDE
DUMFRIES
Barr
Corserine 813 m
Bogrie Hill 432 m
Dunscore
Bennane Head
Ballantrae
Colmonell
Barrhill
Benerald 439 m
Glentrool
Lamachan Hill 716 m
New Galloway
Locharbriggs
Crocketford
Milleur Point
Corsewall Point
SCOTLAND
Southern Uplands
Kirkcolm
Cairnryan
Leswalt
Stranraer
Castle Kennedy
Cairn Pat 182 m
Portpatrick
Dunragit
Lochans
Glenluce
Kirkcowan
Minnigaff
Newton Stewart
Creetown
Gatehouse-of-Fleet
Laurieston
Crossmichael
New Abbey
Criffell 596 m
Castle Douglas
Dalbeattie
Palnackie
Wigtown
The Machars
Kirkinner
Twynholm
Kirkcudbright
Auchencairn
Balcary Point
The Rhinns
Sandhead
Money Head
Luce Bay
Garlieston
Port William
Whithorn
Wigtown Bay
Abbey Head
Mull of Logan
Isle of Whithorn
Burrow Head
Drummore
Mull of Galloway
Solway Firth
Workington
Distington
Whitehaven
Saint Bees Head
Saint Bees
Point of Ayre
Bride
Jurby Head
Ramsey Bay
Ramsey
Sulby
Ballaugh
Kirkmichael
Maughold
Maughold Head
North Barrule 565 m
Snaefell 621 m
Laxey
Peel
Clay Head
Onchan
South Barrule 483 m
Douglas
Isle of Man (U.K.)
Bradda Head
Port Erin
Port St. Mary
Castletown
ISLE OF MAN (RONALDSWAY)
Calf of Man
IRISH SEA
UNITED KINGDOM
IRELAND
St. George's Channel
Cardigan Bay
Malin
Ballyliffin
Clonmany
Carndonagh
Culdaff
Raghtin More 505 m
Inishowen
Slieve Snaght 615 m
Inishowen Head
Greencastle
Moville
DONEGAL
Crana
Pen.
Carrowkeel
Lough Foyle
Muff
Culmore
IRELAND
U.K.
Londonderry
LONDONDERRY
LONDONDERRY (EGLINTON)
Eglinton
New Buildings
Ballykelly
Limavady
LIMAVADY
Magilligan Point
Castlerock
Magilligan
Round Knowe 384 m
Macosquin
Coleraine
COLERAINE
Agivey
Ringsend
Garvagh
Kilrea
Dungiven
Portrush
Portstewart
Bushmills
GIANT'S CAUSEWAY
Benbane Head
Dunseverick
Ballintoy
Ballycastle
MOYLE
Moss-side
Armoy
Carnanmore 379 m
Knocklayd 517 m
Fair Head
Torr Head
Runabay Head
Cushendall
Red Bay
Garron Point
Trostan 551 m
Bull Point
Rue Point
Dervock
Stranocum
Ballymoney
BALLYMONEY
Kilraghts
Dunloy
Cloughmills
Rasharkin
Carnlough
Glenarm
LARNE
Carncastle
Larne
Kilwaughter
Glaudy
Feeny
Glenshane Pass
Dunnamanagh
Sawel Mtn. 678 m
Mullaghmore 555 m
Swatragh
Maghera
MAGHERAFELT
Tobermore
Portglenone
Upperlands
Cullybackey
Ahoghill
Broughshane
Galgorm
Ballymena
BALLYMENA
Kells
Knockcloghrim
Draperstown
Bellaghy
L. Beg
Castledawson
Sperrin Mts.
STRABANE
Plumbridge
Glenelly
Newtownstewart
Gortin
Owenkillew
ULSTER AMERICAN FOLK PARK
Killyclogher
OMAGH
Omagh
Drumnakilly
Sixmilecross
Beragh
Fintona
Magherafelt
Randalstown
ANTRIM
Antrim
Ballyclare
Ballyeaston
Ballynure
Ballycarry
Parkgate
Woodburn
Carrickfergus
CARRICKFERGUS
Whitehead
Black Head
Island Magee
Glynn
Lorne Lough
Greenisland
NORTHERN IRELAND
Moneymore
Dunnamore
Gulladuff
The Loup
Cookstown
COOKSTOWN
Coagh
Pomeroy
Carrickmore
Stewartstown
Coalisland
Donaghmore
Dungannon
Moygashel
Castlecaulfield
DUNGANNON
Moy
Charlemont
Ballygawley
Augher
Aughnacloy
Benburb
Lough Neagh
Aldergrove
BELFAST (ALDERGROVE)
Crumlin
Muckamore Abbey
Templepatrick
Mossley
Mallusk
Newtownabbey
BELFAST (CITY)
Belfast Lough
NORTH DOWN
Holywood
Bangor
Grey Point
Craigavad
Copeland I.
Donaghadee
Divis 480 m
BELFAST
Belfast
STORMONT
Newtownards
Conlig
Millisle
Glenavy
Dunmurry
Lambeg
Lisburn
Moneyreagh
Carryduff
Comber
ARDS
Grey Abbey
Ballywalter
Ballyferis Point
Carrowdore
Drumbeg
Hillhall
LISBURN
Hillsborough
Saintfield
Ballygowan
Killinchy
Strangford Lough
Ards Pen.
Kircubbin
Ballyhalbert
Portavogie
Ringboy Point
Cloghy
Portaferry
Kearny Point
Strangford
Derryboy
Crossgar
Killyleagh
Aghagallon
Lurgan
Maze
CRAIGAVON
Craigavon
Portadown
Waringstown
Dromore
Loughgall
Richhill
Laurelvale
Tandragee
Lawrencetown
Gilford
Banbridge
BANBRIDGE
Ballynahinch
Drumaness
Slieve Croob 535 m
DOWN
Downpatrick
Ballyquintin Point
Fivemiletown
Slieve Beagh 382 m
N. IRELAND
IRELAND
U.K.
Emyvale
Armagh
Milford
ARMAGH
Markethill
Middletown
Loughbrickland
Annaclone
Seaforde
Castlewellan
Ardglass
Killough
Saint John's Point
Scotstown
FERMANAGH
Monaghan
Rossle
Keady
Carrigatuke 365 m
Bessbrook
Rathfriland
Dundrum
Dundrum Bay
Ulster
Clones
Newbliss
MONAGHAN
Newtownhamilton
Belleek
Newry
Hilltown
Newcastle
Slieve Donard 852 m
Slieve Binnian 746 m
Annalong
Ballybay
Rockcorry
Castleblayney
Slieve Gullion 577 m
MOURNE
Mourne Mts.
Warrenpoint
Rostrevor
Jonesborough
Forkill
Crossmaglen
Cootehill
Omeath
Carlingford Lough
Lisnacree
Kilkeel
Ballyhaise
Annalee
Carlingford Mtn. 587 m
Carlingford
Greenore
Ballagan Point
Shercock
Cavan
CAVAN
Carrickmacross
Dundalk
Dundalk Bay
Cooley Point
Bailieborough
Louth
LOUTH
Tallanstown
Dromiskin
Castlebellingham
Kingscourt
Glyde
Kilnaleck
L. Sheelin
Ballyjamesduff
Virginia
L. Ramor
Mullagh
Drumcondra
Ardee
Drumcar
Dunany Point
Oldcastle
Nobber
Moynalty
Dee
Dunleer
Collon
Clogher Head
Clogherhead
Slíabh na Caillíghe 278 m
Ceanannus Mór (Kells)
Termonfeckin
Drogheda
Baltray
Mornington
Betaghstown
Laytown
Kilberry
Slane
Boyne
Blackwater
Castlepollard
Clonmellon
L. Derrevaragh
Delvin
Athboy
Navan (An Uaimh)
Duleek
Gormanston
Stamullin
Balbriggan
Skerries
MEATH
HILL OF TARA
WESTMEATH
Ballivor
Rathwire
Trim
Laracor
Dunshaughlin
Ratoath
Ashbourne
Lusk
Rush
Donabate
Lambay I.
Killucan
Kinnegad
IRELAND
Swords
DUBLIN (COLLINSTOWN)
Malahide
Ireland's Eye
Rochfortbridge
Royal Canal
Dunboyne
Portmarnock
Kilcock
Blanchardstown
DUBLIN
Maynooth
Leixlip
PHOENIX PARK
Rhode
Edenderry
Carbury
Celbridge
Lucan
Dublin Bay
Drumleck Point
Philipstown
Bog of Allen
Grand Canal
Clondalkin
Dublin
Prosperous
Clane
Straffan
Newcastle
Rathcoole
Saggart
Tallaght
Dún Laoghaire
OFFALY
Clonbullogue
Robertstown
Sallins
Kill
Rathangan
KILDARE
Naas
Rathmore
Stepaside
Enniskerry
Bray
Bray Head
Brackagh
Portarlington
Droichead Nuadh
Kildare
Monasterevin
THE CURRAGH
Blessington
Kippure 754 m
Poulaphouca Res.
Kilcullen
Ballymore Eustace
Sally Gap
Mullaghcleevaun 850 m
Djouce Mtn. 726 m
Kilmacanoge
Delgany
Greystones
Kilcoole
Newtown Mount Kennedy
Leinster
Wicklow Mts.
Dunlavin
Wicklow Gap
Togher
Vartry Res.
Stradbally
Ballitore
Athy
Barrow
Lugnaquilla 926 m
Rathnew
Wicklow
Glenealy
Wicklow Head
LAOIS (LEIX)
Baltinglass
Castledermot
Rathdrum
Rathvilly
Avonbeg
Avonmore
WICKLOW
Clogh
Carlow
Hacketstown
Aughrim
Avoca
Mizen Head
Castlecomer
Tullow
Woodenbridge
Tinahely
CARLOW
Croghan Mtn. 607 m
Arklow
Leighlinbridge
Oldleighlin
Shillelagh
Slaney
Derry
Kilmichael Point
KILKENNY
Carnew
Clonegall
WEXFORD
Carmel Head
Amlwch
Point Lynas
Llyn Alaw
Llanerchymedd
Benllech
Puffin I.
Pen-y-Gogarth
Holyhead Mtn. 220 m
Holyhead
Anglesey
Llandudno
Deganwy
Colwyn Bay
Penrhyn Mawr
Holy I.
Conwy Bay
Conwy
Abergele
Beaumaris
Penmaenmawr
Llanfairfechan
Menai Bridge
Llanfair-Pwllgwyngyll
Bangor
Aber
Bethesda
Carnedd Llewelyn 1,062 m
Carnedd Dafydd 1,044 m
Llanrwst
Caernarfon
CAERNARFON CASTLE
Llanberis
Pass of Llanberis
Capel-Curig
Snowdon 1,085 m
Caernarfon Bay
Menai Strait
Betws-y-Coed
GWYNEDD
SNOWDONIA
WALES
Cambrian Mts.
Llanllyfni
Beddgelert
Cerrig-y-Druidion
Blaenau Ffestiniog
Garreg
Yr Eifl 564 m
Carreg Ddu
Nefyn
Criccieth
Porthmadog
Ffestiniog
Arenig Fawr 854 m
Trawsfynydd
Bala
Lleyn Pen.
Pwllheli
Harlech
Trawsfynydd
NAT'L PARK
Penrhyn Mawr
Aberdaron
Abersoch
Tremadoc Bay
Y Llethr 754 m
Aran Fawddwy 905 m
Braich-y-Pwll
Trwyn Cilan
Llanenddwyn
Bardsey I.
Dyffryn
Llanelltyd
Dolgellau

Northeastern Ireland, Northern England and Wales

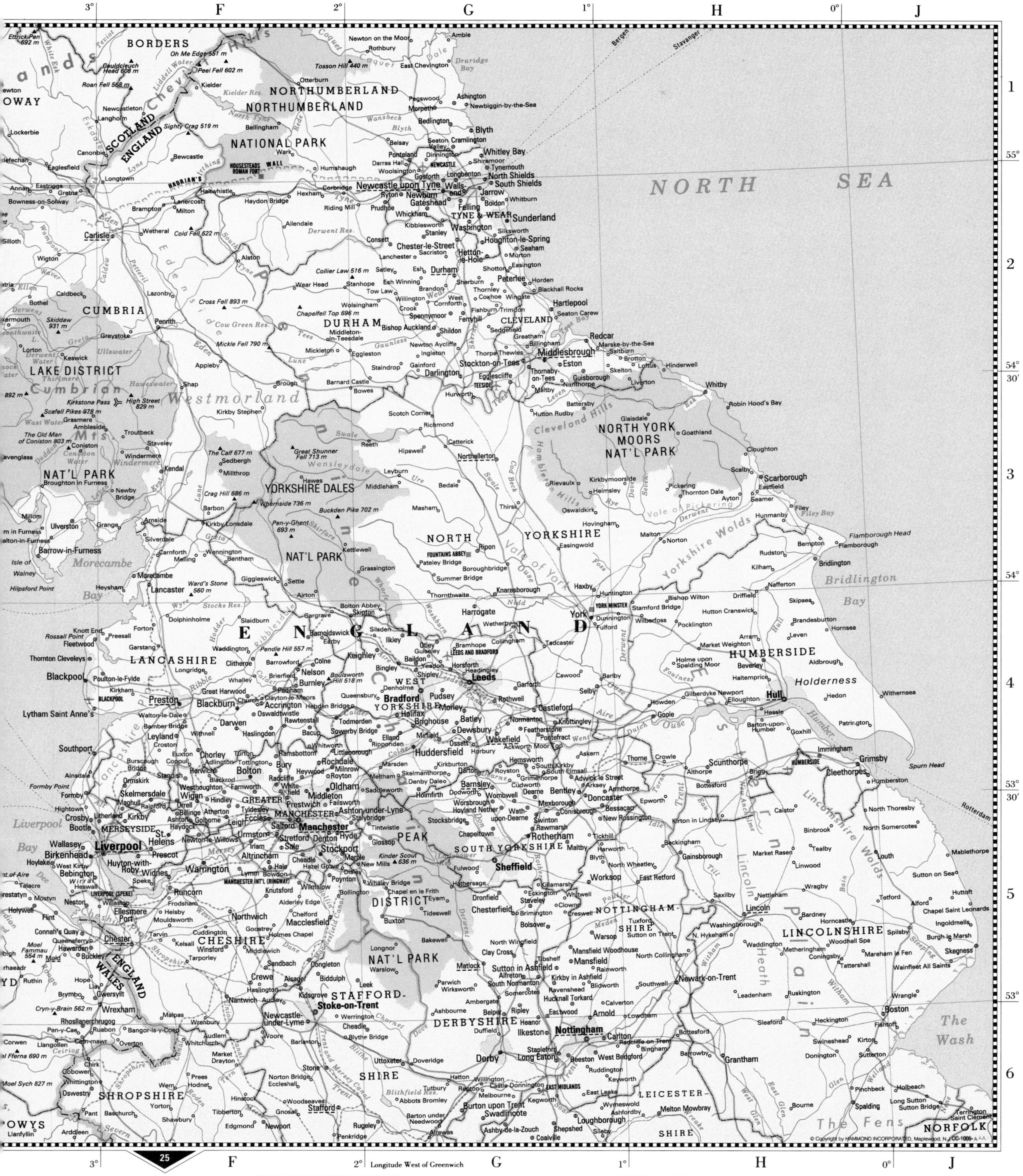

3° F 2° G 1° H 0° J

NORTH SEA

BORDERS · NORTHUMBERLAND · NORTHUMBERLAND NATIONAL PARK · DURHAM · CLEVELAND · CUMBRIA · LAKE DISTRICT NAT'L PARK · NORTH YORK MOORS NAT'L PARK · YORKSHIRE DALES NAT'L PARK · NORTH YORKSHIRE · LANCASHIRE · WEST YORKSHIRE · HUMBERSIDE · GREATER MANCHESTER · MERSEYSIDE · SOUTH YORKSHIRE · PEAK DISTRICT NAT'L PARK · CHESHIRE · STAFFORDSHIRE · DERBYSHIRE · NOTTINGHAMSHIRE · LINCOLNSHIRE · LEICESTERSHIRE · SHROPSHIRE · NORFOLK · ENGLAND · WALES · SCOTLAND

3° F 2° Longitude West of Greenwich G 1° H 0° J

25

POPULATION OF CITIES AND TOWNS

OVER 2,000,000	500,000 - 999,999	100,000 - 249,999	10,000 - 29,999
1,000,000 - 1,999,999	250,000 - 499,999	30,000 - 99,999	UNDER 10,000

SCALE 1:1,170,000 LAMBERT CONFORMAL CONIC PROJECTION

MILES 0 10 20 30 40 50

KILOMETERS 0 10 20 30 40 50

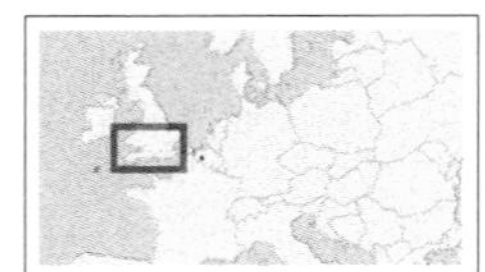

Southern England and Wales

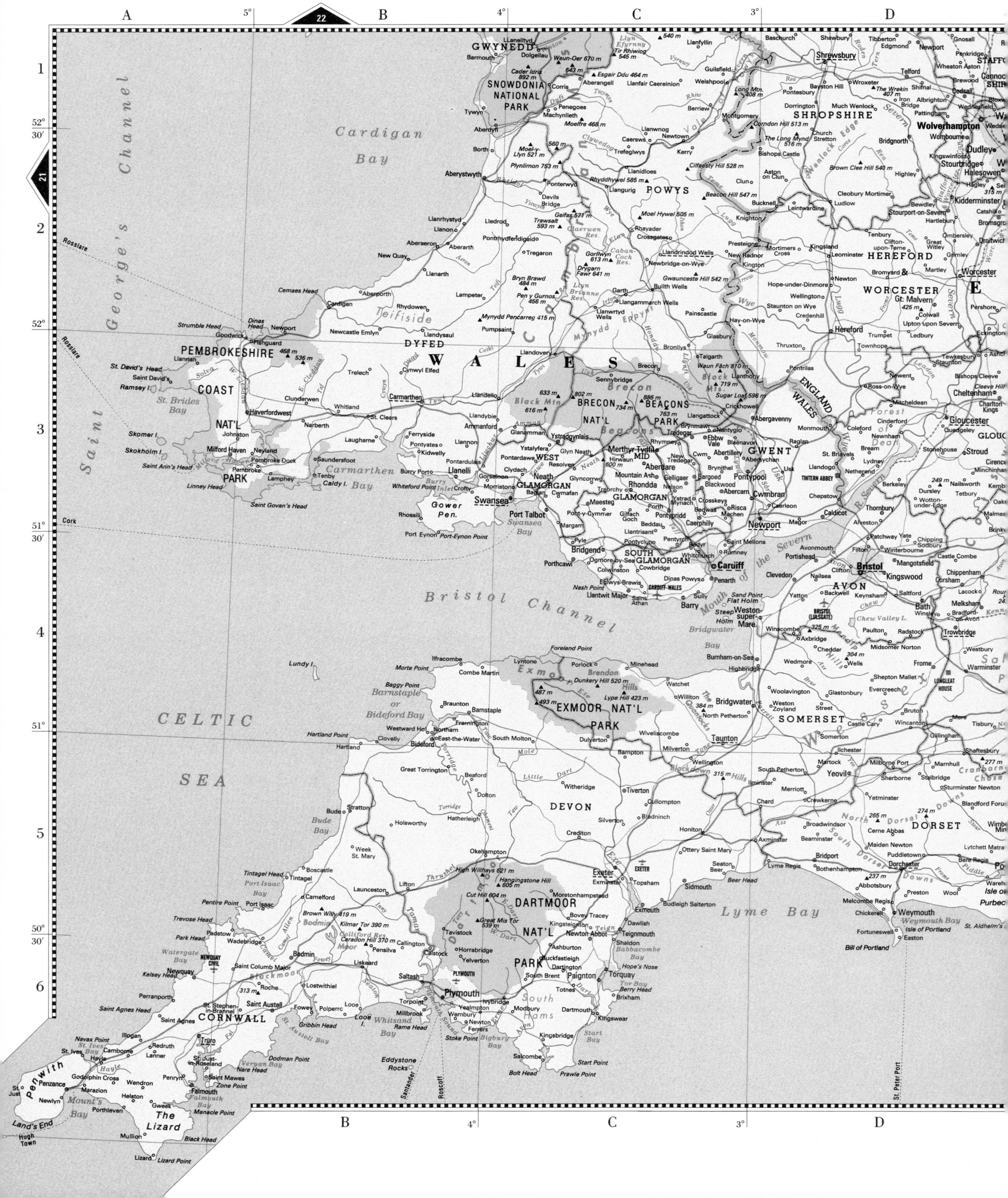

A 5° B 4° C 3° D

22 21

1 2 3 4 5 6

52° 30′ 52° 51° 30′ 51° 50° 30′

GWYNEDD
SNOWDONIA NATIONAL PARK
Cardigan Bay
Saint George's Channel
Rosslare
Cork
POWYS
SHROPSHIRE
Shrewsbury
Wolverhampton
Dudley
Kidderminster
HEREFORD & WORCESTER
Worcester
Hereford
Aberystwyth
Cardigan
Teifiside
DYFED
WALES
PEMBROKESHIRE COAST NAT'L PARK
St. David's Head
Ramsey I.
St. Brides Bay
Skomer I.
Skokholm I.
Haverfordwest
Milford Haven
Carmarthen
Carmarthen Bay
BRECON BEACONS NAT'L PARK
Black Mts.
GWENT
Abergavenny
Newport
MID GLAMORGAN
WEST GLAMORGAN
SOUTH GLAMORGAN
Swansea
Gower Pen.
Swansea Bay
Port Talbot
Cardiff
ENGLAND WALES
Gloucester
Cheltenham
Forest of Dean
Mouth of the Severn
Bristol
AVON
Bath
Bristol Channel
Lundy I.
Barnstaple or Bideford Bay
Ilfracombe
Barnstaple
Bideford
EXMOOR NAT'L PARK
Minehead
Bridgwater Bay
Bridgwater
Taunton
SOMERSET
Yeovil
Wells
CELTIC SEA
DEVON
Exeter
Tiverton
Lyme Bay
DORSET
Dorchester
Weymouth
Isle of Portland
Bill of Portland
DARTMOOR NAT'L PARK
High Willhays 621 m
Torquay
Plymouth
Start Bay
CORNWALL
Bodmin Moor
Bude Bay
Tintagel Head
Newquay
Truro
Saint Austell
Falmouth
Penzance
Mount's Bay
Land's End
The Lizard
Lizard Point
Eddystone Rocks

E
F
G
H
23
28
32
1
2
3
4
1°
0°
52°
52° 30′
51° 30′
ENGLAND
NORTH SEA
ENGLISH CHANNEL
Strait of Dover
The Wash
LINCOLNSHIRE
LEICESTERSHIRE
NORFOLK
NORTHAMPTONSHIRE
CAMBRIDGESHIRE
WARWICKSHIRE
BEDFORDSHIRE
SUFFOLK
BUCKINGHAMSHIRE
HERTFORDSHIRE
ESSEX
OXFORDSHIRE
GREATER LONDON
LONDON
BERKSHIRE
SURREY
KENT
HAMPSHIRE
WEST SUSSEX
EAST SUSSEX
ISLE OF WIGHT
FRANCE
UNITED KINGDOM
FRANCE
NORD-P.-DE-C.
PICARDIE
The Fens
East Anglia
Breckland
North Downs
South Downs
The Weald
Birmingham
Coventry
Leicester
Northampton
Peterborough
Cambridge
Norwich
Great Yarmouth
Lowestoft
Ipswich
Colchester
Chelmsford
Oxford
Reading
Luton
Southend-on-Sea
Brighton
Southampton
Portsmouth
Canterbury
Dover
Folkestone
Hastings
Eastbourne
Calais
Boulogne-sur-Mer
Dunkerque
Hoek Van Holland
Vlissingen
Zeebrugge
Oostende
Cherbourg
Le Havre
Dieppe
Longitude West of Greenwich
Longitude East of Greenwich
© Copyright by HAMMOND INCORPORATED, Maplewood, N.J.
POPULATION OF CITIES AND TOWNS
OVER 2,000,000
1,000,000 - 1,999,999
500,000 - 999,999
250,000 - 499,999
100,000 - 249,999
30,000 - 99,999
10,000 - 29,999
UNDER 10,000
SCALE 1:1,170,000
LAMBERT CONFORMAL CONIC PROJECTION
MILES 0 10 20 30 40 50
KILOMETERS 0 10 20 30 40 50

A
B
C
D
E
F
1
2
3
4
5
2°
4°
6°
8°
10°
12°
54°
52°
50°
48°
20
25
32
33
Longitude East of Greenwich
NORTH SEA
North Frisian Islands
East Frisian Islands
West Frisian Islands
Helgoländer Bucht
DENMARK
Copenhagen
Odense
FYN
SØNDERJYLLAND
RIBE
VEJLE
VEST-SJÆLLAND
STORSTRØM
Lolland
Falster
Fehmarn
Kiel Bay
Great Britain
U.K.
NETHERLANDS
Amsterdam
The Hague
Rotterdam
BELGIUM
Brussels
Antwerp
LUXEMBOURG
Luxembourg
GERMANY
Hamburg
Bremen
Hannover
LOWER SAXONY
SCHLESWIG-HOLSTEIN
MECKLENBURG-WESTE
SAXONY-ANHALT
Magdeburg
Leipzig
THURINGIA
HESSE
NORTH RHINE-WESTPHALIA
Düsseldorf
Cologne
Dortmund
Essen
Duisburg
Bonn
RHINELAND-PALATINATE
SAARLAND
Frankfurt am Main
Stuttgart
BADEN-WÜRTTEMBERG
BAVARIA
Munich
Nürnberg
FRANCE
PARIS
NORD-PAS-DE-CALAIS
PICARDIE
CHAMPAGNE-ARDENNE
ILE-DE-FRANCE
LORRAINE
ALSACE
Strasbourg
BOURGOGNE
FRANCHE-COMTÉ
CENTRE
SWITZERLAND
AUSTRIA
TIROL
VORARLBERG

North Central Europe

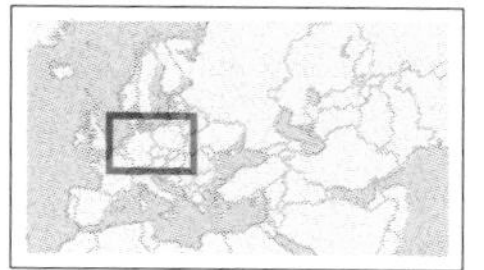

POPULATION OF CITIES AND TOWNS

- OVER 2,000,000
- 1,000,000 - 1,999,999
- 500,000 - 999,999
- 250,000 - 499,999
- 100,000 - 249,999
- 30,000 - 99,999
- 10,000 - 29,999
- UNDER 10,000

SCALE 1:3,500,000

LAMBERT CONFORMAL CONIC PROJECTION

MILES 0 50 100

KILOMETERS 0 50 100 150

Netherlands, Northwestern Germany

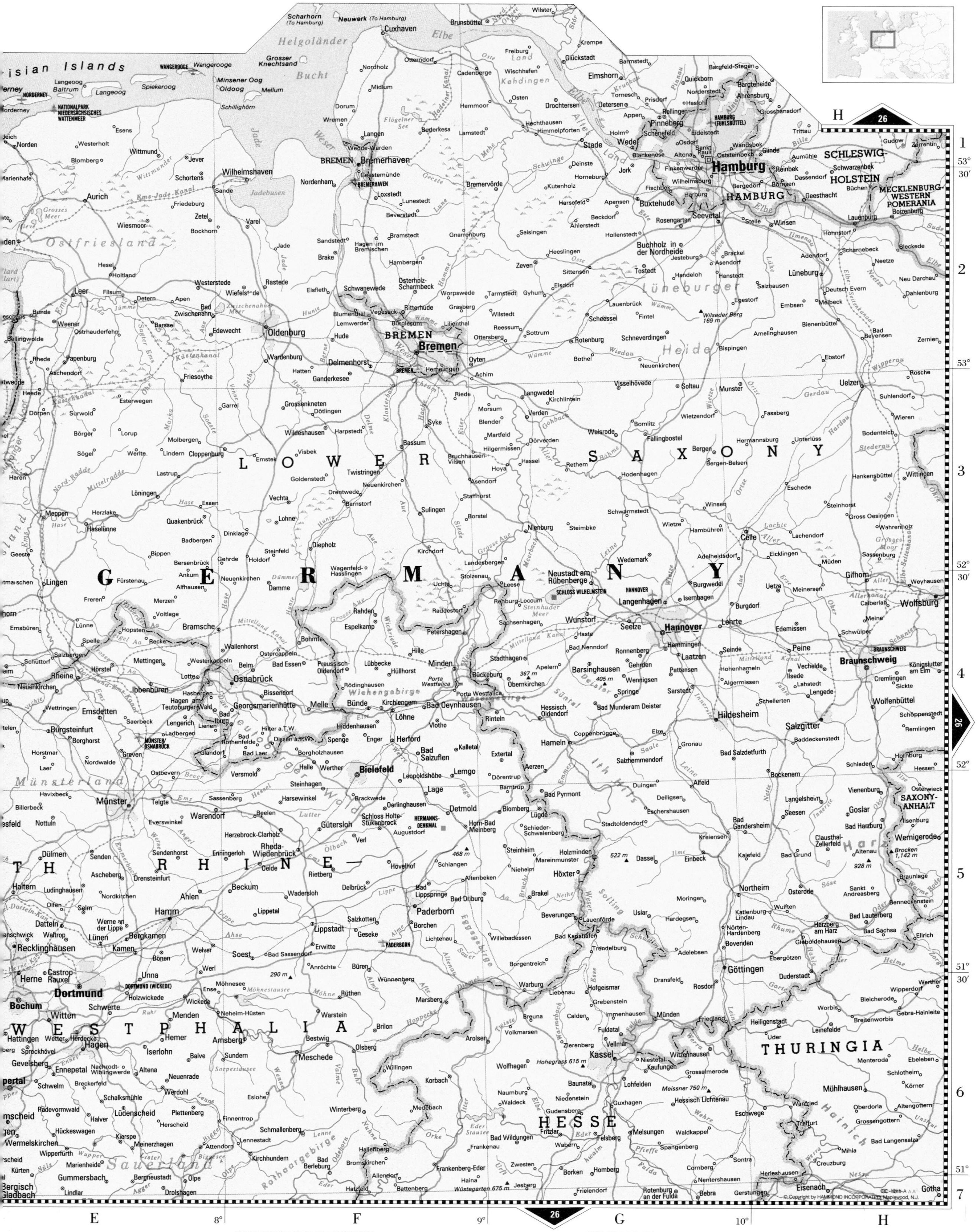

LOWER SAXONY

GERMANY

NORTH RHINE–WESTPHALIA

HESSE

THURINGIA

SAXONY-ANHALT

SCHLESWIG-HOLSTEIN

MECKLENBURG-WESTERN POMERANIA

HAMBURG

BREMEN

POPULATION OF CITIES AND TOWNS

- OVER 2,000,000
- 1,000,000 - 1,999,999
- 500,000 - 999,999
- 250,000 - 499,999
- 100,000 - 249,999
- 30,000 - 99,999
- 10,000 - 29,999
- UNDER 10,000

SCALE 1:1,170,000 LAMBERT CONFORMAL CONIC PROJECTION

MILES 0 10 20 30 40 50

KILOMETERS 0 10 20 30 40 50

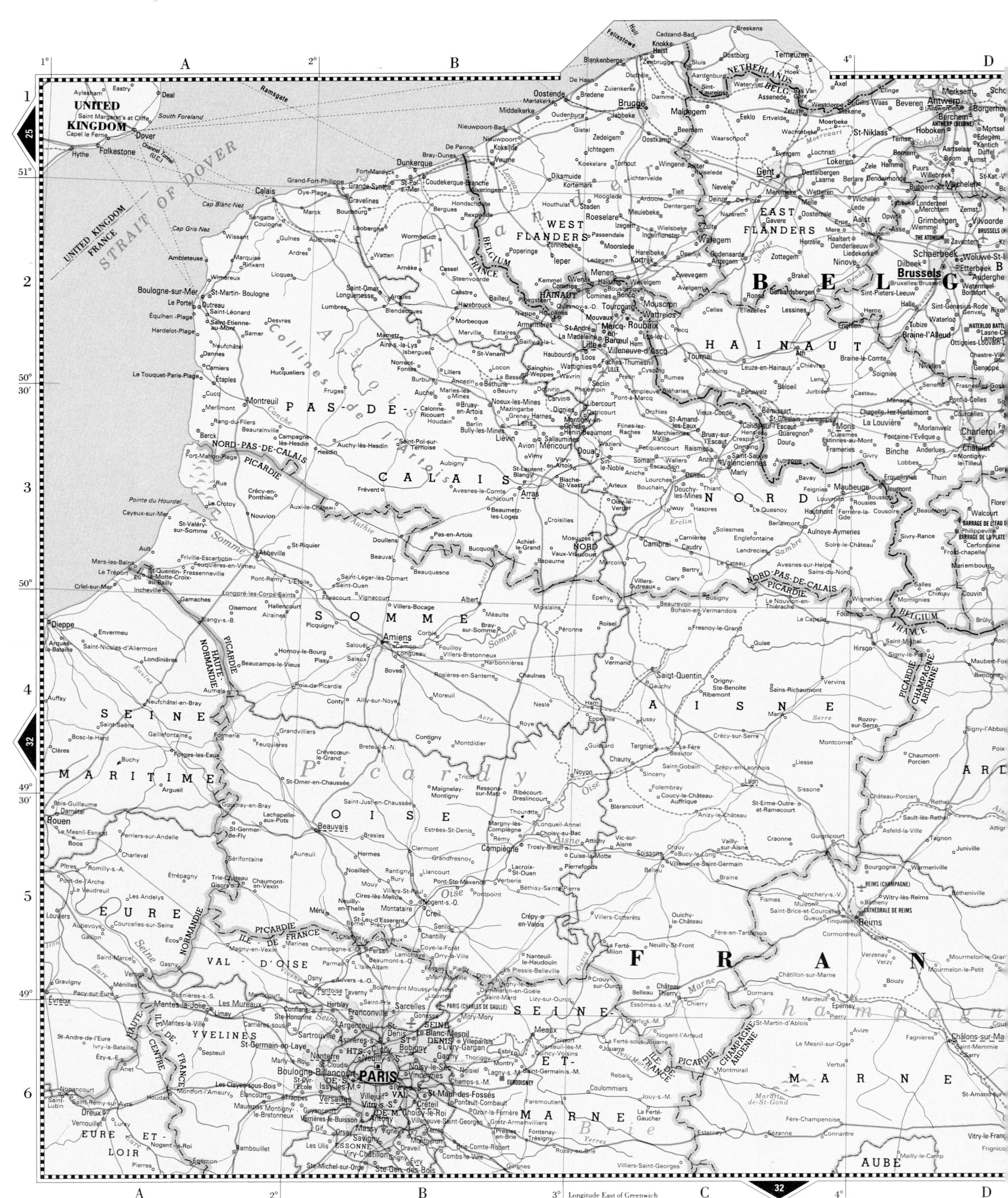

1°
A
2°
B
4°
D
1
2
3
4
5
6
51°
50° 30′
50°
49° 30′
49°
25
32
UNITED KINGDOM
STRAIT OF DOVER
UNITED KINGDOM
FRANCE
NETHERLANDS
BELG.
WEST FLANDERS
EAST FLANDERS
HAINAUT
B E L G
Brussels
Flanders
BELGIUM
FRANCE
NORD-PAS-DE-CALAIS
PICARDIE
PAS-DE-CALAIS
Collines de l'Artois
NORD
SOMME
AISNE
Picardy
OISE
SEINE-MARITIME
HAUTE-NORMANDIE
EURE
VAL-D'OISE
ILE-DE-FRANCE
YVELINES
PARIS
SEINE-ET-MARNE
EURE-ET-LOIR
ESSONNE
AUBE
MARNE
CHAMPAGNE-ARDENNE
Champagne
FRANCE
Dover
Calais
Dunkerque
Lille
Boulogne-sur-Mer
Arras
Amiens
Rouen
Beauvais
Reims
Saint-Quentin
Gent
Brugge
Antwerp
Oostende
Compiègne
Mons
Charleroi
Meaux
Dieppe
Abbeville
Evreux
2°
B
3°
Longitude East of Greenwich
C
32
4°
D

Belgium, Northern France, Western Germany

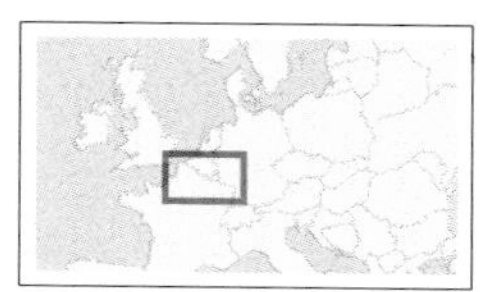

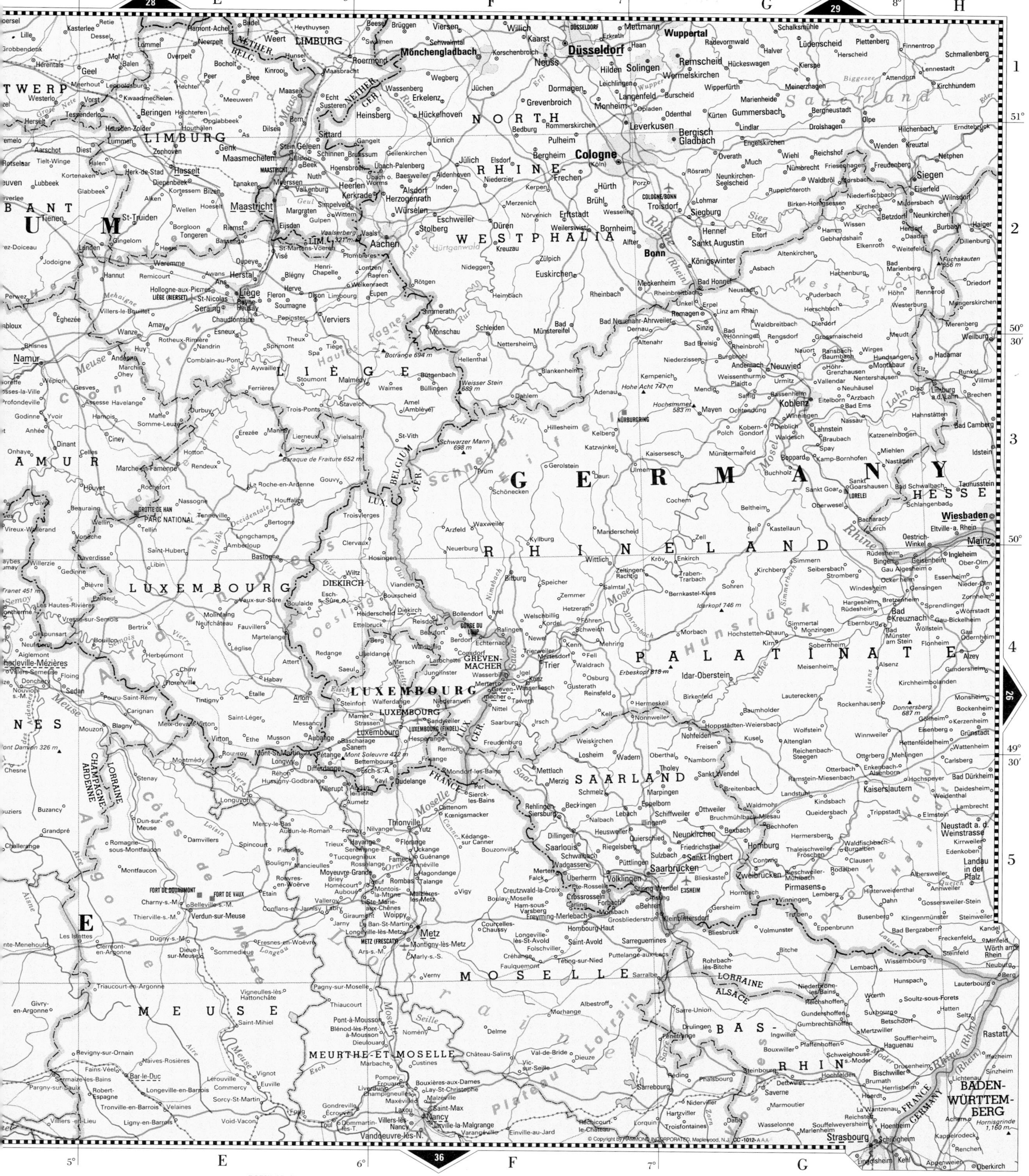

POPULATION OF CITIES AND TOWNS

■ OVER 2,000,000	◉ 500,000 - 999,999
▣ 1,000,000 - 1,999,999	◎ 250,000 - 499,999
● 100,000 - 249,999	◦ 10,000 - 29,999
⊙ 30,000 - 99,999	○ UNDER 10,000

SCALE 1:1,170,000 — LAMBERT CONFORMAL CONIC PROJECTION

MILES 0 10 20 30 40 50

KILOMETERS 0 10 20 30 40 50

English Channel
BAY OF BISCAY
Gulf of Lions
Channel Islands (U.K.)
U.K.
FRANCE
BELGIUM
SPAIN
ANDORRA
F R A N C E
NORD-PAS-DE-CALAIS
PICARDIE
HAUTE-NORMANDIE
BASSE-NORMANDIE
BRETAGNE
PAYS DE LA LOIRE
CENTRE
ILE-DE-FRANCE
CHAMPAGNE-ARDENNE
BOURGOGNE
POITOU-CHARENTES
LIMOUSIN
AUVERGNE
RHONE-ALPES
AQUITAINE
MIDI-PYRÉNÉES
LANGUEDOC-ROUSSILLON
CANTABRIA
BASQUE PROVS.
NAVARRE
ARAGÓN
CASTILE & LEÓN
LA RIOJA
CATALONIA
Massif Central
PARIS
Brussels
Lille
Amiens
Rouen
Le Havre
Caen
Cherbourg
Rennes
Brest
Nantes
Angers
Le Mans
Tours
Orléans
Reims
Troyes
Dijon
Lyon
Poitiers
Limoges
Clermont-Ferrand
Bordeaux
Toulouse
Montpellier
Nîmes
Marseille
Perpignan
Bilbao
San Sebastián
Pamplona
Vitoria
Logroño
Plymouth
Southampton
Portsmouth
Brighton
Dover
Calais
Boulogne-sur-Mer
Dunkerque
B
C
D
E
F
2°
0°
4°
44°
46°
3
4
5
26
34
35
Longitude West of Greenwich
Longitude East of Greenwich

West Central Europe

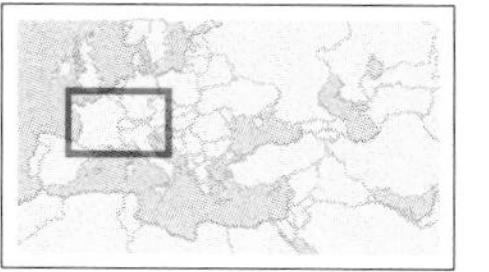

POPULATION OF CITIES AND TOWNS

- OVER 2,000,000
- 1,000,000 - 1,999,999
- 500,000 - 999,999
- 250,000 - 499,999
- 100,000 - 249,999
- 30,000 - 99,999
- 10,000 - 29,999
- UNDER 10,000

SCALE 1:3,500,000 LAMBERT CONFORMAL CONIC PROJECTION

MILES 0 50 100 150

KILOMETERS 0 50 100 150

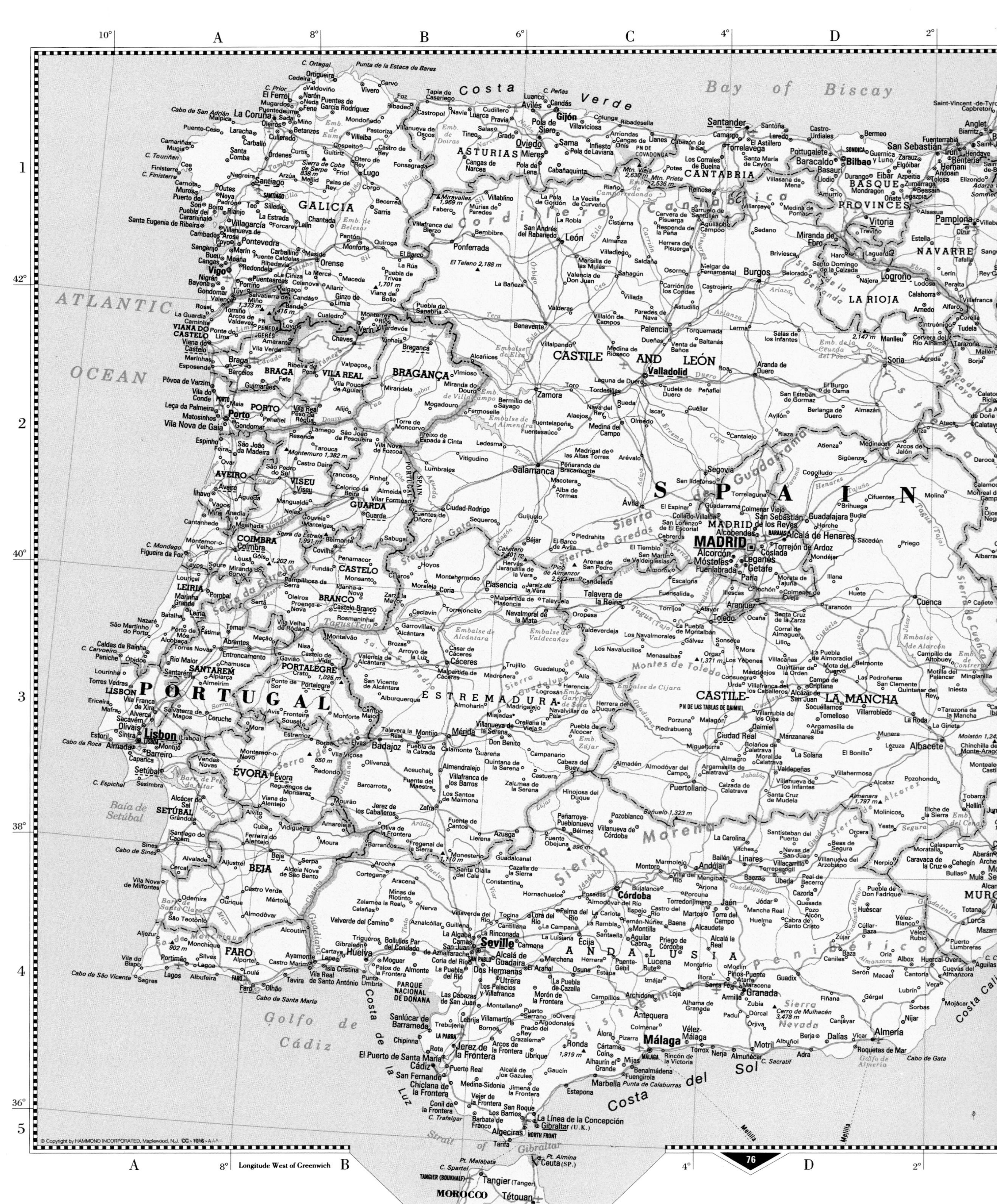

10°
A
8°
B
6°
C
4°
D
2°
1
2
3
4
5
42°
40°
38°
36°
Bay of Biscay
Costa Verde
ATLANTIC
OCEAN
GALICIA
ASTURIAS
CANTABRIA
BASQUE PROVINCES
NAVARRE
LA RIOJA
CASTILE AND LEÓN
SPAIN
PORTUGAL
ESTREMADURA
CASTILE-LA MANCHA
ANDALUSIA
MADRID
Lisbon
Porto
Seville
Córdoba
Granada
Málaga
Valladolid
Salamanca
Toledo
Badajoz
Cádiz
Gibraltar (U.K.)
Golfo de Cádiz
Costa de la Luz
Costa del Sol
Strait of Gibraltar
Sierra Morena
Sierra Nevada
Montes de Toledo
Sierra de Gredos
Sierra de Guadarrama
Cordillera Cantábrica
Sistema Ibérico
Sistema Penibético
Baía de Setúbal
Tangier (Tanger)
Ceuta (SP.)
Tétouan
MOROCCO
Melilla
© Copyright by HAMMOND INCORPORATED, Maplewood, N.J. CC - 1016
Longitude West of Greenwich
76

Spain, Portugal

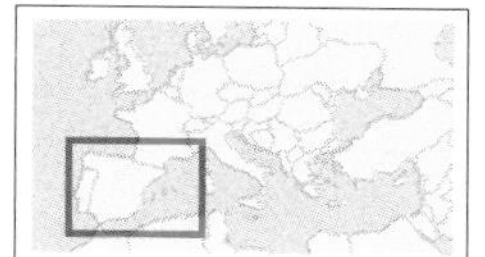

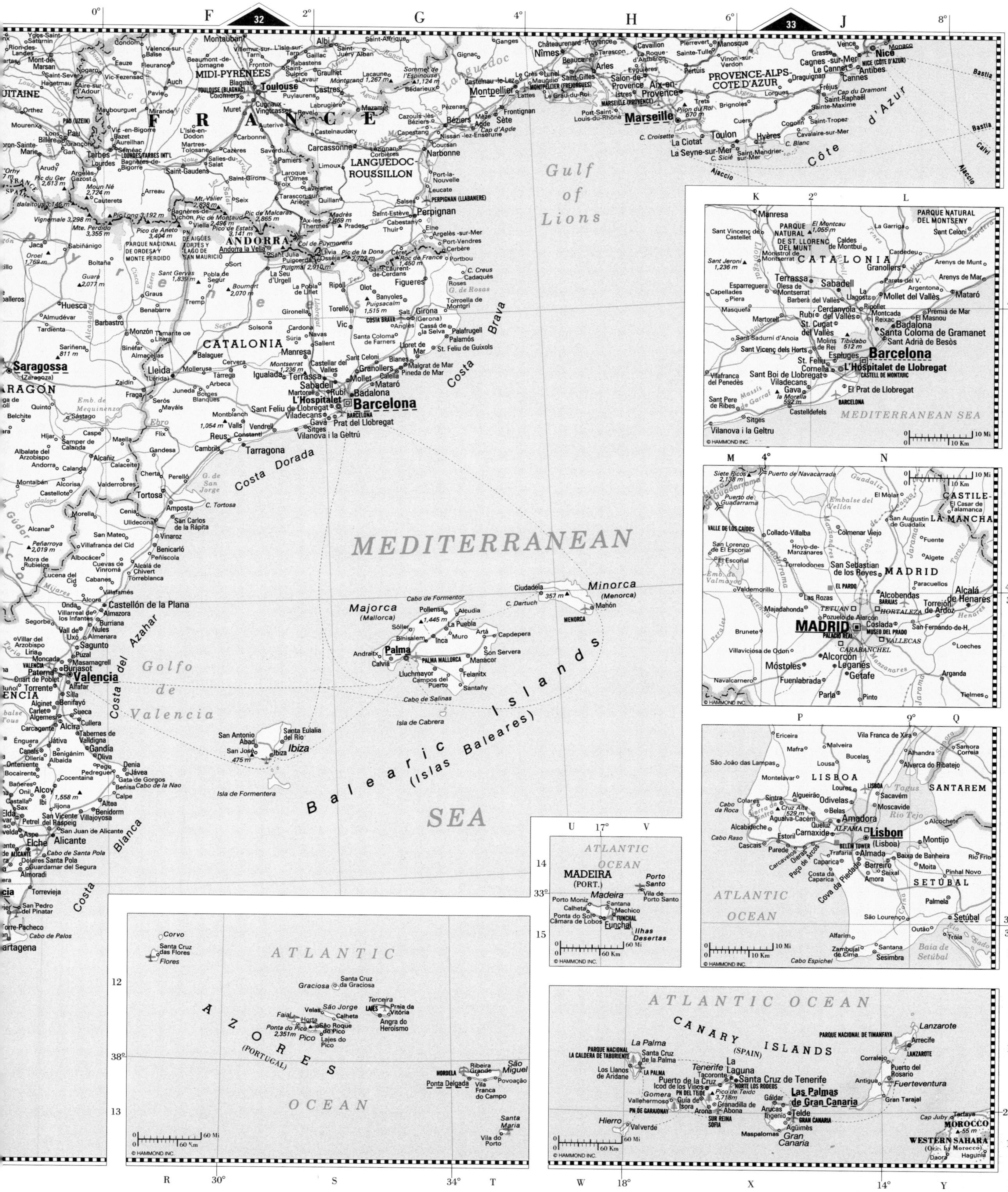

POPULATION OF CITIES AND TOWNS

OVER 2,000,000	500,000 - 999,999	100,000 - 249,999	10,000 - 29,999
1,000,000 - 1,999,999	250,000 - 499,999	30,000 - 99,999	UNDER 10,000

SCALE 1:3,500,000 LAMBERT CONFORMAL CONIC PROJECTION

MILES 0 50 100 150

KILOMETERS 0 50 100 150

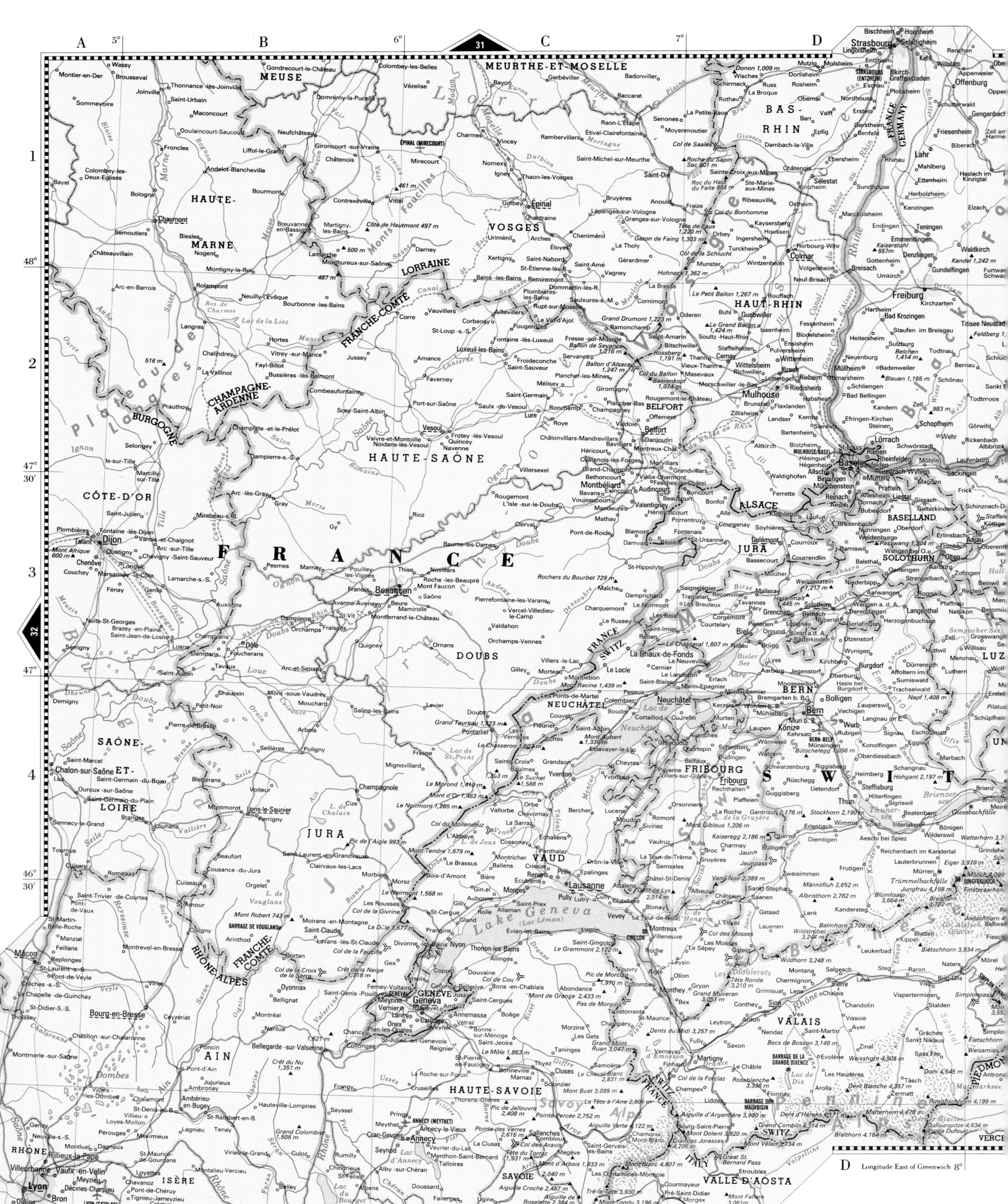

A
5°
B
6°
31
C
7°
D
1
2
3
4
48°
47° 30′
47°
46° 30′
32
FRANCE
MEUSE
MEURTHE-ET-MOSELLE
HAUTE-MARNE
VOSGES
LORRAINE
FRANCHE-COMTÉ
CHAMPAGNE-ARDENNE
BURGOGNE
HAUTE-SAÔNE
CÔTE-D'OR
DOUBS
JURA
SAÔNE-ET-LOIRE
AIN
HAUTE-SAVOIE
SAVOIE
ISÈRE
RHÔNE
RHÔNE-ALPES
BAS-RHIN
HAUT-RHIN
ALSACE
BELFORT
NEUCHÂTEL
FRIBOURG
VAUD
VALAIS
BERN
SOLOTHURN
BASELLAND
JURA
VALLE D'AOSTA
ITALY
SWITZ.
FRANCE
GERMANY
Strasbourg
Colmar
Mulhouse
Freiburg
Basel
Épinal
Chaumont
Langres
Dijon
Besançon
Vesoul
Belfort
Montbéliard
Dôle
Lons-le-Saunier
Bourg-en-Bresse
Mâcon
Lyon
Villeurbanne
Geneva
Genève
Annecy
Lausanne
Neuchâtel
La Chaux-de-Fonds
Bern
Biel
Thun
Fribourg
Sion
Montreux
Vevey
Chamonix-Mont-Blanc
Lake Geneva (Lac Léman)
Lac de Neuchâtel
Plateau de Langres
Monts Faucilles
Mont Blanc 4,807 m
Matterhorn 4,478 m
Jungfrau 4,158 m
Grand Ballon 1,424 m
Le Crêt de la Neige 1,718 m
Pennine Alps
Black Forest
Longitude East of Greenwich 8°

Central Alps Region

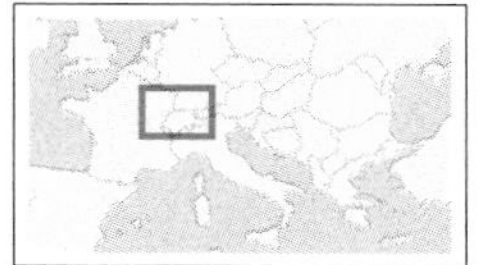

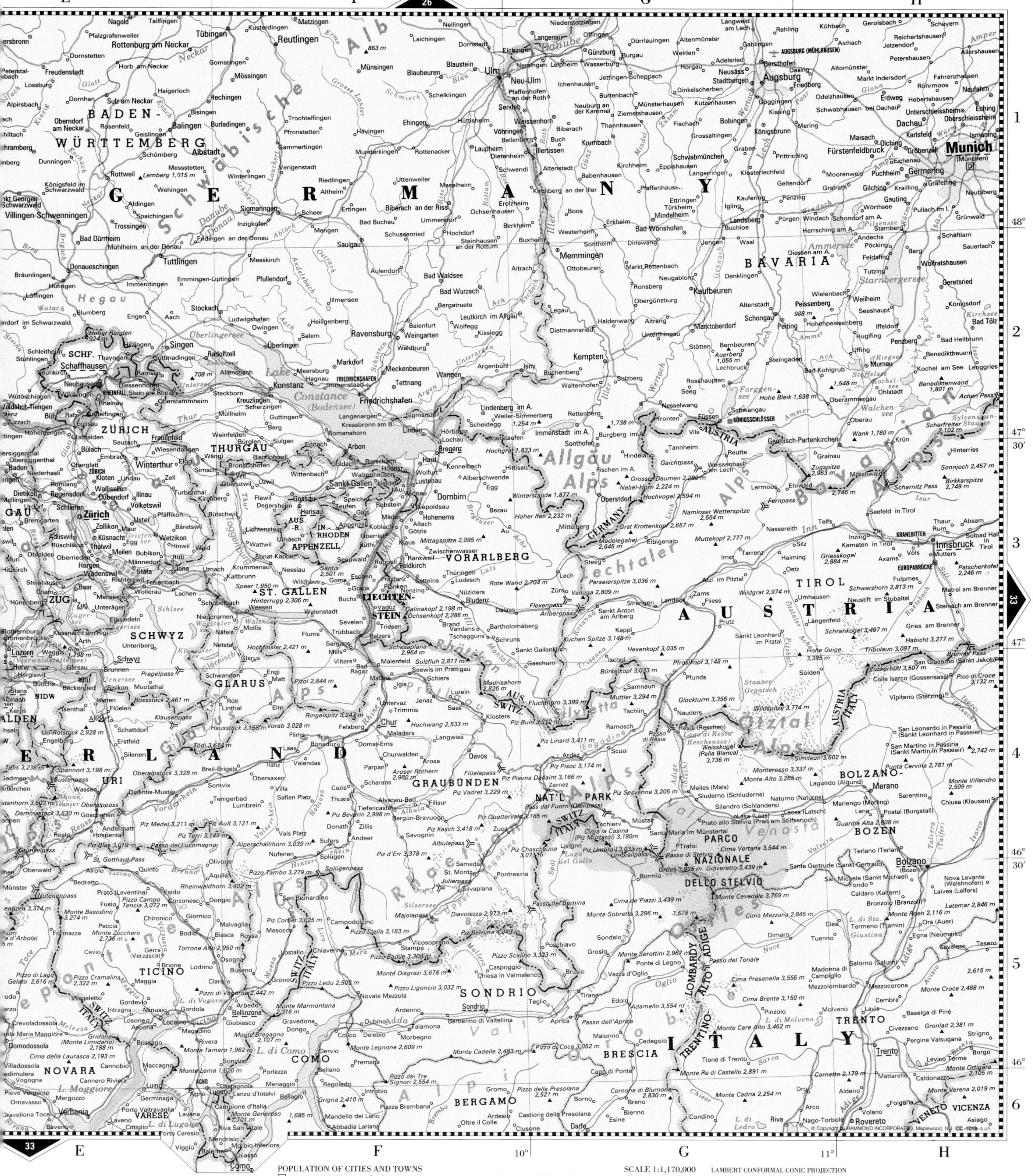

POPULATION OF CITIES AND TOWNS

- ▣ OVER 2,000,000
- ◻ 1,000,000 - 1,999,999
- ◉ 500,000 - 999,999
- ◎ 250,000 - 499,999
- ● 100,000 - 249,999
- ⊕ 30,000 - 99,999
- ⊙ 10,000 - 29,999
- ○ UNDER 10,000

SCALE 1:1,170,000 LAMBERT CONFORMAL CONIC PROJECTION

MILES 0 10 20 30 40 50

KILOMETERS 0 10 20 30 40 50

33
76
TYRRHENIAN SEA
MEDITERRANEAN
ADRIATIC
ITALY
CORSE
Corsica
SARDEGNA
Sardinia
Sicily
SICILIA
MALTA
TUNISIA
CROATIA
TUSCANY
UMBRIA
MARCHE
LAZIO
ABRUZZI
MOLISE
CAMPANIA
PUGLIA
BASILICATA
CALABRIA
ROME
(Roma)
Vatican City
(Città del Vaticano)
Naples
(Napoli)
Palermo
Catania
Messina
Bari
Cagliari
Tūnis
Bastia
Ajaccio
Sassari
Foggia
Taranto
Cosenza
Catanzaro
Reggio di Calabria
Siracusa
Agrigento
Trapani
Marsala
Pescara
Perugia
Salerno
Valletta
Strait of Bonifacio
Strait of Sicily
Malta Channel
Lipari Islands
Arcipelago Toscano
Golfo di Gaeta
Golfo di Taranto
Gulf of Tunis
Khalīj al Ḩammāmāt
Isole Ponziane
Isole Egadi
Isole de Pelagie (IT.)
I. di Pantelleria (IT.)
Lampedusa
Linosa
I. di Ustica
I. Stromboli
Monte Cinto 2,710 m
M. Etna 3,323 m
Monte Corno Grande 2,912 m
ITALY FRANCE
ITALY TUNISIA
ITALY MALTA
A
B
C
D
E
1
4
5
8°
10°
12°
14°
16°
42°
38°
36°
Longitude East of Greenwich
© Copyright by HAMMOND INCORPORATED, Maplewood, N.J.
SCALE 1:3,500,000
LAMBERT CONFORMAL CONIC PROJECTION
MILES 0 50 100 150
KILOMETERS 0 50 100 150
POPULATION OF CITIES AND TOWNS
OVER 2,000,000
1,000,000 - 1,999,999
500,000 - 999,999
250,000 - 499,999
100,000 - 249,999
30,000 - 99,999
10,000 - 29,999
UNDER 10,000

Southern Italy, Albania, Greece

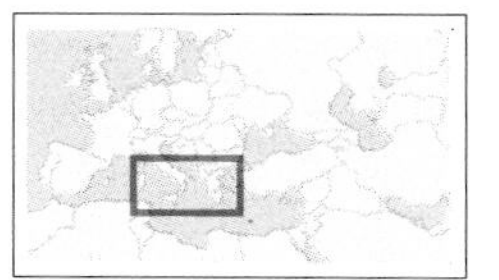

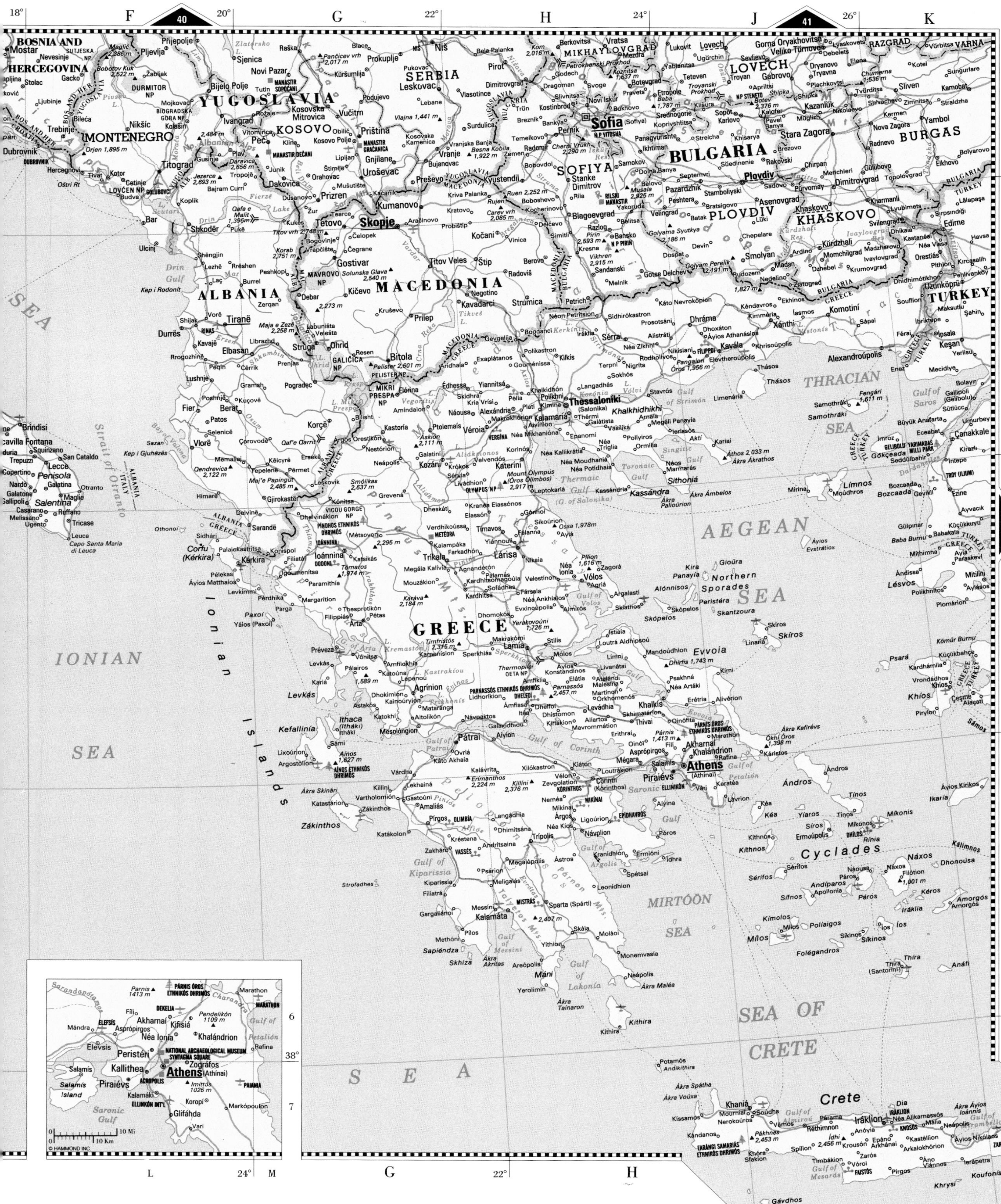

BOSNIA AND HERCEGOVINA
YUGOSLAVIA
SERBIA
KOSOVO
MONTENEGRO
MACEDONIA
ALBANIA
BULGARIA
SOFIYA
PLOVDIV
KHASKOVO
LOVECH
BURGAS
TURKEY
GREECE
ADRIATIC SEA
IONIAN SEA
Ionian Islands
AEGEAN SEA
THRACIAN SEA
MIRTÓON SEA
SEA OF CRETE
Crete
Cyclades
Northern Sporades
Sofia
Skopje
Tiranë
Athens (Athínai)
Thessaloníki (Salonika)

Parnis 1413 m
PÁRNIS ÓROS ETHNIKÓS DHRIMÓS
DEKELIA
MARATHON
Marathon
Fili
Mándra
ELEFSÍS
Akharnaí
Kifisiá
Pendelikón 1109 m
Aspropirgos
Néa Ionía
Khalándrion
Gulf of Petalión
Elevsís
Peristéri
NATIONAL ARCHAEOLOGICAL MUSEUM
SYNTAGMA SQUARE
Rafina
Salamís
Kallithéa
Athens (Athínai)
Zográfos
ACROPOLIS
Imittós 1026 m
PAIANIA
Salamís Island
Piraiévs
Kalamáki
ELLINIKÓN INT'L
Koropí
Markópoulon
Saronic Gulf
Glifáda
Vari
© HAMMOND INC.

SCALE 1:3,500,000 LAMBERT CONFORMAL CONIC PROJECTION

MILES 0 | 50 | 100 | 150

KILOMETERS 0 | 50 | 100 | 150

POPULATION OF CITIES AND TOWNS

- OVER 2,000,000
- 1,000,000 - 1,999,999
- 500,000 - 999,999
- 250,000 - 499,999
- 100,000 - 249,999
- 30,000 - 99,999
- 10,000 - 29,999
- UNDER 10,000

* WHILE THERE IS NO OTHER OFFICIALLY RECOGNIZED NAME FOR THIS AREA, THE NAME "MACEDONIA" DERIVES FROM ITS FORMER STATUS AS A YUGOSLAV REPUBLIC, AND IS NOT RECOGNIZED BY MANY NATIONS.

Hungary, Northern Balkan States

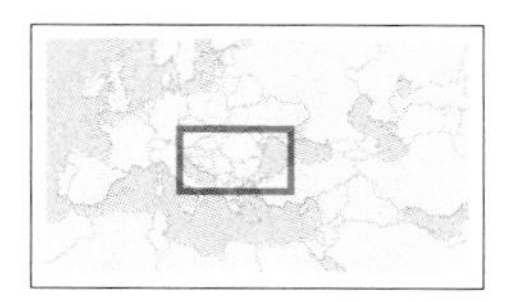

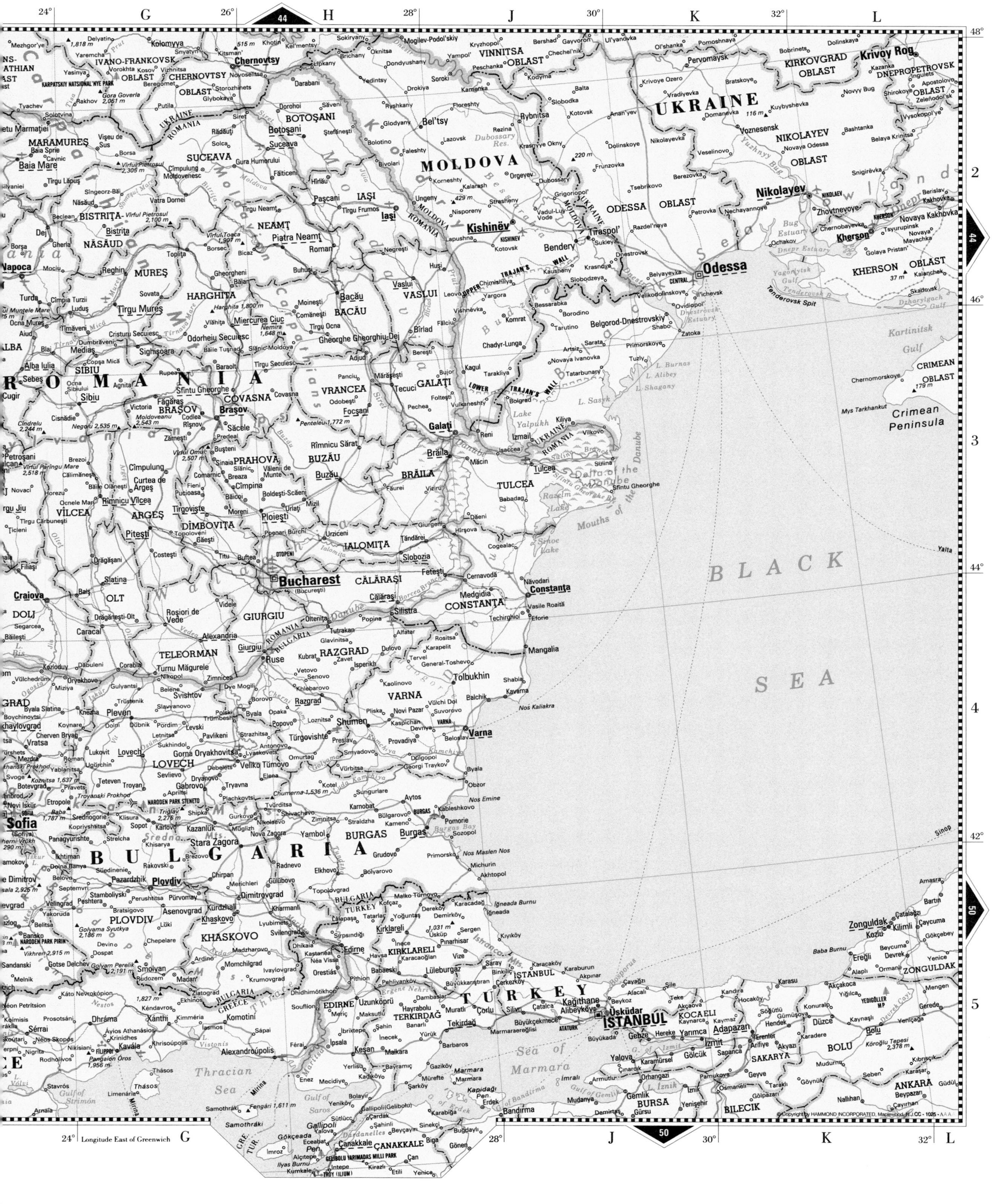

UKRAINE
MOLDOVA
ROMANIA
BULGARIA
TURKEY
BLACK SEA
Sea of Marmara
Thracian Sea
Crimean Peninsula

24° Longitude East of Greenwich

8°
A
12°
B
16°
C
20°
D
24°
E
28°
F
32°
G
36°
H
40°
J
2
3
4
5
64°
60°
56°
20
27
44
20°
D
24°
E
28°
Longitude East F of Greenwich
32°
G
36°
H
40°
J
NORWEGIAN SEA
Arctic Circle
Vestfjorden
NORWAY
NORDLAND
NORD TRØNDELAG
SWEDEN
NORRBOTTEN
VÄSTERBOTTEN
JAMTLAND
VÄSTERNORRLAND
KOPPARBERG
GÄVLEBORG
UPPSALA
VÄSTMANLAND
SÖDERMANLAND
ÖSTERGÖTLAND
KALMAR
GOTLAND
GOTSKA SANDÖN NP
BALTIC SEA
Gulf of Bothnia
Åland
AHVENANMAA
FINLAND
LAPPI
OULU
VAASA
KUOPIO
KESKI-SUOMI
POHJOIS-KARJALA
MIKKELI
HÄME
TURKU PORI
KYMI
UUSIMAA
Gulf of Finland
FINNMARK
TROMS
KARELIAN AUT. REPUBLIC
MURMANSK OBLAST
Kola Peninsula
BARENTS
White Sea
Kandalaksha Gulf
Onega Bay
Dvina Bay
Onega Pen.
ARCHANGEL
VOLOGDA OBL.
Lake Ladoga
Lake Onega
SAINT PETERSBURG OBLAST
ESTONIA
Gulf of Riga
LATVIA
LITHUANIA
RUSSIA
KALININGRAD OBL.
POLAND
BELARUS
VITEBSK OBL.
MINSK OBL.
GRODNO OBL.
MOGILEV OBL.
PSKOV OBLAST
NOVGOROD OBL.
TVER OBLAST
YAROSLAVL' OBL.
IVANOVO OBL.
SMOLENSK OBLAST
KALUGA OBL.
MOSCOW OBL.
RYAZAN' OBL.
VLADIMIR OBL.
R
U
Lake Peipus
Rybinsk Res.
Murmansk
Archangel
Petrozavodsk
ST. PETERSBURG
Helsinki
Stockholm
Tallinn
Riga
Vilnius
Minsk
MOSCOW
Novgorod
Pskov
Smolensk
Vitebsk
Tver
Yaroslavl'
Vologda
Cherepovets
Kaliningrad
Kaunas
Grodno
Białystok
Mogilev
Kaluga
Ryazan'
Kostroma
Ivanovo
Vladimir
Oulu
Kuopio
Tampere
Turku
Vaasa
Jyväskylä
Luleå
Umeå
Gdańsk
Gdynia
Olsztyn
Daugavpils
Tartu
Pärnu
Liepāja
Klaipėda
Šiauliai
Panevėžys
Bodø

Northeastern Europe

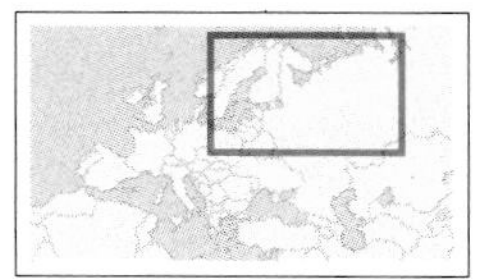

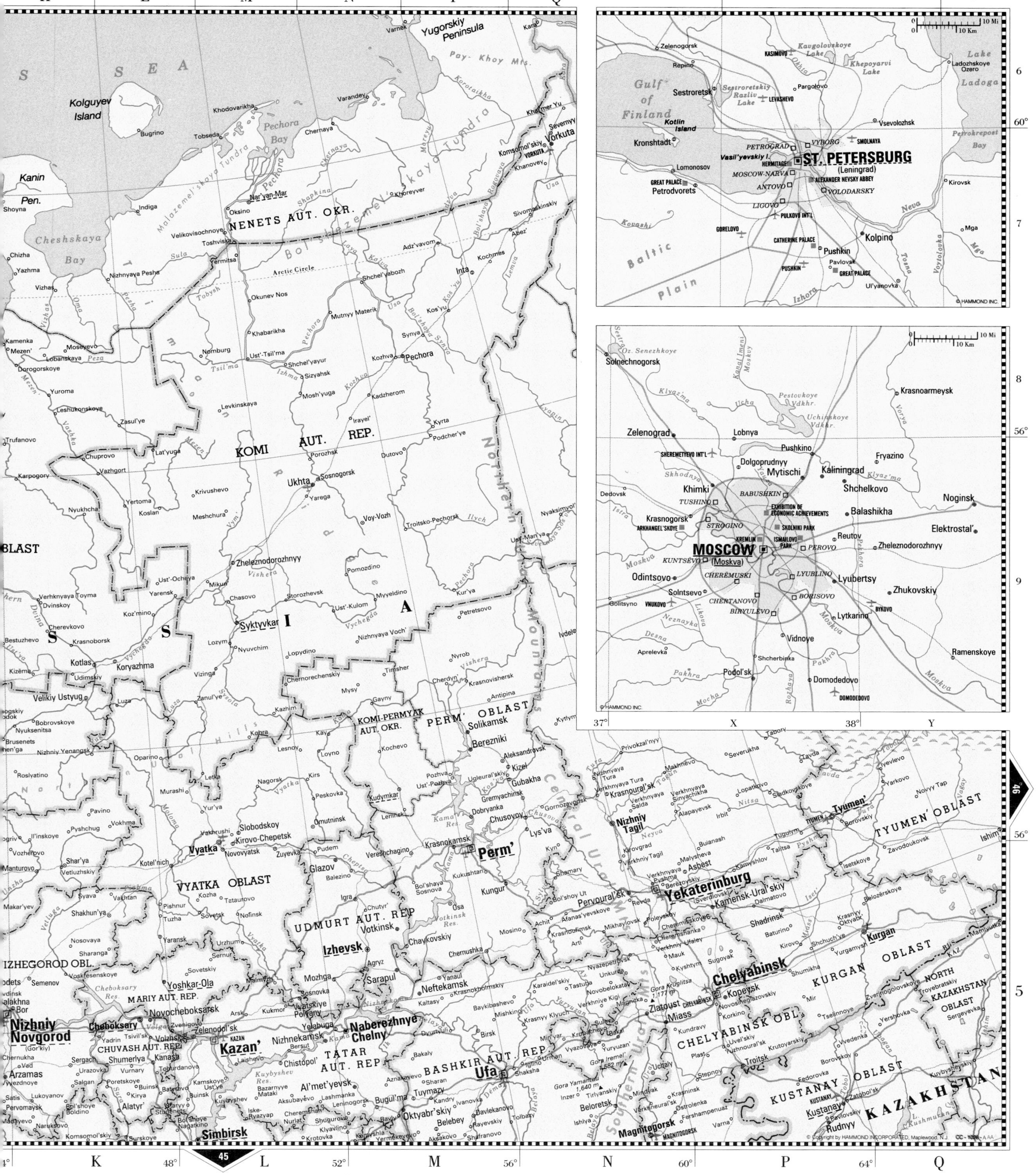

POPULATION OF CITIES AND TOWNS

■ OVER 2,000,000	◉ 500,000 - 999,999	● 100,000 - 249,999
▣ 1,000,000 - 1,999,999	◎ 250,000 - 499,999	⊕ 30,000 - 99,999
⊙ 10,000 - 29,999	○ UNDER 10,000	

SCALE 1:7,000,000 LAMBERT CONFORMAL CONIC PROJECTION

MILES 0 100 200 300

KILOMETERS 0 100 200 300

A
B
C
D
E
20°
24°
28°
32°
42
52°
48°
44°
40°
1
2
3
4
5
27
39
50
POLAND
Warsaw
(Warszawa)
BELARUS
Minsk
UKRAINE
KIEV
MOSCOW
(Moskva)
MOLDOVA
Kishinëv
ROMANIA
Bucharest
(Bucureşti)
HUNGARY
SLOVAKIA
YUGOSLAVIA
Belgrade
(Beograd)
BULGARIA
Sofia
(Sofiya)
MACEDONIA
GREECE
Athens
(Athinai)
TURKEY
ANKARA
ISTANBUL
BLACK SEA
AEGEAN SEA
Sea of Azov
Sea of Marmara
Crimean Pen.
Karkinit'sk Gulf
Mouths of the Danube
Kraków
Lublin
Brest
Gomel'
Chernigov
Smolensk
Kursk
Khar'kov
Dnepropetrovsk
Zaporozh'ye
Donetsk
Odessa
Nikolayev
Kherson
Simferopol'
Sevastopol'
Cluj-Napoca
Iaşi
Constanţa
Varna
Burgas
Plovdiv
Thessaloníki
İzmir
Bursa
Eskişehir
B 24°
C
Longitude East 28° of Greenwich
D
32°
E
36°
F
40°
SCALE 1:7,000,000
LAMBERT CONFORMAL CONIC PROJECTION
MILES 0 100 200 300
KILOMETERS 0 100 200 300
POPULATION OF CITIES AND TOWNS
OVER 2,000,000
1,000,000 - 1,999,999
500,000 - 999,999
250,000 - 499,999
100,000 - 249,999
30,000 - 99,999
10,000 - 29,999
UNDER 10,000

Southeastern Europe

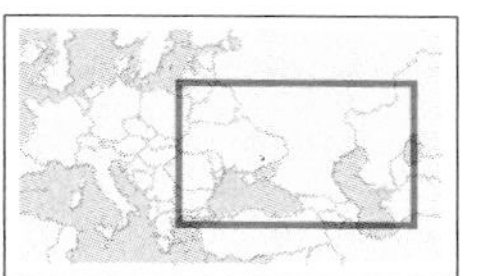

4
0°
3
2
30°
Spitsbergen
SVALBARD (NORWAY)
Northeast Land
Edge I.
Bear I. (NOR.)
ARCTIC
FRANZ JOSEF LAND
George Land
Graham Bell I.
Wilczek I.
Rudolf I.
Wiese I.
Pioner I.
SEVERNAYA ZEMLYA
Sergeya Kirova Is.
Nordenskjöld Arch.
Arkticheskiy Institut Is.
Sverdrup I.
Mys Zhelaniya
Barents Sea
Novaya Zemlya
Kara Sea
Mezhdusharskiy I.
Kolguyev I.
Vaygach I.
Kanin Pen.
Mys Kanin Nos
Kola Pen.
Murmansk
White Sea
Arkhangel'sk
Severodvinsk
North Cape (Nordkapp)
Hammerfest
Tromsø
Norwegian Sea
North Sea
NORWAY
SWEDEN
FINLAND
Gulf of Bothnia
Trondheim
Bergen
Oslo
Stockholm
Helsinki
Tallinn
ESTONIA
LATVIA
Riga
LITH.
Vilnius
Minsk
BELARUS
Warsaw
POLAND
Gdańsk
Baltic Sea
DENMARK
Copenhagen
Malmö
Göteborg
Berlin
GERMANY
Hamburg
Bremen
NETH.
Amsterdam
Rotterdam
The Hague
London
U.K.
Antwerp
BEL.
Brussels
Cologne
Düsseldorf
Dortmund
Frankfurt am Main
Leipzig
Dresden
Prague
CZECH REP.
AUST.
Bratislava
SLOVAKIA
Budapest
HUNGARY
ROMANIA
Cluj-Napoca
Iași
Brăila
Constanța
MOLDOVA
Kishinev
Odessa
UKRAINE
Kiev
Kharkov
Dnepropetrovsk
Zaporozh'ye
Donetsk
Simferopol'
Sevastopol'
Black Sea
Sea of Azov
Rostov
Krasnodar
Volgograd
Saratov
Samara
Kazan'
Nizhniy Novgorod
Moscow
St. Petersburg
Novgorod
Pskov
Smolensk
Tula
Yaroslavl'
Vologda
Kostroma
Ivanovo
Vladimir
Ryazan'
Voronezh
Lipetsk
Penza
Ul'yanovsk
Tol'yatti
Izhevsk
Perm'
Kirov
Ufa
Orenburg
Chelyabinsk
Yekaterinburg
Magnitogorsk
Kurgan
Tyumen'
Petropavlovsk
Omsk
Novosibirsk
Barnaul
Tomsk
Kemerovo
Novokuznetsk
Krasnoyarsk
Astrakhan'
Caspian Sea
Makhachkala
Baku
AZERBAIJAN
Tbilisi
GEORGIA
ARMENIA
Yerevan
Sukhumi
Batumi
Grozny
Vladikavkaz
TURKEY
Trabzon
Samsun
Erzurum
IRAQ
IRAN
Tabrīz
Tehrān
Qom
Eşfahān
Shīrāz
Mashhad
Ahvāz
Kermān
Yazd
Dasht-e Kavīr
Dasht-e Lūt
Zagros Mts.
Elburz Mts.
Persian Gulf
KARELIAN AUT. REP.
KOMI AUT. REP.
NENETS AUT. OKRUG
YAMAL-NENETS AUT. OKRUG
KHANTY-MANSIYSK AUT. OKRUG
TAYMYR AUT. OKRUG
Yamal Pen.
Gyda Pen.
Ural Mts.
Vorkuta
Syktyvkar
Ukhta
Salekhard
Noril'sk
Surgut
Nizhnevartovsk
West Siberian Plain
RUSSIA
KAZAKHSTAN
TURGAY OBLAST
MANGISTAUZ OBLAST
Aral Sea
Kazakh Uplands
Karaganda
Tselinograd
Semipalatinsk
Ust'-Kamenogorsk
Pavlodar
Aktyubinsk
Gur'yev
Ural'sk
Kzyl-Orda
Dzhambul
Chimkent
Alma-Ata
KYRGYZSTAN
Bishkek
Lake Balkhash
Taldy-Kurgan
UZBEKISTAN
Tashkent
Samarkand
Bukhara
Namangan
Andizhan
Fergana
Osh
TURKMENISTAN
Ashkhabad
Chardzhou
BALKHAN OBLAST
Krasnovodsk
Nebit-Dag
KARAKALPAK AUT. REP.
Nukus
Urgench
Kara Kum
Kyzyl Kum
TAJIKISTAN
Dushanbe
GORNO-BADAKHSTAN AUT. OBL.
Communism Peak 7,495 m
Pik Pobedy 7,439 m
AFGHANISTAN
Herāt
Mazār-e Sharīf
Hindu Kush
PAKISTAN
CHINA
Tian Shan
Ürümqi
Kashi
Tarim Basin
Dzungarian Basin
Yining
Karamay
Altai Mountains
ALTAY KRAY
GORNO-ALTAY AUT. OBL.
Gora Belukha 4,506 m
MONGOLIA
Abakan
Minusinsk
Kyzyl
TUVA AUT. REP.
33
41
52
53
F
60°
G
70°
H
80° Longitude East of Greenwich
J
90°
K
50°
5
40°
6
30°
7

Russia and Neighboring Countries

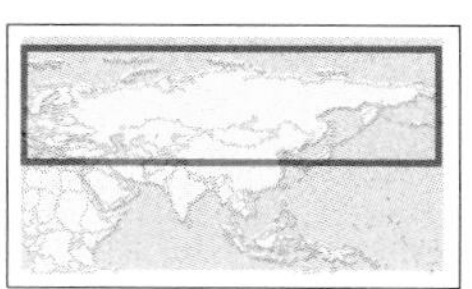

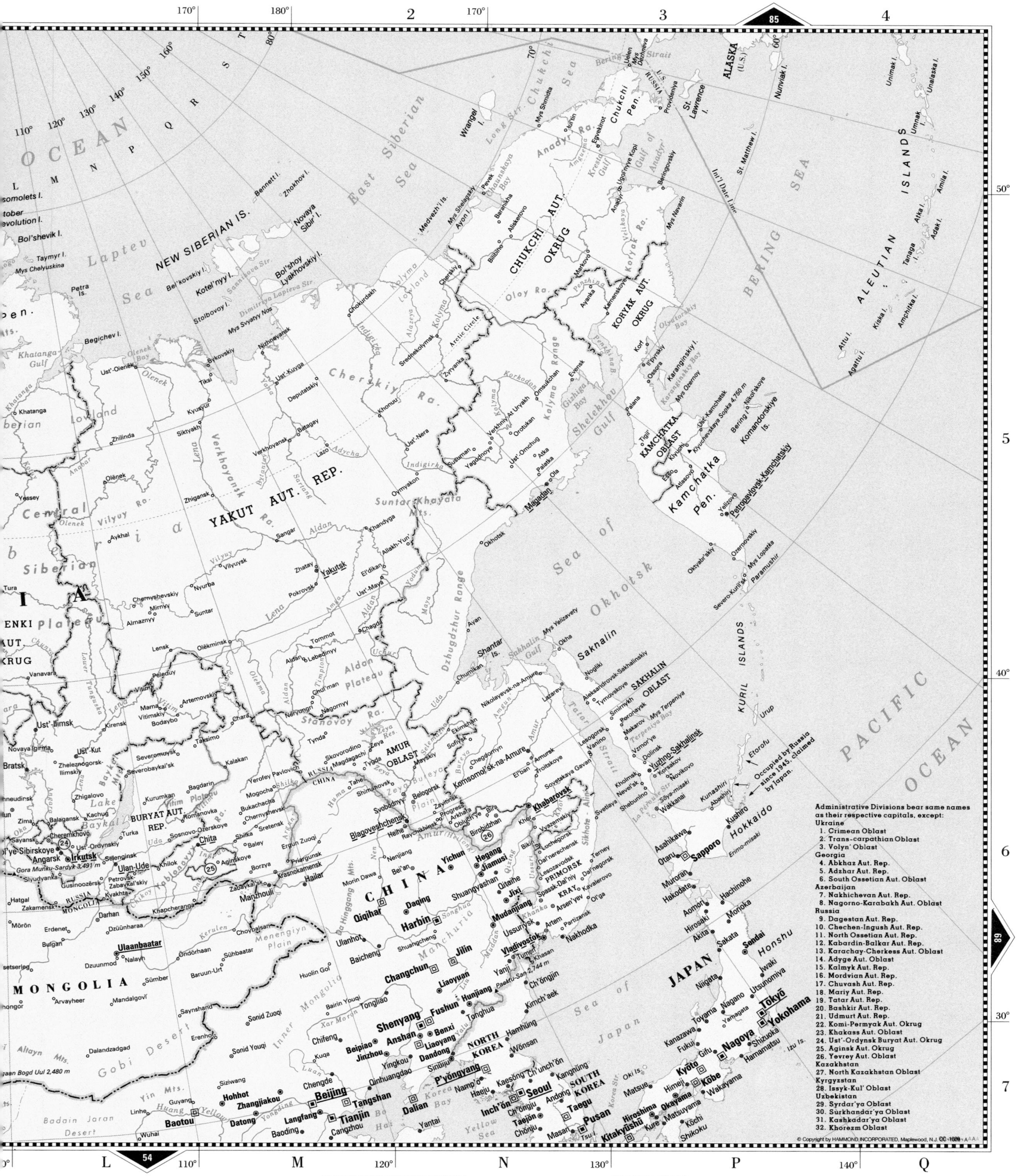

Administrative Divisions bear same names as their respective capitals, except:

Ukraine
1. Crimean Oblast
2. Trans-carpathian Oblast
3. Volyn' Oblast

Georgia
4. Abkhaz Aut. Rep.
5. Adzhar Aut. Rep.
6. South Ossetian Aut. Oblast

Azerbaijan
7. Nakhichevan Aut. Rep.
8. Nagorno-Karabakh Aut. Oblast

Russia
9. Dagestan Aut. Rep.
10. Chechen-Ingush Aut. Rep.
11. North Ossetian Aut. Rep.
12. Kabardin-Balkar Aut. Rep.
13. Karachay-Cherkess Aut. Oblast
14. Adyge Aut. Oblast
15. Kalmyk Aut. Rep.
16. Mordvian Aut. Rep.
17. Chuvash Aut. Rep.
18. Mariy Aut. Rep.
19. Tatar Aut. Rep.
20. Bashkir Aut. Rep.
21. Udmurt Aut. Rep.
22. Komi-Permyak Aut. Okrug
23. Khakass Aut. Oblast
24. Ust'-Ordynsk Buryat Aut. Okrug
25. Aginsk Aut. Okrug
26. Yevrey Aut. Oblast

Kazakhstan
27. North Kazakhstan Oblast

Kyrgyzstan
28. Issyk-Kul' Oblast

Uzbekistan
29. Syrdar'ya Oblast
30. Surkhandar'ya Oblast
31. Kashkadar'ya Oblast
32. Khorezm Oblast

POPULATION OF CITIES AND TOWNS
- OVER 2,000,000
- 1,000,000 - 1,999,999
- 500,000 - 999,999
- 100,000 - 499,999
- 50,000 - 99,999
- UNDER 50,000

SCALE 1:21,000,000 LAMBERT CONFORMAL CONIC PROJECTION

MILES 0 300 600 900

KILOMETERS 0 300 600 900

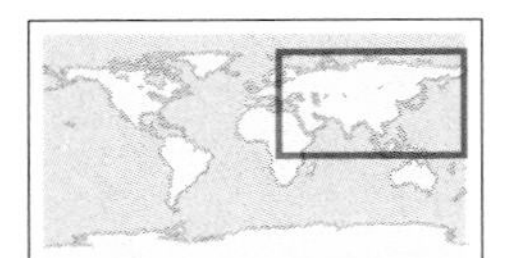

Asia

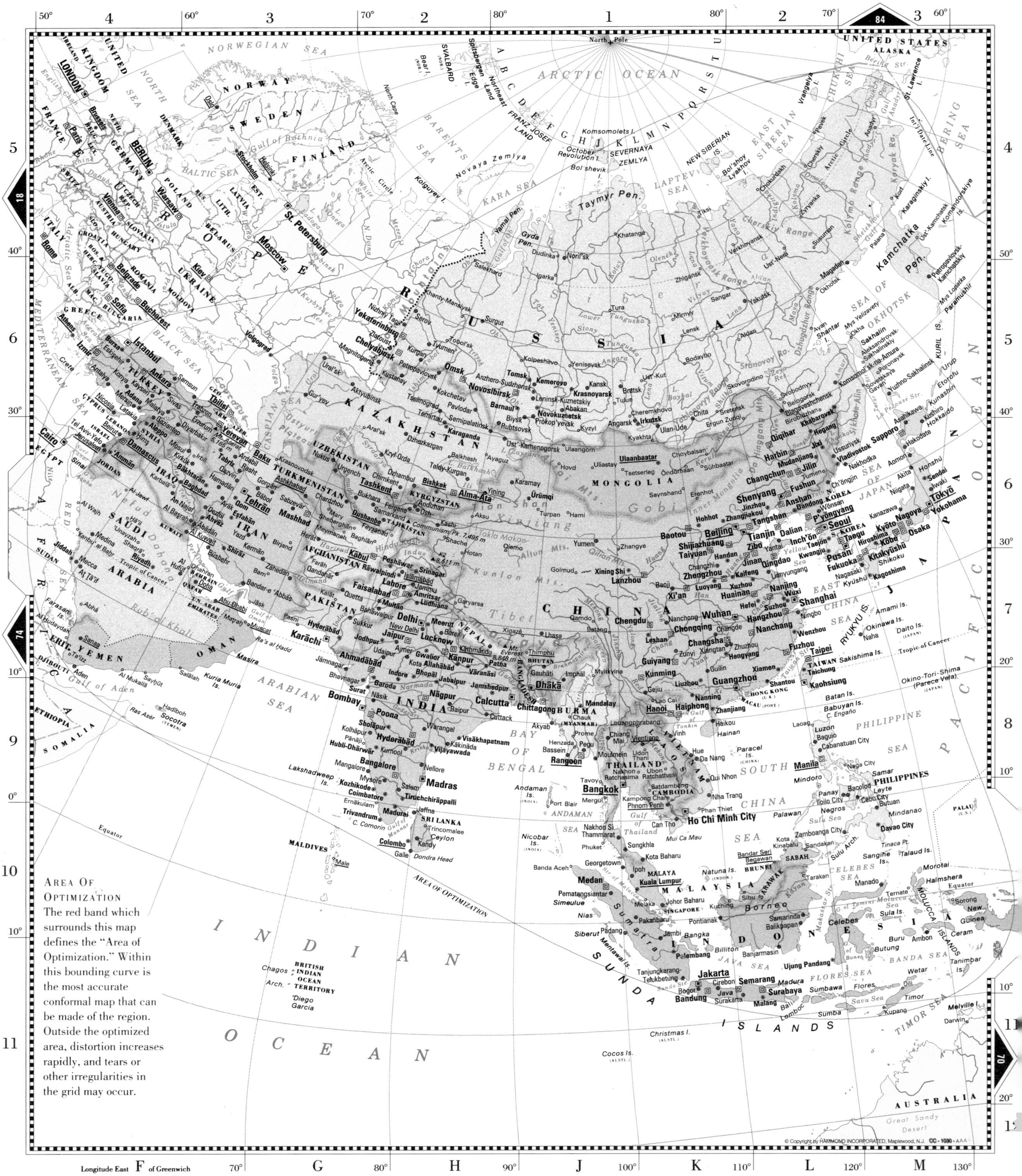

AREA OF OPTIMIZATION

The red band which surrounds this map defines the "Area of Optimization." Within this bounding curve is the most accurate conformal map that can be made of the region. Outside the optimized area, distortion increases rapidly, and tears or other irregularities in the grid may occur.

Longitude East F of Greenwich

SCALE 1:49,000,000 OPTIMAL CONFORMAL PROJECTION

MILES 0 700 1400 2100

KILOMETERS 0 700 1400 2100

POPULATION OF CITIES AND TOWNS

- OVER 3,000,000
- 1,000,000 - 2,999,999
- 500,000 - 999,999
- 100,000 - 499,999
- UNDER 100,000

Eastern Mediterranean Region

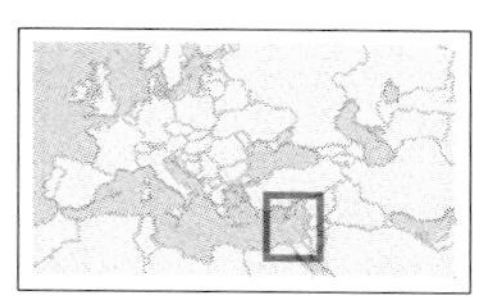

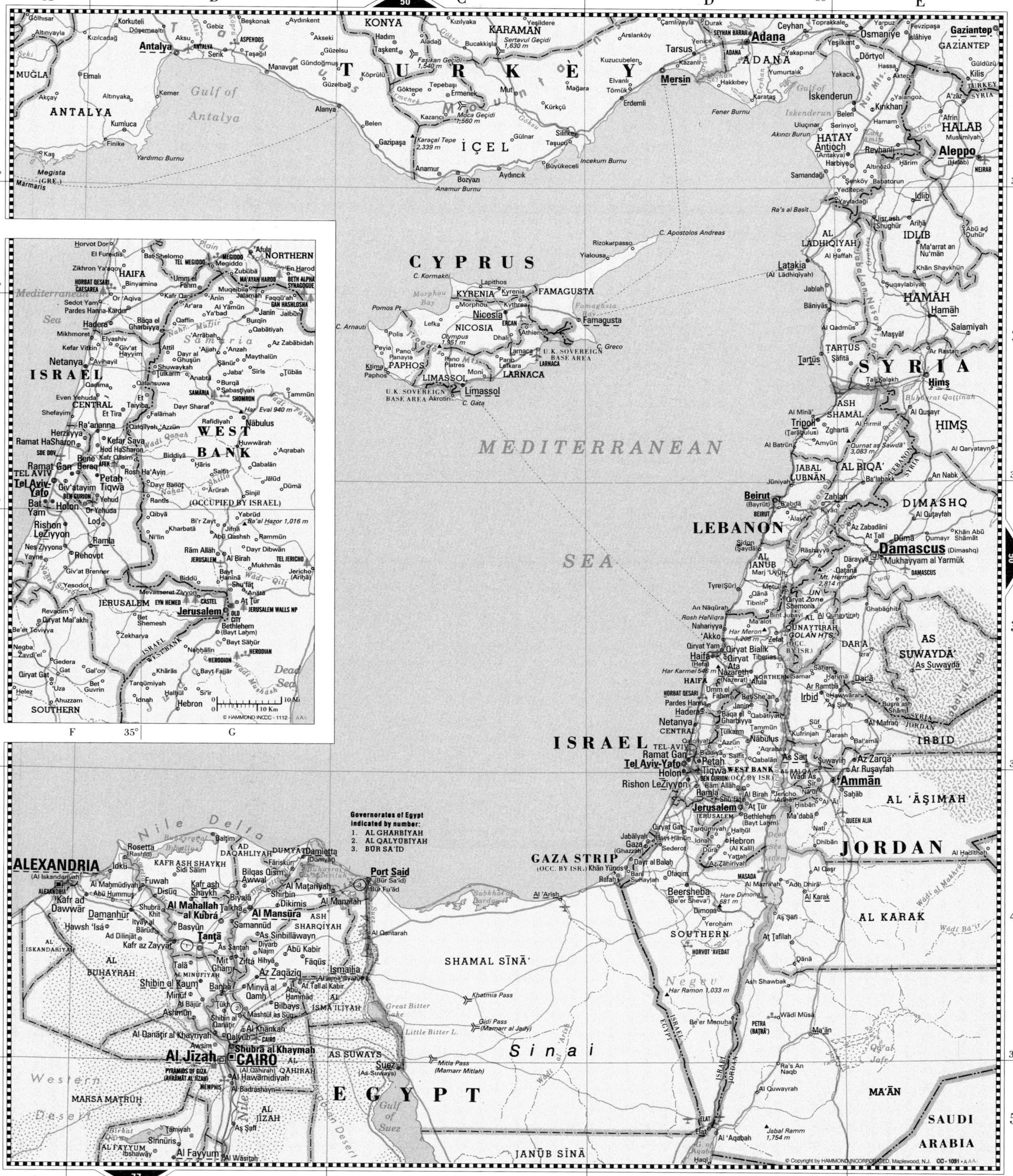

Governorates of Egypt indicated by number:

1. AL GHARBĪYAH
2. AL QALYŪBĪYAH
3. BŪR SA'ĪD

Longitude East of Greenwich

POPULATION OF CITIES AND TOWNS

- OVER 2,000,000
- 1,000,000 - 1,999,999
- 500,000 - 999,999
- 250,000 - 499,999
- 100,000 - 249,999
- 30,000 - 99,999
- 10,000 - 29,999
- UNDER 10,000

SCALE 1:3,500,000 POLYCONIC PROJECTION

MILES 0 50 100 150

KILOMETERS 0 50 100 150

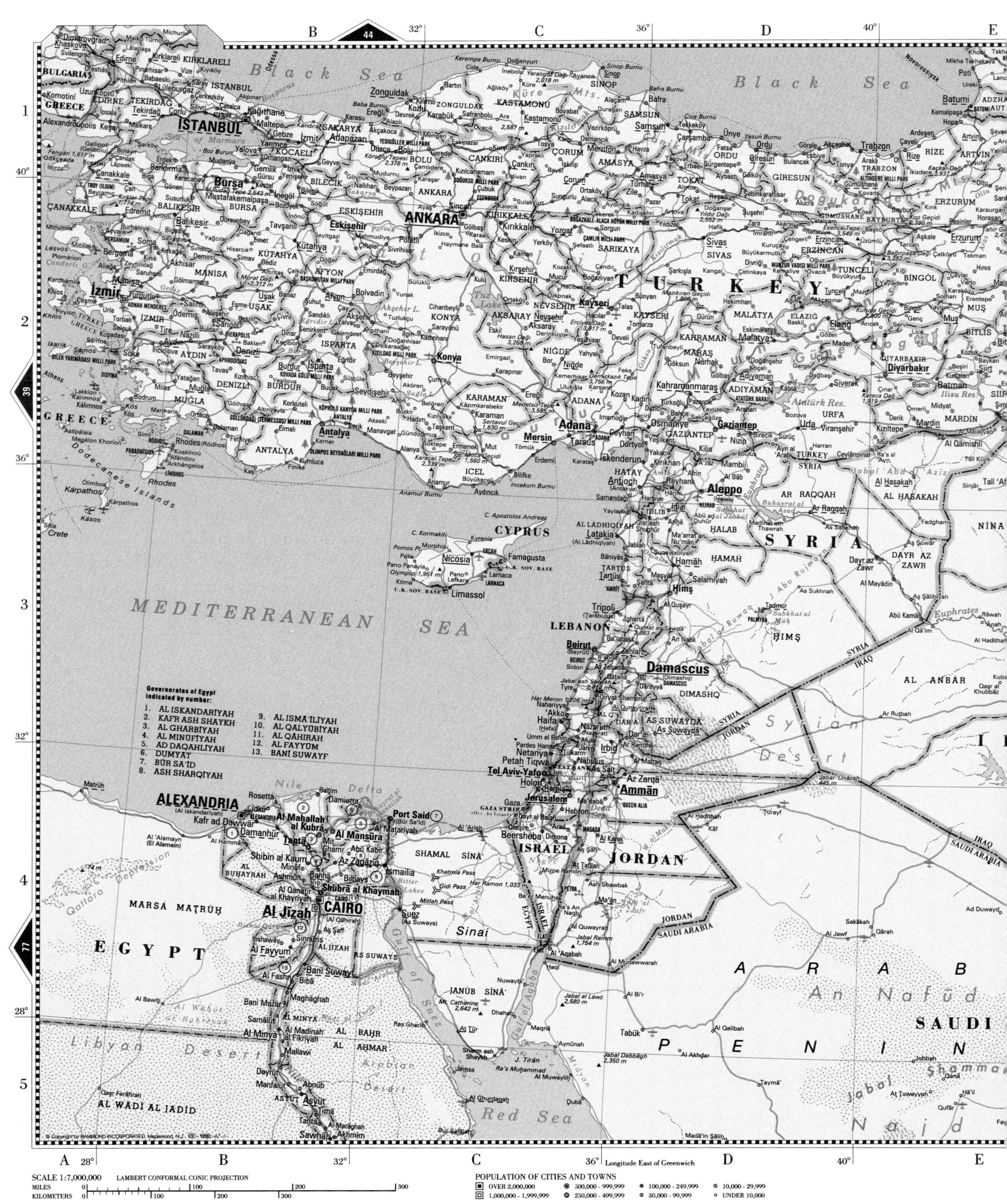

Black Sea
TURKEY
SYRIA
CYPRUS
LEBANON
ISRAEL
JORDAN
EGYPT
GREECE
BULGARIA
MEDITERRANEAN SEA
Red Sea
Sinai
ARAB PENINSULA
SAUDI
ISTANBUL
ANKARA
İzmir
Bursa
Adana
Konya
Aleppo
Damascus
Beirut
Nicosia
Tel Aviv-Yafo
Jerusalem
Ammān
ALEXANDRIA
CAIRO
Port Said
Suez
Governorates of Egypt indicated by number:
1. AL ISKANDARĪYAH
2. KAFR ASH SHAYKH
3. AL GHARBĪYAH
4. AL MINŪFĪYAH
5. AD DAQAHLĪYAH
6. DUMYĀṬ
7. BŪR SAʻĪD
8. ASH SHARQĪYAH
9. AL ISMAʻĪLĪYAH
10. AL QALYŪBĪYAH
11. AL QĀHIRAH
12. AL FAYYŪM
13. BANĪ SUWAYF
© Copyright by HAMMOND INCORPORATED, Maplewood, N.J.
Longitude East of Greenwich
SCALE 1:7,000,000
LAMBERT CONFORMAL CONIC PROJECTION
MILES 0 100 200 300
KILOMETERS 0 100 200 300
POPULATION OF CITIES AND TOWNS
OVER 2,000,000
1,000,000 - 1,999,999
500,000 - 999,999
250,000 - 499,999
100,000 - 249,999
30,000 - 99,999
10,000 - 29,999
UNDER 10,000

Northern Middle East

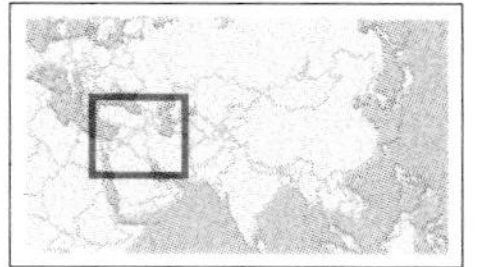

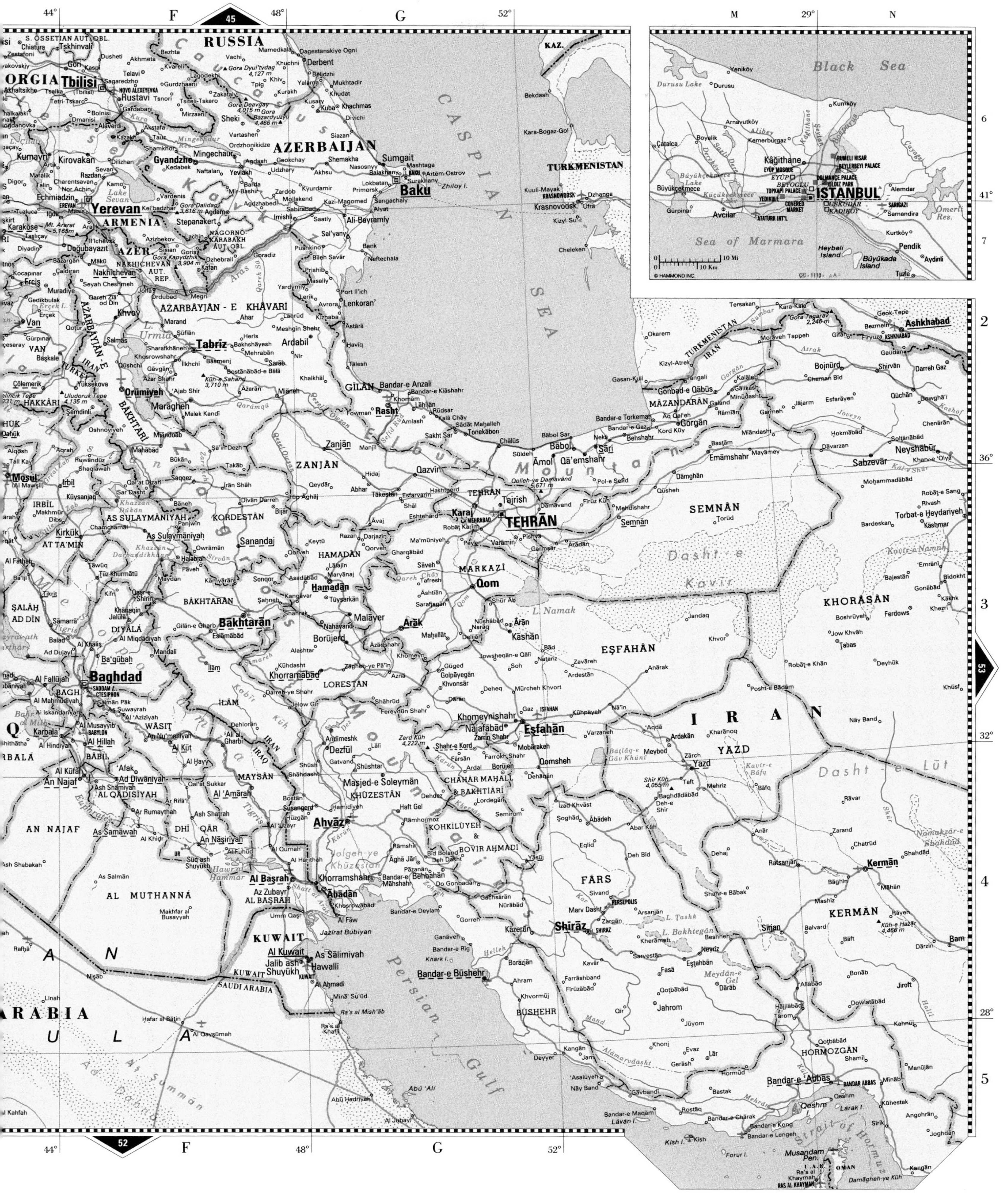

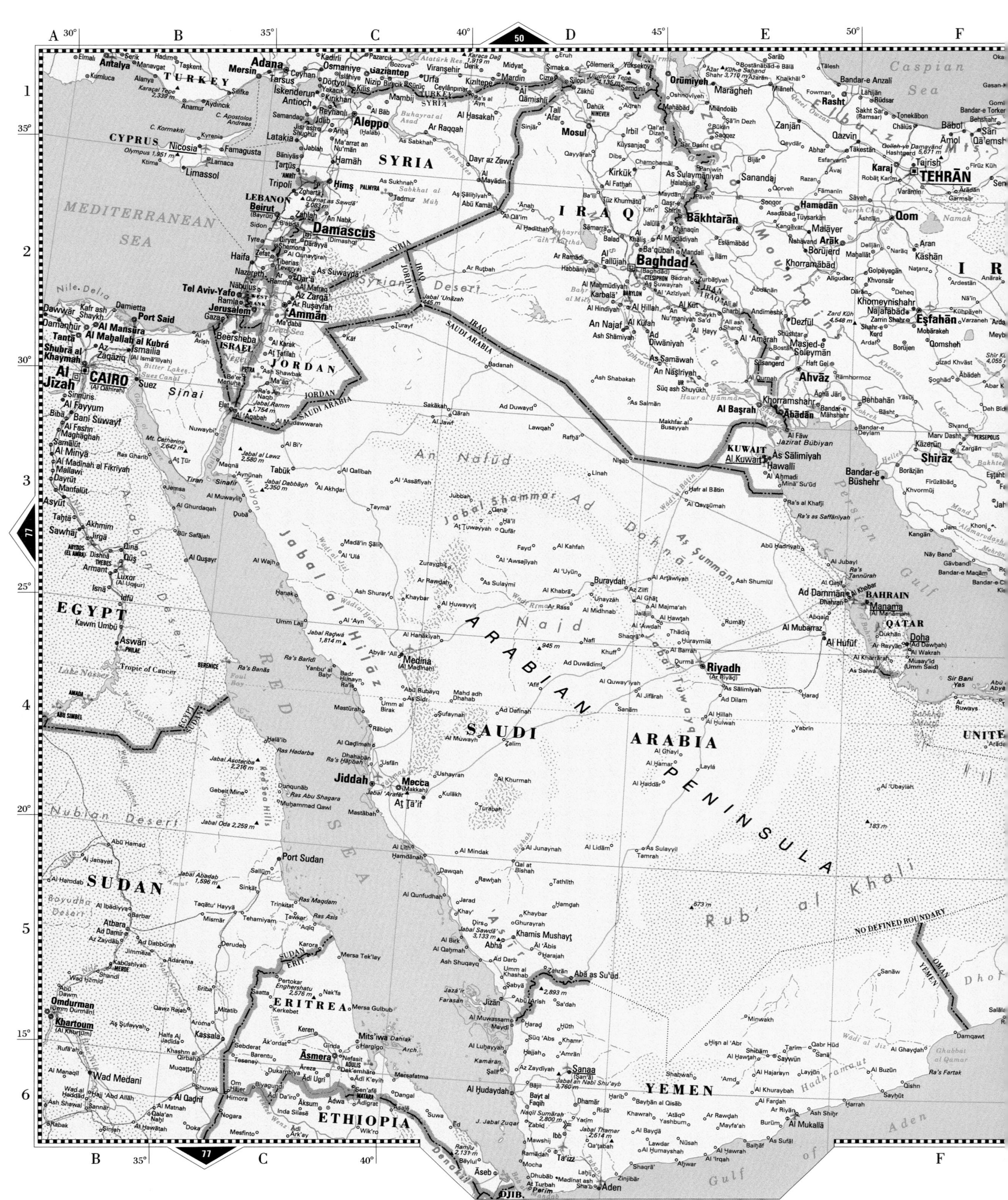

A
B
C
D
E
F
30°
35°
40°
45°
50°
50
77
1
2
3
4
5
6
TURKEY
Antalya
Adana
Mersin
Tarsus
Ceyhan
Osmaniye
Gaziantep
İskenderun
Antioch
Urfa
Viranşehir
Kilis
Mardin
Cizre
Şırnak
Siirt
Kiziltepe
Al Qāmishlī
Zākhū
Dahūk
Mosul
Tall 'Afar
Sinjār
Irbil
Kirkūk
Orūmīyeh
Marāgheh
Mahābād
Miāndoāb
Saqqez
Zanjān
Qazvīn
Rasht
Bandar-e Anzalī
Karaj
TEHRĀN
Qom
Caspian Sea
Elburz Mts.
CYPRUS
Nicosia
Famagusta
Larnaca
Limassol
Kyrenia
Olympus 1,951 m
Aleppo
(Halab)
Idlib
Latakia
Jablah
Bāniyās
Ţarţūs
Ḩamāh
Ḩimş
Tripoli
Ar Raqqah
Al Ḩasakah
Dayr az Zawr
Al Mayādīn
Abū Kamāl
Tadmur
PALMYRA
SYRIA
Syrian Desert
LEBANON
Beirut
(Bayrūt)
Sidon
Tyre
Zahlah
Damascus
(Dimashq)
Haifa
Tiberias
Nazareth
Nābulus
Tel Aviv-Yafo
Jerusalem
Gaza
Beersheba
ISRAEL
WEST BANK
Amman
Az Zarqā'
JORDAN
Al Karak
Ma'ān
Al 'Aqabah
Elat
Ar Rutbah
IRAQ
Ar Ramādī
Al Fallūjah
Baghdad
(Baghdād)
Karbalā'
Al Ḩillah
An Najaf
Al Kūfah
Ad Dīwānīyah
As Samāwah
An Nāşirīyah
Al 'Amārah
Al Başrah
Ba'qūbah
As Sulaymānīyah
Sanandaj
Bākhtarān
Hamadān
Malāyer
Arāk
Borūjerd
Khorramābād
Dezfūl
Ahvāz
Khorramshahr
Ābādān
Eşfahān
Kāshān
Shīrāz
Bandar-e Būshehr
Zagros Mountains
Euphrates
Tigris
KUWAIT
Al Kuwait
Hawallī
MEDITERRANEAN SEA
Nile Delta
Damietta
Port Said
Al Manşūrah
Al Maḩallah al Kubrá
Ţanţā
Shubrā al Khaymah
Az Zaqāzīq
Ismailia
Al Jīzah
CAIRO
(Al Qāhirah)
Suez
Suez Canal
Sinai
Mt. Catherine 2,642 m
Al Fayyūm
Banī Suwayf
Al Minyā
Asyūţ
Sawhāj
Qinā
Luxor
(Al Uqşur)
Isnā
Idfū
Aswān
EGYPT
Arabian Desert
Tropic of Cancer
Lake Nasser
ABU SIMBEL
Nubian Desert
Wādī Ḩalfā
SUDAN
Atbara
Omdurman
(Umm Durmān)
Khartoum
(Al Kharţūm)
Wad Medani
Kassala
Port Sudan
ERITREA
Āsmera
Mits'iwa
Āseb
ETHIOPIA
RED SEA
Jabal al Ḩijāz
Tabūk
Taymā'
Al Wajh
Umm Lajj
Yanbu' al Baḩr
Medina
(Al Madīnah)
Jiddah
Mecca
(Makkah)
Aţ Ţā'if
Al Līth
Al Qunfudhah
Abhā
Khamīs Mushayţ
Jīzān
Najrān
An Nafūd
Ḩā'il
Buraydah
'Unayzah
Najd
ARABIAN PENINSULA
SAUDI ARABIA
Riyadh
(Ar Riyāḑ)
Al Kharj
Al Hufūf
Ad Dammām
Az Zahrān
Al Jubayl
BAHRAIN
Manama
(Al Manāmah)
QATAR
Doha
(Ad Dawḩah)
Persian Gulf
Rub' al Khālī
As Summān
Ad Dahnā'
NO DEFINED BOUNDARY
OMAN
YEMEN
Sanaa
(Şan'ā')
Al Ḩudaydah
Ta'izz
Aden
Al Mukallā
Gulf of Aden
Ḩaḑramawt
Ma'rib
DJIB.

Southwestern Asia

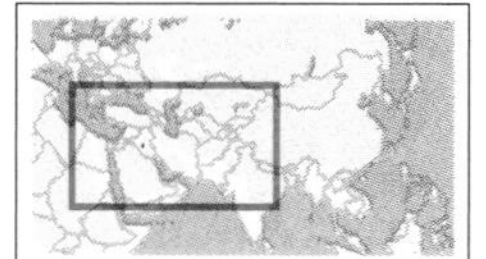

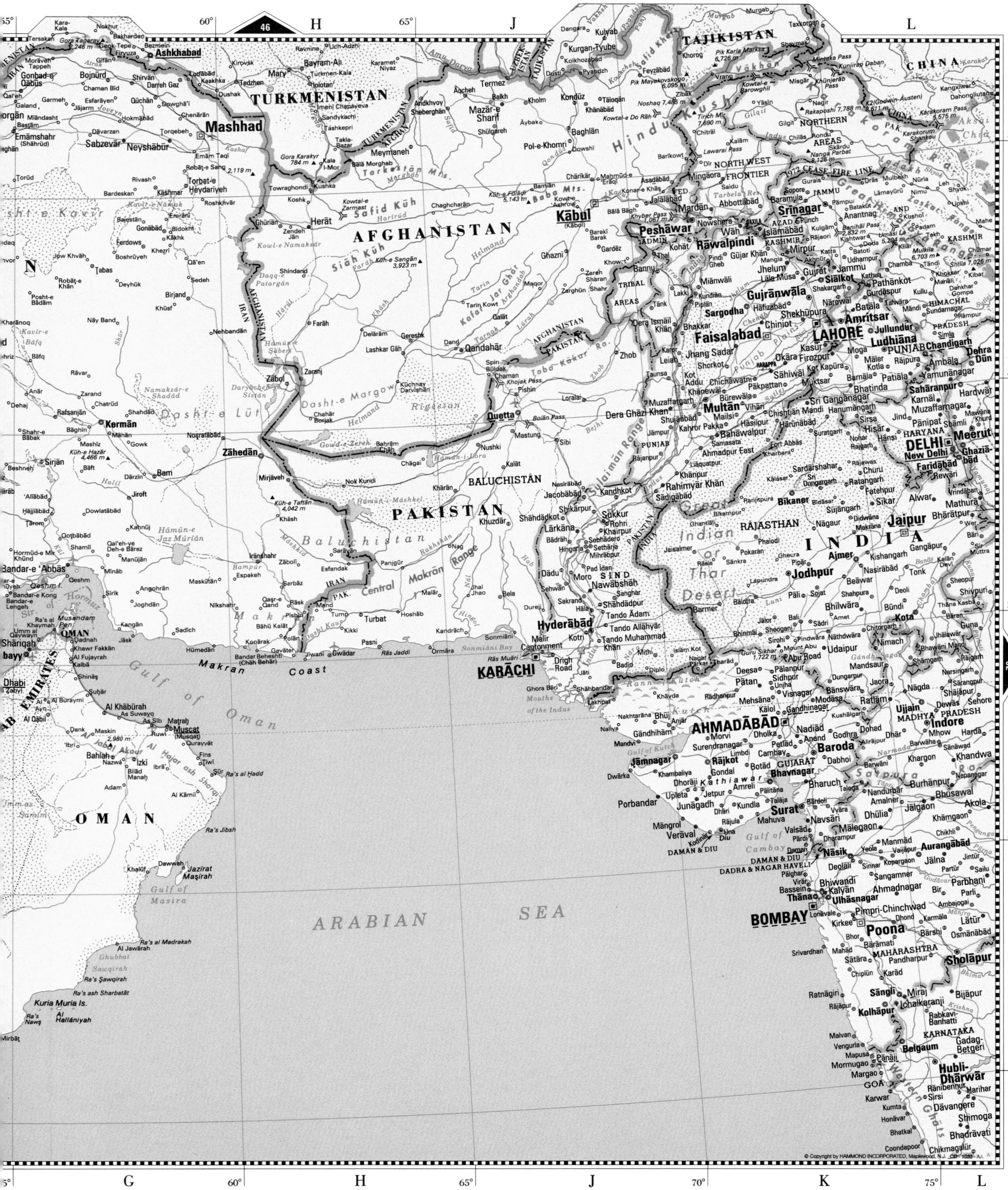

POPULATION OF CITIES AND TOWNS

- OVER 2,000,000
- 1,000,000 - 1,999,999
- 500,000 - 999,999
- 250,000 - 499,999
- 100,000 - 249,999
- 30,000 - 99,999
- 10,000 - 29,999
- UNDER 10,000

SCALE 1:10,500,000 LAMBERT CONFORMAL CONIC PROJECTION

MILES 0 150 300 450

KILOMETERS 0 150 300 450

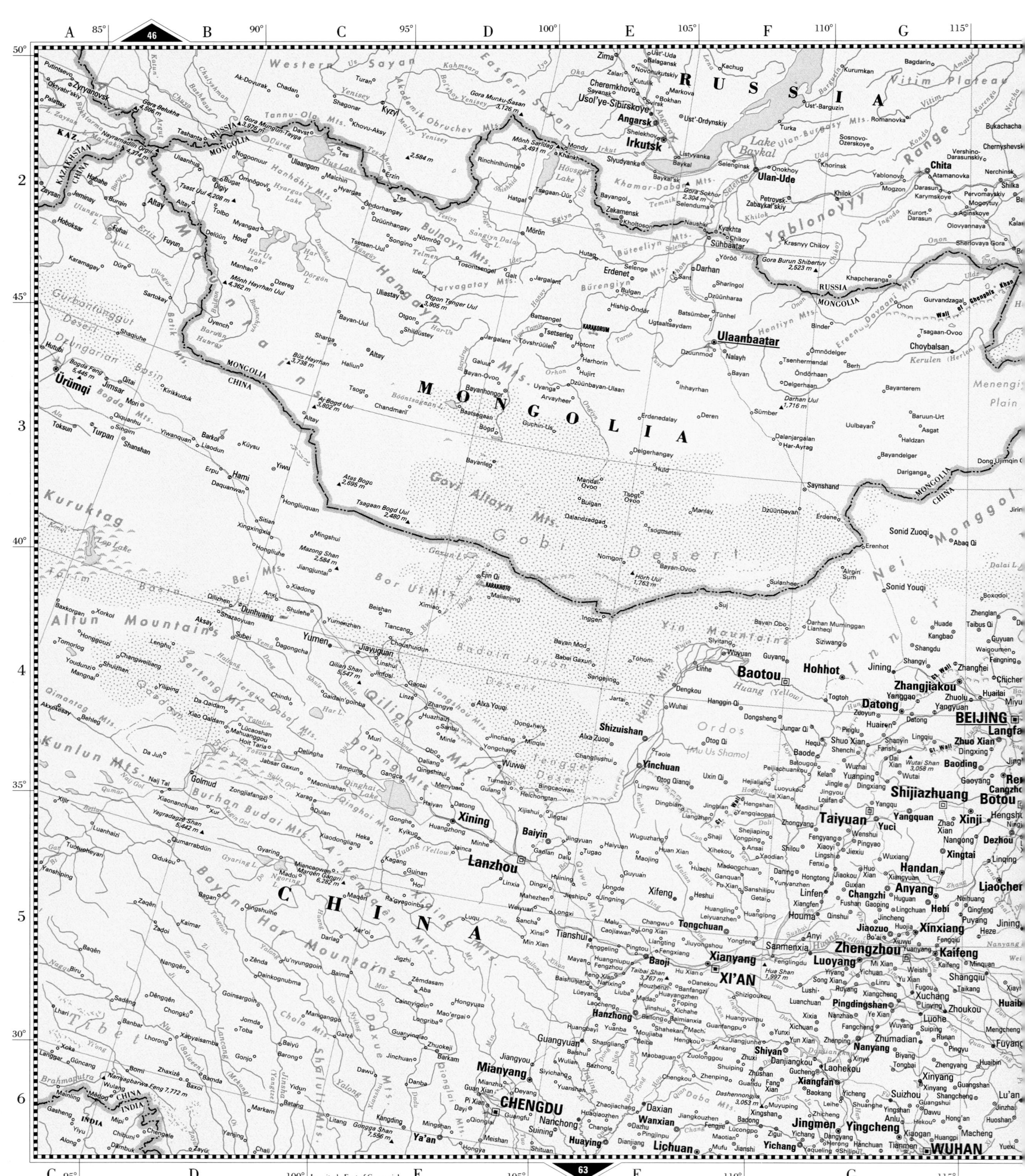

46
63
Longitude East of Greenwich
RUSSIA
MONGOLIA
CHINA
KAZAKHSTAN
KAZ.
INDIA
Western Sayan
Eastern Sayan
Tannu-Ola Mts.
Akademik Obruchev Mts.
Lake Baykal
Ulan-Burgasy Mts.
Khamar-Daban Mts.
Vitim Plateau
Yablonovyy Range
Bulnayn Mts.
Hangayn Mts.
Tarvagatay Mts.
Büteeliyn Mts.
Bürengiyn Mts.
Hentiyn Mts.
Mongol Altayn Mts.
Gurbantunggut Desert
Dzungarian Basin
Bogda Mts.
Kuruktag
Lop Lake
Tarim Basin
Bei Mts.
Bor Ul Mts.
Gobi Desert
Gobi Altayn Mts.
Yin Mountains
Badain Jaran Desert
Tengger Desert
Ordos
Helan Mts.
Altun Mountains
Qilian Mts.
Datong Mts.
Serteng Mts.
Qaidam Basin
Kunlun Mts.
Burhan Budai Mts.
Qinghai Lake
Bayan Har Mountains
A'nyêmaqên Mts.
Qinling Mts.
Daba Mts.
Tibet
Chola Mts.
Daxue Mts.
Shaluli Mts.
Qionglai Mts.
Nei Monggol
Inner
Menengiyn Plain
Huang (Yellow)
Brahmaputra
Irkutsk
Angarsk
Ulan-Ude
Chita
Ulaanbaatar
Darhan
Erdenet
Ürümqi
Turpan
Hami
Dunhuang
Jiayuguan
Yumen
Xining
Lanzhou
Baiyin
Yinchuan
Shizuishan
Baotou
Hohhot
Zhangjiakou
Datong
BEIJING
Langfang
Baoding
Shijiazhuang
Taiyuan
Xinji
Handan
Anyang
Xingtai
Dezhou
Liaocheng
Hebi
Xinxiang
Kaifeng
Zhengzhou
Luoyang
Jiaozuo
Tongchuan
Xianyang
XI'AN
Baoji
Tianshui
Hanzhong
Shiyan
Xiangfan
Nanyang
Pingdingshan
Xuchang
Zhoukou
Zhumadian
Guangyuan
Mianyang
CHENGDU
Ya'an
Nanchong
Huaying
Daxian
Wanxian
Lichuan
Jingmen
Yingcheng
Yichang
WUHAN
Laohekou
Karakorum
Wall of Chenghis Khan
Gt. Wall
Gora Belukha 4,506 m
Gora Munku-Sasan 3,126 m
Mönh Sarīdag 3,491 m
Otgon Tenger Uul 3,905 m
Mönh Hayrhan Uul 4,362 m
Tsast Uul 4,208 m
Bogda Feng 5,445 m
Ih Bogd Uul 3,802 m
Tsagaan Bogd Uul 2,480 m
Hörh Uul 1,763 m
Qilian Shan 5,547 m
Yagradagzê Shan 5,442 m
Mianxu Shan 3,058 m
Hua Shan 1,997 m
Taibai Shan 3,767 m
Gongga Shan 7,556 m
Namjagbarwa Feng 7,772 m
Dashennongjia 3,053 m

Eastern Asia

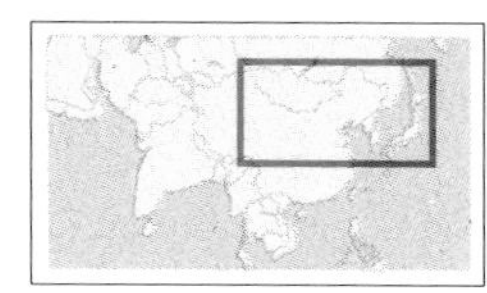

POPULATION OF CITIES AND TOWNS

■ OVER 2,000,000	◉ 500,000 - 999,999	● 100,000 - 249,999	◦ 10,000 - 29,999
▣ 1,000,000 - 1,999,999	◎ 250,000 - 499,999	◉ 30,000 - 99,999	○ UNDER 10,000

SCALE 1:10,500,000 LAMBERT CONFORMAL CONIC PROJECTION

MILES 0 150 300 450

KILOMETERS 0 150 300 450

Longitude East of Greenwich

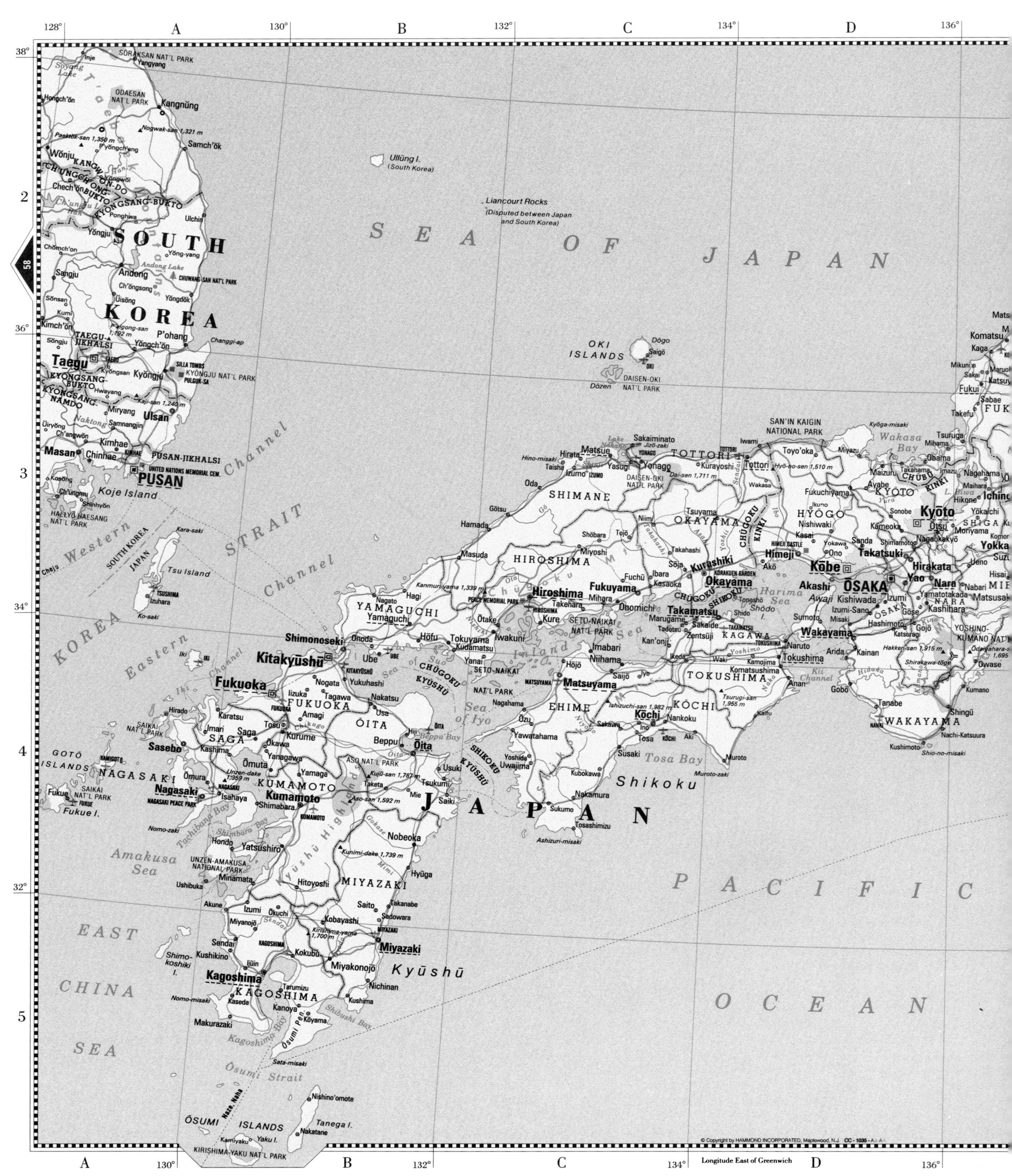
SEA OF JAPAN
SOUTH KOREA
JAPAN
PACIFIC OCEAN
EAST CHINA SEA
KOREA STRAIT
Western Channel
Eastern Channel
Ullŭng I. (South Korea)
Liancourt Rocks (Disputed between Japan and South Korea)
OKI ISLANDS
Kyūshū
Shikoku
Tosa Bay
Harima Sea
Inland Sea
Sea of Iyo
Amakusa Sea
Ōsumi Strait
ŌSUMI ISLANDS
Tanega I.
Yaku I.
Tsu Island
Koje Island
GOTŌ ISLANDS
Fukue I.
PUSAN
Taegu
Ulsan
Masan
Fukuoka
Kitakyūshū
Shimonoseki
Nagasaki
Kumamoto
Kagoshima
Miyazaki
Ōita
Hiroshima
Okayama
Kōbe
ŌSAKA
Kyōto
Nara
Wakayama
Tokushima
Takamatsu
Matsuyama
Kōchi
Tottori
Matsue
Yamaguchi
Saga
HIROSHIMA
OKAYAMA
SHIMANE
TOTTORI
YAMAGUCHI
FUKUOKA
SAGA
NAGASAKI
KUMAMOTO
ŌITA
MIYAZAKI
KAGOSHIMA
EHIME
KŌCHI
TOKUSHIMA
KAGAWA
HYŌGO
WAKAYAMA
128° 130° 132° 134° 136°
38° 36° 34° 32°
A B C D
2 3 4 5
58
Longitude East of Greenwich
© Copyright by HAMMOND INCORPORATED, Maplewood, N.J.

Central and Southern Japan

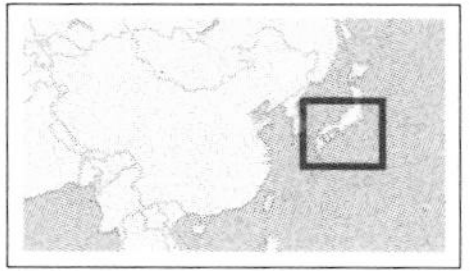

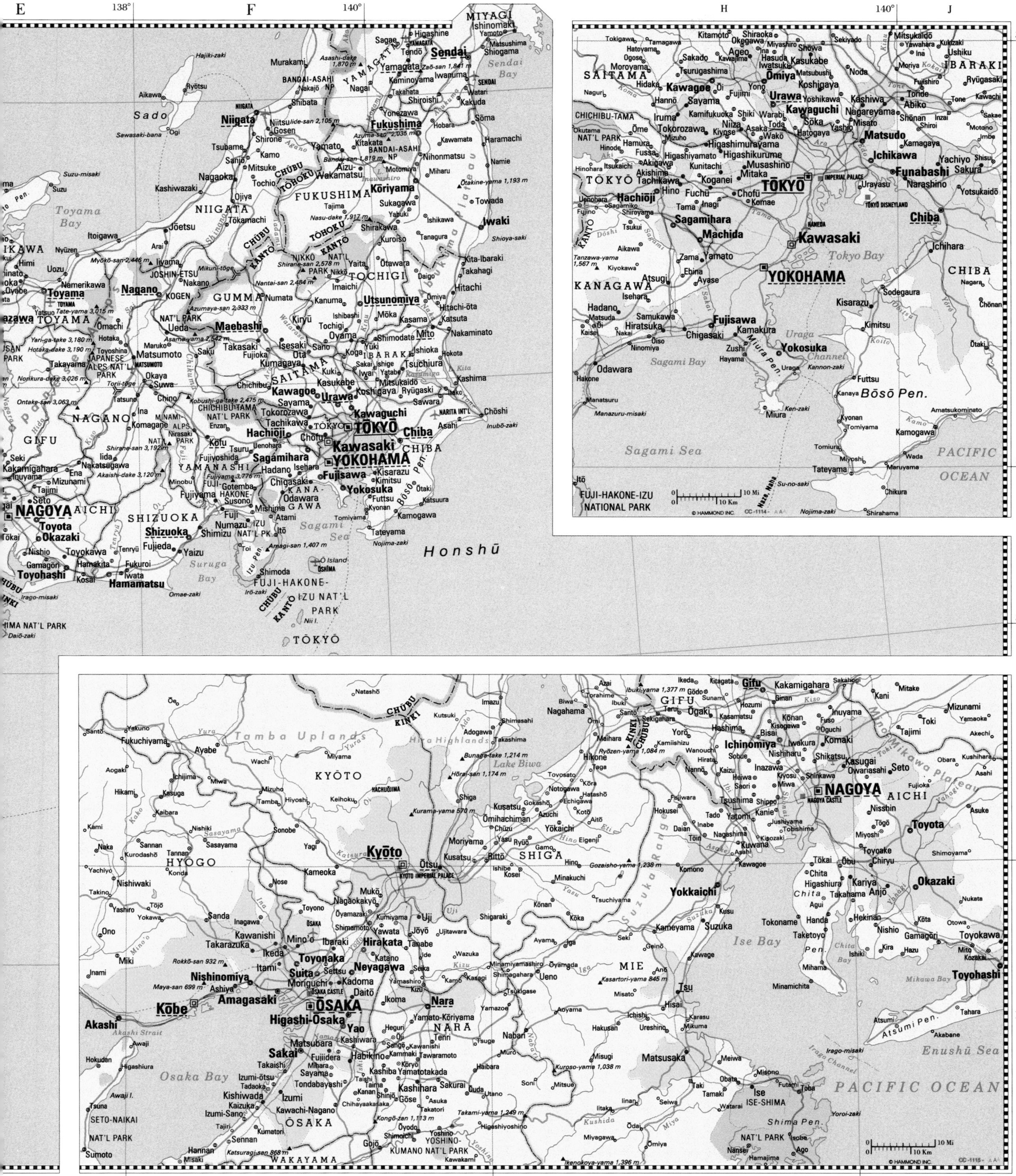

POPULATION OF CITIES AND TOWNS

- OVER 2,000,000
- 1,000,000 - 1,999,999
- 500,000 - 999,999
- 250,000 - 499,999
- 100,000 - 249,999
- 30,000 - 99,999
- 10,000 - 24,999
- UNDER 10,000

SCALE 1:3,500,000 LAMBERT CONFORMAL CONIC PROJECTION

MILES 0 10 20 30 40 50

KILOMETERS 0 10 20 30 40 50

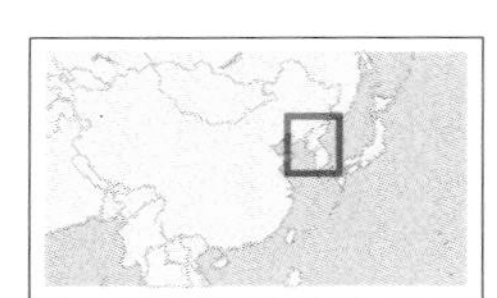

Korea

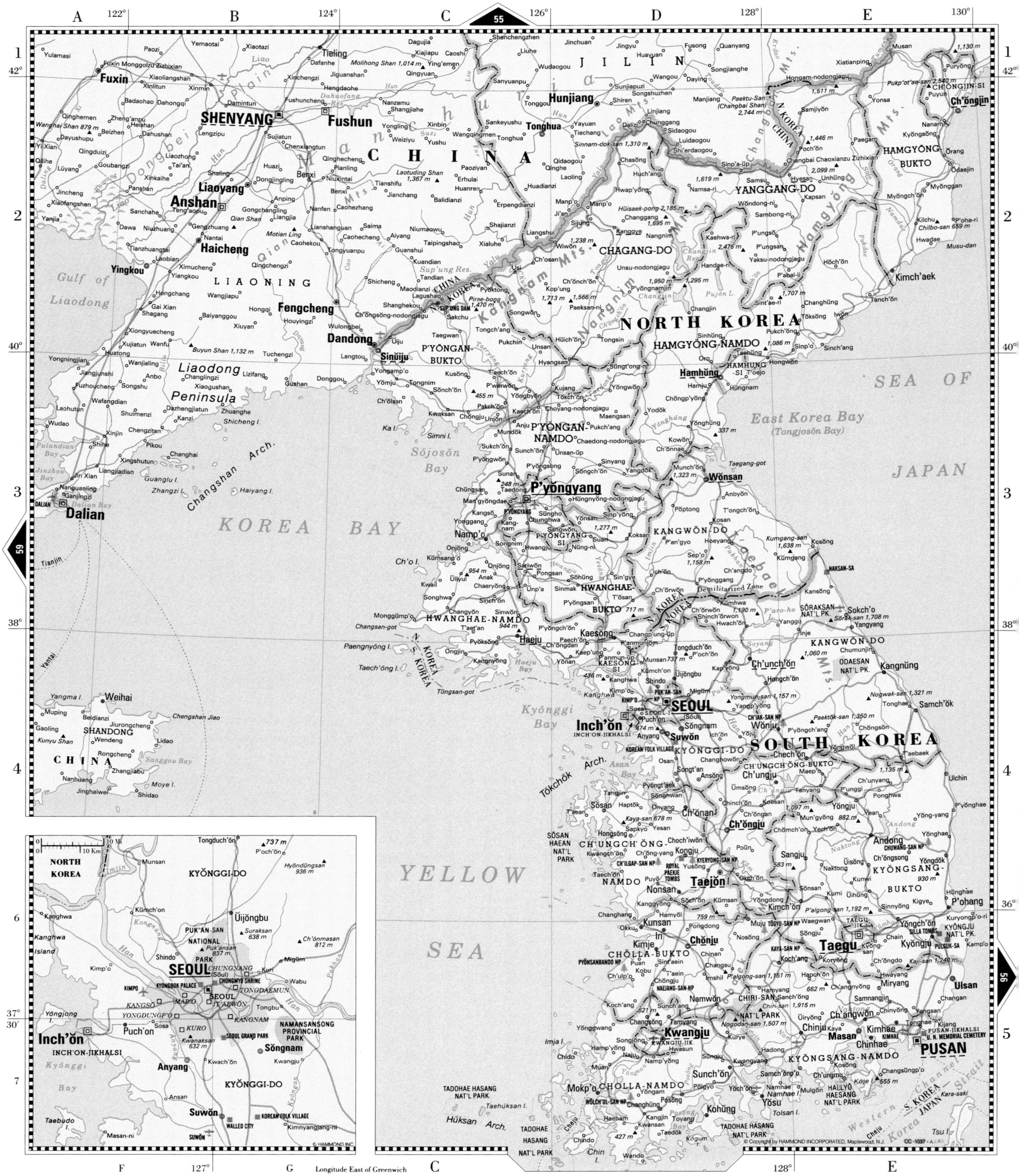

SCALE 1:3,500,000 LAMBERT CONFORMAL CONIC PROJECTION

MILES 0 50 100 150

KILOMETERS 0 50 100 150

Longitude East of Greenwich

POPULATION OF CITIES AND TOWNS

- OVER 2,000,000
- 1,000,000 - 1,999,999
- 500,000 - 999,999
- 250,000 - 499,999
- 100,000 - 249,999
- 30,000 - 99,999
- 10,000 - 29,999
- UNDER 10,000

Northeastern China

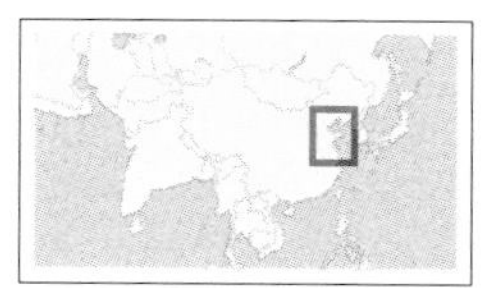

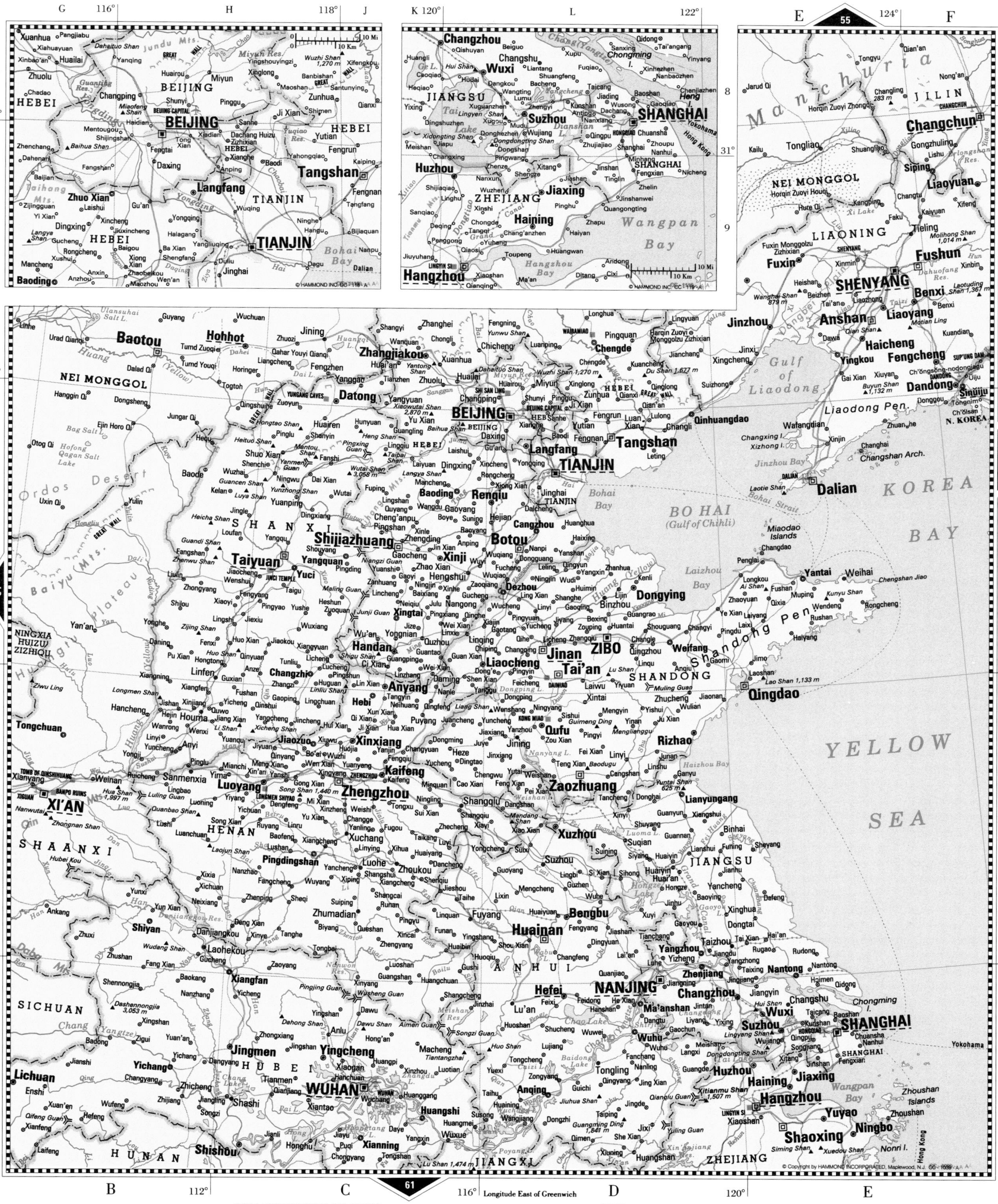

POPULATION OF CITIES AND TOWNS

- OVER 2,000,000
- 1,000,000 - 1,999,999
- 500,000 - 999,999
- 250,000 - 499,999
- 100,000 - 249,999
- 30,000 - 99,999
- 10,000 - 29,999
- UNDER 10,000

SCALE 1:7,000,000 LAMBERT CONFORMAL CONIC PROJECTION

MILES 0 100 200 300

KILOMETERS 0 100 200 300

Longitude East of Greenwich

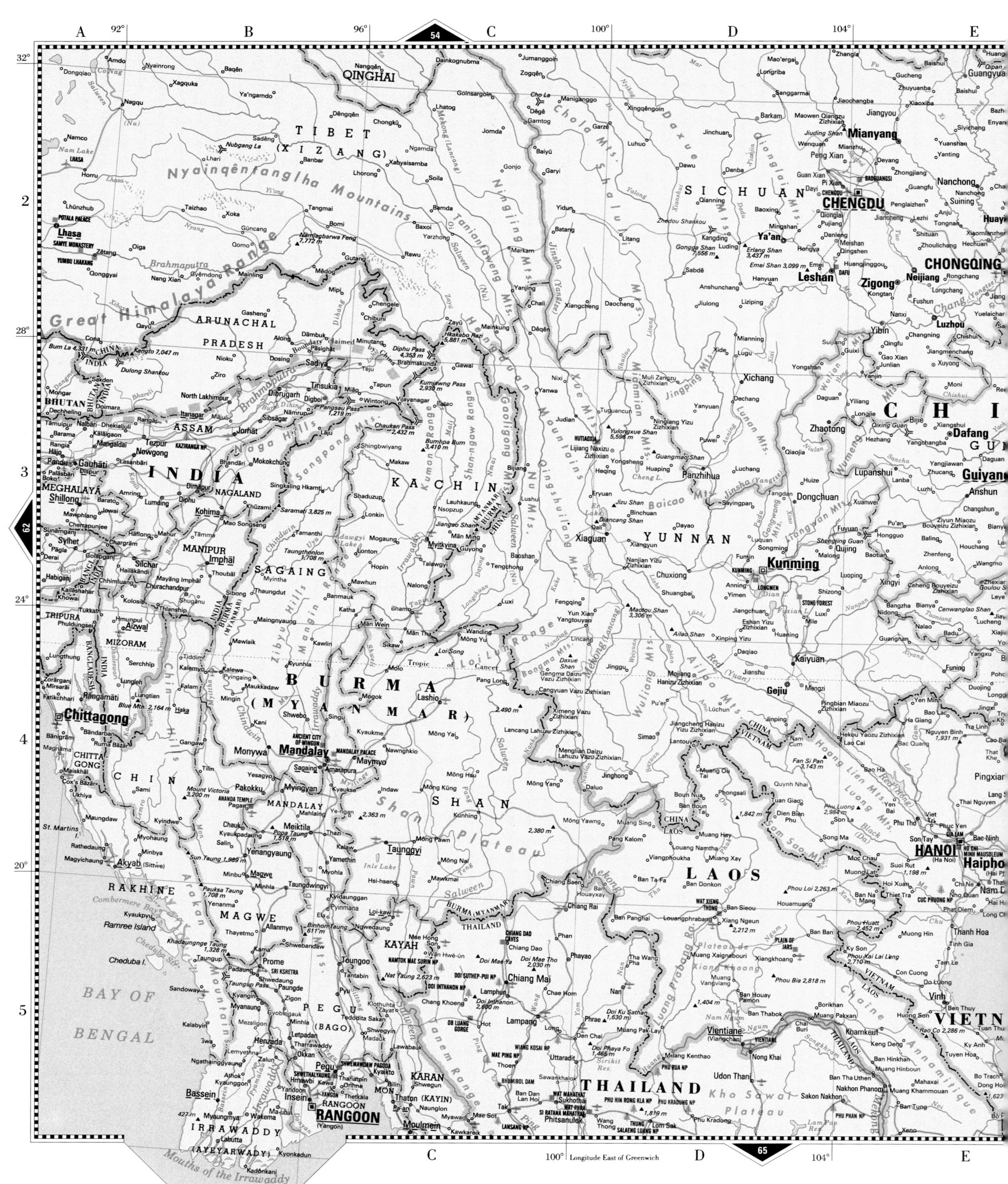
A
92°
B
96°
54
C
100°
D
104°
E
32°
28°
24°
20°
2
3
4
5
62
QINGHAI
TIBET
(XIZANG)
Nyainqêntanglha Mountains
Lhasa
Great Himalaya Range
Brahmaputra
ARUNACHAL
PRADESH
BHUTAN
ASSAM
INDIA
MEGHALAYA
Shillong
NAGALAND
MANIPUR
Imphal
MIZORAM
TRIPURA
BANGLADESH
Chittagong
CHITTAGONG
CHIN
RAKHINE
Akyab (Sittwe)
Ramree Island
Cheduba I.
BAY OF
BENGAL
KACHIN
SAGAING
BURMA
(MYANMAR)
Mandalay
MANDALAY
MAGWE
SHAN
Shan Plateau
Taunggyi
KAYAH
PEGU
(BAGO)
KARAN
Shwegun
Thaton (KAYIN)
RANGOON
(Yangon)
Bassein
IRRAWADDY
(AYEYARWADY)
Mouths of the Irrawaddy
Moulmein
Tropic of Cancer
SICHUAN
CHENGDU
CHONGQING
Leshan
Zigong
Mianyang
Kunming
YUNNAN
Gejiu
LAOS
THAILAND
Chiang Mai
Vientiane
(Viangchan)
Kho Sawat Plateau
HANOI
Haipho
VIETN
Hengduan Mountains
Qingshuilang Mts.
Daxue Mts.
Ailao Mts.
Wuliang Mts.
C
100° Longitude East of Greenwich
D
65
104°
E

Southeastern China, Burma

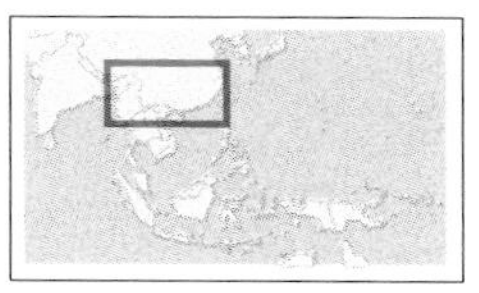

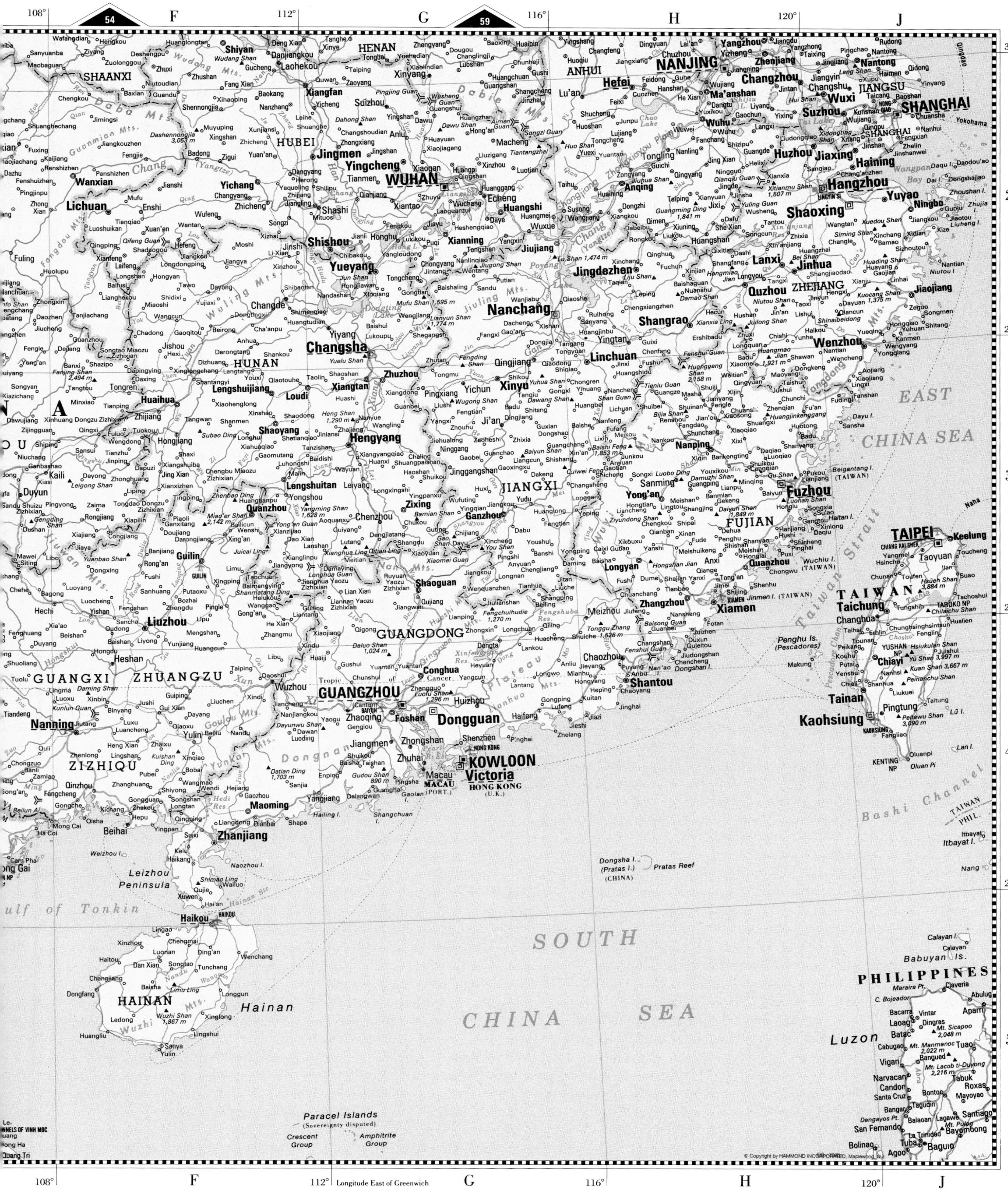

108° F 112° G 116° H 120° J

54 59

HENAN ANHUI HUBEI SHAANXI JIANGSU HUNAN JIANGXI ZHEJIANG FUJIAN GUANGDONG GUANGXI ZHUANGZU ZIZHIQU HAINAN TAIWAN PHILIPPINES

NANJING SHANGHAI WUHAN Changsha Nanchang Hangzhou Fuzhou Guangzhou KOWLOON Victoria HONG KONG (U.K.) Macau MACAU (PORT.) TAIPEI Nanning Haikou

EAST CHINA SEA

SOUTH CHINA SEA

Taiwan Strait

Bashi Channel

Gulf of Tonkin

Paracel Islands (Sovereignty disputed)

Luzon

Tropic of Cancer

32° 28° 24° 20°

2 3 4 5

108° F 112° Longitude East of Greenwich G 116° H 120° J

POPULATION OF CITIES AND TOWNS

- OVER 2,000,000
- 1,000,000 - 1,999,999
- 500,000 - 999,999
- 250,000 - 499,999
- 100,000 - 249,999
- 30,000 - 99,999
- 10,000 - 29,999
- UNDER 10,000

SCALE 1:7,000,000 LAMBERT CONFORMAL CONIC PROJECTION

MILES 0 100 200 300

KILOMETERS 0 100 200 300

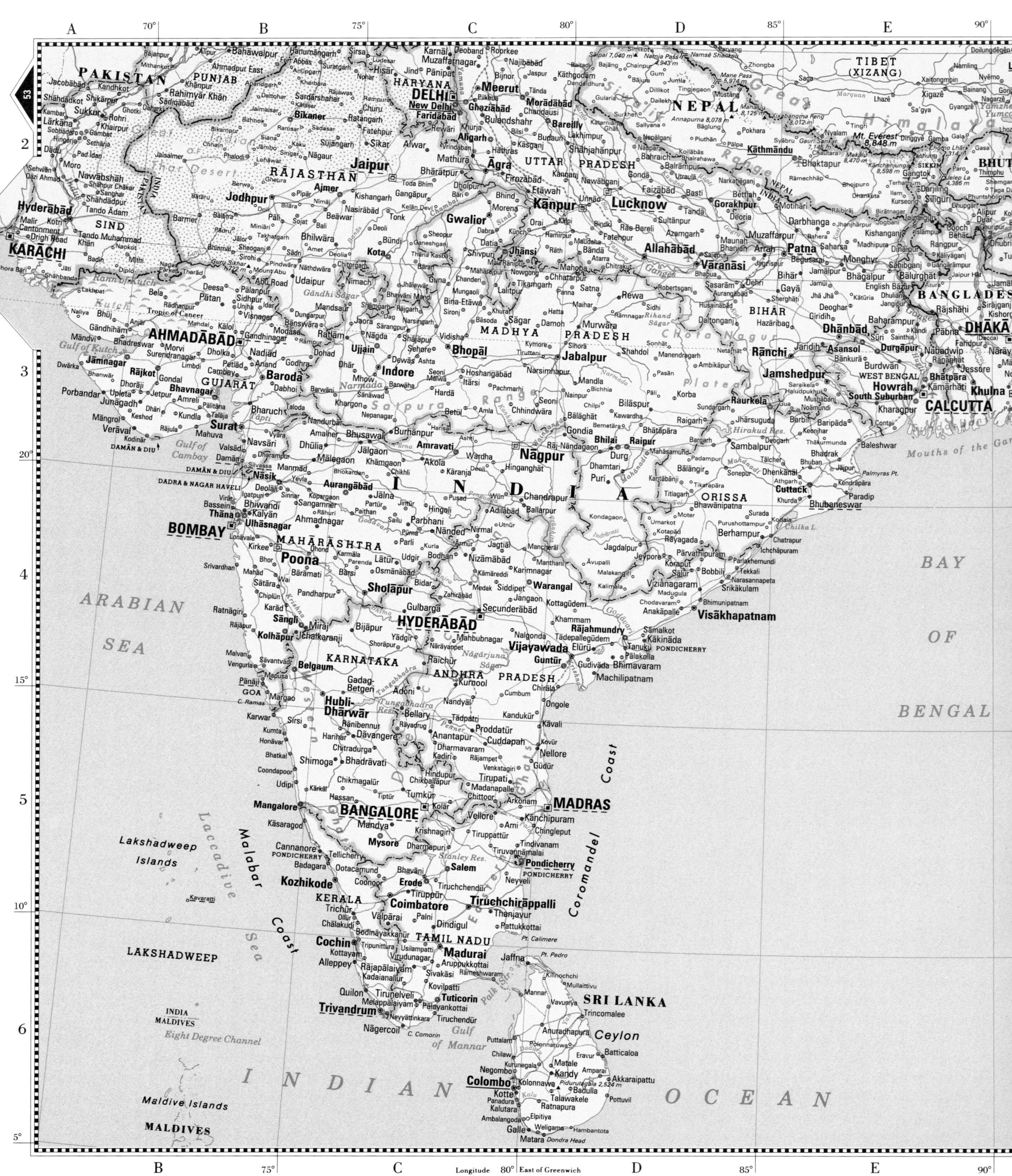

A
70°
B
75°
C
80°
D
85°
E
90°
53
2
3
4
5
6
20°
15°
10°
5°
Longitude 80° East of Greenwich
PAKISTAN
PUNJAB
SIND
KARĀCHI
Hyderābād
Jacobābād
Sukkur
Bahāwalpur
Rahimyār Khān
TIBET (XIZANG)
NEPAL
Kāthmāndu
Mt. Everest 8,848 m
BHUT
Thimphu
BANGLADES
DHĀKĀ
HARYANA
DELHI
New Delhi
Farīdābād
Meerut
Morādābād
Bareilly
Āgra
UTTAR PRADESH
Lucknow
Kānpur
Allahābād
Vārānasi
Gorakhpur
Patna
BIHĀR
Rānchi
Jamshedpur
Dhānbād
Asansol
Durgāpur
WEST BENGAL
Howrah
CALCUTTA
Khulna
RĀJASTHĀN
Jaipur
Jodhpur
Ajmer
Bikaner
Kota
Udaipur
Great Indian Thar Desert
Rann of Kutch
Gulf of Kutch
Tropic of Cancer
GUJARĀT
AHMADĀBĀD
Rājkot
Jāmnagar
Bhavnagar
Baroda
Surat
DAMĀN & DIU
Gulf of Cambay
MADHYA PRADESH
Gwalior
Jhānsi
Bhopāl
Indore
Ujjain
Jabalpur
Sāgar
Narmada
Satpura Range
Nāgpur
INDIA
Raipur
Bhilai
Durg
Chota Nagpur Plateau
ORISSA
Cuttack
Bhubaneswar
Sambalpur
Raurkela
Hirakud Res.
Mouths of the Ganges
MAHĀRĀSHTRA
BOMBAY
Thāna
Ulhāsnagar
Poona
Nāsik
Aurangābād
Sholāpur
Kolhāpur
Sāngli
DADRA & NAGAR HAVELI
HYDERĀBĀD
Secunderābād
Warangal
ANDHRA PRADESH
Vijayawada
Guntūr
Rājahmundry
Visākhapatnam
Kākināda
PONDICHERRY
Godāvari
Krishna
KARNATAKA
Belgaum
Hubli-Dhārwār
GOA
Panāji
BANGALORE
Mysore
Mangalore
MADRAS
Kānchipuram
Pondicherry
Salem
Coimbatore
Tiruchchirāppalli
Madurai
TAMIL NADU
KERALA
Kozhikode
Cochin
Trivandrum
C. Comorin
ARABIAN SEA
BAY OF BENGAL
Malabar Coast
Coromandel Coast
Laccadive Sea
Lakshadweep Islands
LAKSHADWEEP
Kavaratti
INDIA
MALDIVES
Eight Degree Channel
Maldive Islands
MALDIVES
Palk Str.
Gulf of Mannar
SRI LANKA
Ceylon
Jaffna
Trincomalee
Anurādhapura
Batticaloa
Kandy
Colombo
Galle
Matara
Dondra Head
Pidurutalagala 2,524 m
INDIAN OCEAN

Southern Asia

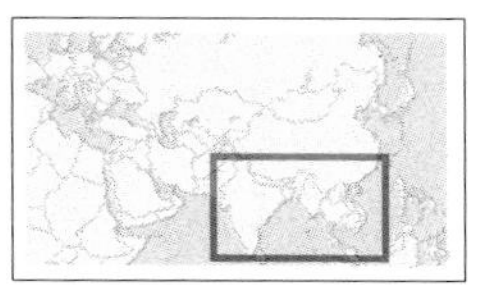

Longitude 100° East of Greenwich

POPULATION OF CITIES AND TOWNS

■ OVER 2,000,000	◉ 500,000 - 999,999	● 100,000 - 249,999	◎ 10,000 - 29,999
▣ 1,000,000 - 1,999,999	◉ 250,000 - 499,999	⊕ 30,000 - 99,999	○ UNDER 10,000

SCALE 1:10,500,000 LAMBERT CONFORMAL CONIC PROJECTION

MILES 0 150 300 450

KILOMETERS 0 150 300 450

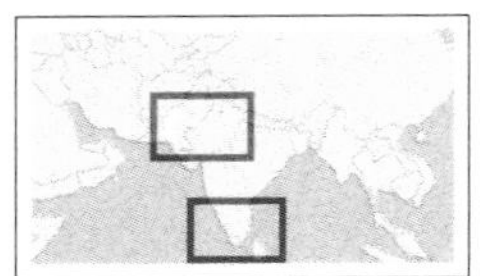

Punjab Plain, Southern India

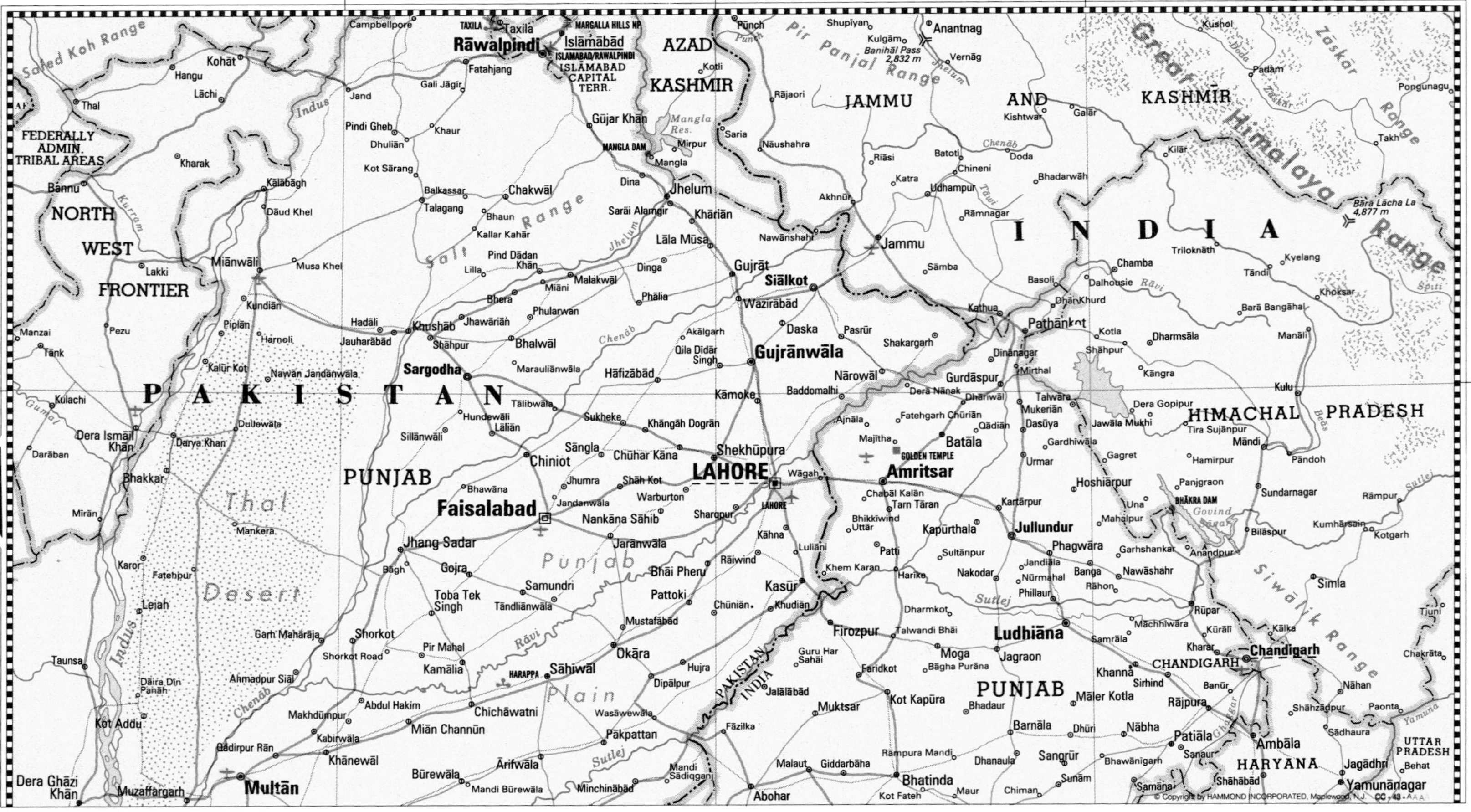

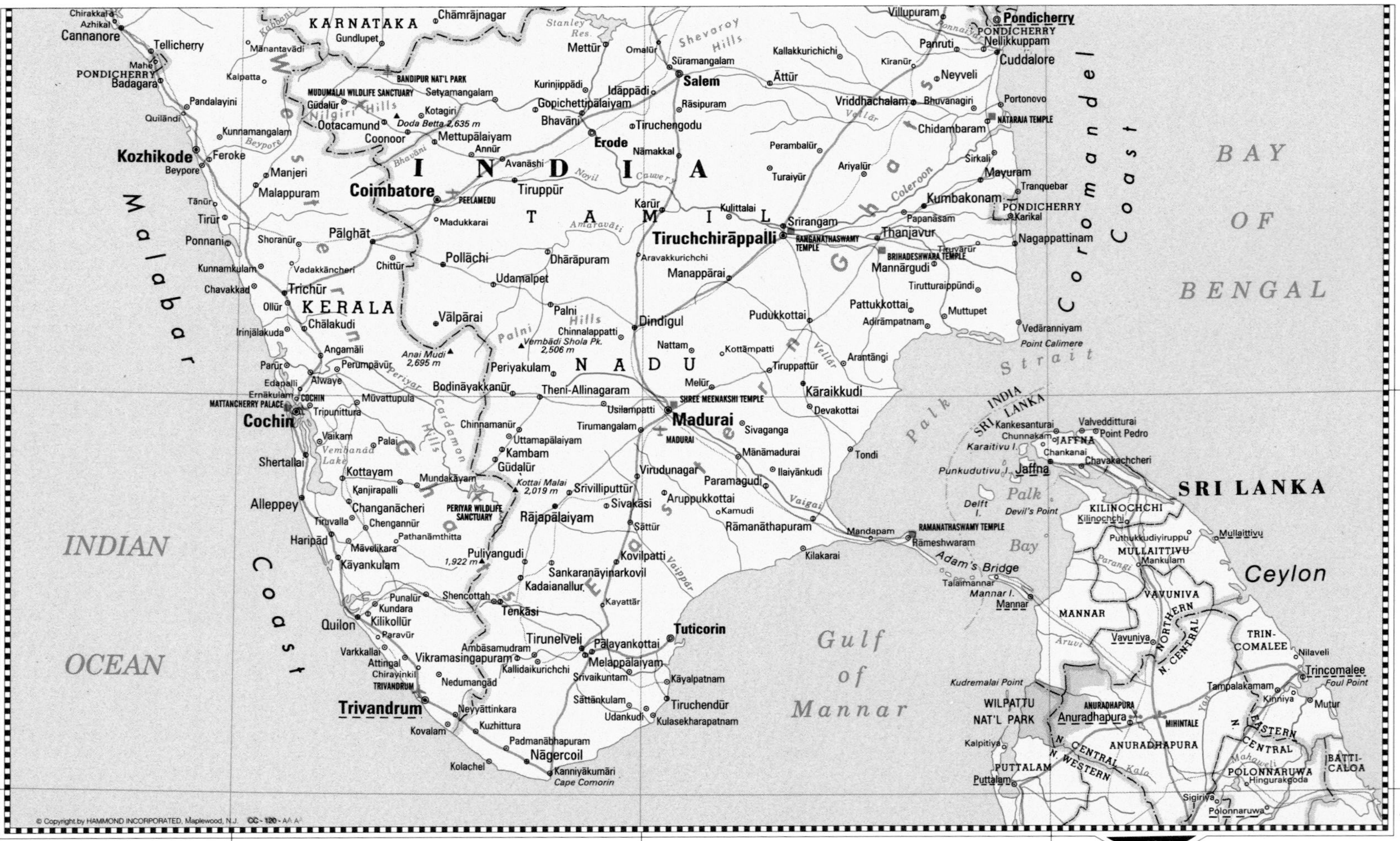

SCALE 1:3,500,000 LAMBERT CONFORMAL CONIC PROJECTION

MILES 0 50 100 150

KILOMETERS 0 50 100 150

Longitude East of Greenwich

POPULATION OF CITIES AND TOWNS

- OVER 2,000,000
- 1,000,000 - 1,999,999
- 500,000 - 999,999
- 250,000 - 499,999
- 100,000 - 249,999
- 30,000 - 99,999
- 10,000 - 29,999
- UNDER 10,000

Eastern Burma, Thailand, Indochina

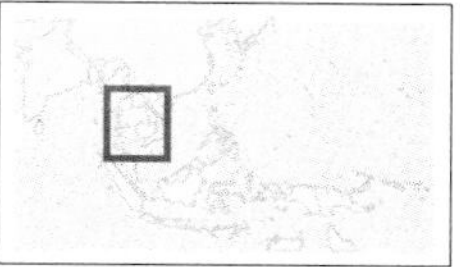

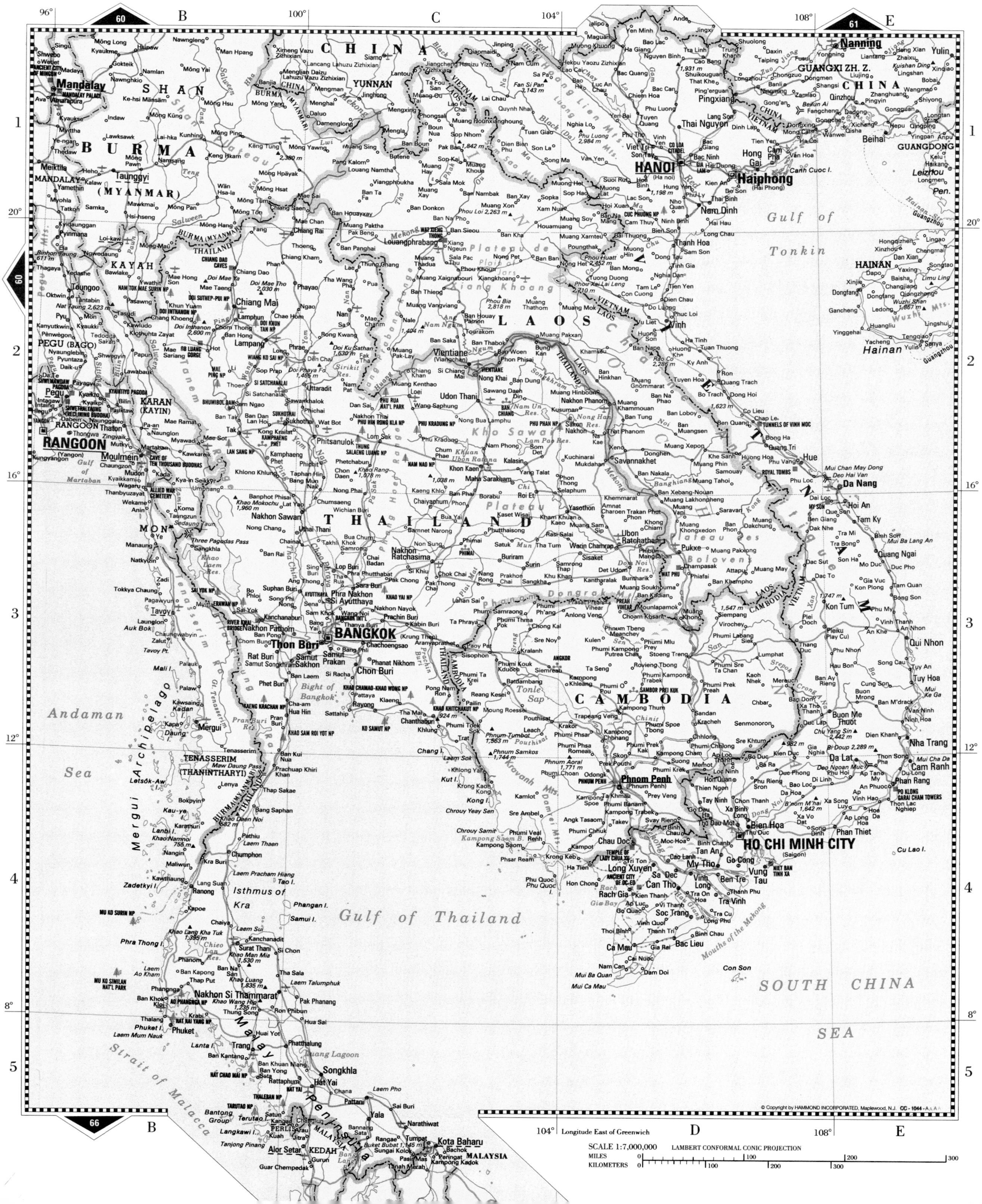

Longitude East of Greenwich

SCALE 1:7,000,000 LAMBERT CONFORMAL CONIC PROJECTION

MILES 0 100 200 300

KILOMETERS 0 100 200 300

65
95° A 100° B 105° C 110° D 115°
1
2
3
4
5
6
10°
5°
0°
Equator
BURMA (MYANMAR)
THAILAND
CAMBODIA
VIETNAM
MALAYSIA
BRUNEI
SINGAPORE
Andaman Sea
Gulf of Thailand
SOUTH C
SEA
Mergui Archipelago
Isthmus of Kra
Malay Peninsula
Strait of Malacca
Spratly Islands
(Sovereignty disputed)
Mergui
Tenasserim
Prachuap Khiri Khan
Ranong
Chumphon
Surat Thani
Nakhon Si Thammarat
Phuket
Trang
Songkhla
Hat Yai
Pattani
Yala
Narathiwat
Kota Baharu
Alor Setar
Sungai Petani
Georgetown
Butterworth
Taiping
Ipoh
Kuala Terengganu
Kuantan
Kuala Lumpur
Seremban
Port Dickson
Melaka
Muar
Batu Pahat
Johor Baharu
Phnom Penh
(Phnom Penh)
Kampong Saom
Phu Quoc I.
Rach Gia
Long Xuyen
Can Tho
Soc Trang
Bac Lieu
Ca Mau
Con Son
Buon Me Thuot
Nha Trang
Cam Ranh
Phan Rang
Bien Hoa
HO CHI MINH CITY
(Saigon)
Vinh Long
Go Cong
Mouths of the Mekong
Natuna Is.
Anambas Is.
Bunguran I.
Bandar Seri Begawan
Kuala Belait
Miri
Sarawak
Kuching
Sibu
Bintulu
Pontianak
Singkawang
Kalimantan
Banjarmasin
Palangkaraya
Sumatra
Medan
Tebingtinggi
Pematangsiantar
Tanjungbalai
Banda Aceh
Sabang
Sigli
Lhokseumawe
Langsa
Sibolga
Padangsidempuan
Nias I.
Simeulue I.
Banyak Islands
Batu Islands
Siberut I.
Mentawai Islands
Mentawai Strait
Bukittinggi
Payakumbuh
Padangpanjang
Pariaman
Padang
Solok
Pekanbaru
Riau Islands
Lingga Is.
Jambi
Palembang
Bangka I.
Pangkalpinang
Muntok
Belitung I.
Tanjungpandan
Karimata Strait
Gaspar Strait
Bengkulu
Lubuklinggau
Lahat
Baturaja
Kotabumi
Tanjungkarang-Telukbetung
Enggano I.
Sunda Strait
Krakatoa
Greater Sunda
JAVA SEA
INDIAN OCEAN
JAKARTA
Bekasi
Serang
Bogor
Sukabumi
Cianjur
Bandung
Garut
Tasikmalaya
Ciamis
Cirebon
Tegal
Pekalongan
Semarang
Kudus
Purwokerto
Cilacap
Magelang
Yogyakarta
Surakarta
Madiun
Kediri
Malang
Jember
Probolinggo
Pasuruan
SURABAYA
Madura
Bawean I.
Java
Longitude East of Greenwich
SCALE 1:10,500,000 LAMBERT CONFORMAL CONIC PROJECTION
MILES 0 150 300 450
KILOMETERS 0 150 300 450
POPULATION OF CITIES AND TOWNS
OVER 2,000,000
1,000,000 - 1,999,999
500,000 - 999,999
250,000 - 499,999
100,000 - 249,999
30,000 - 99,999
10,000 - 29,999
UNDER 10,000

Southeastern Asia

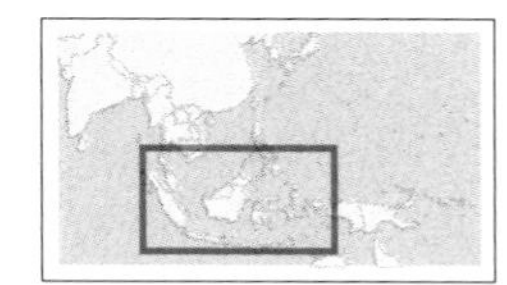

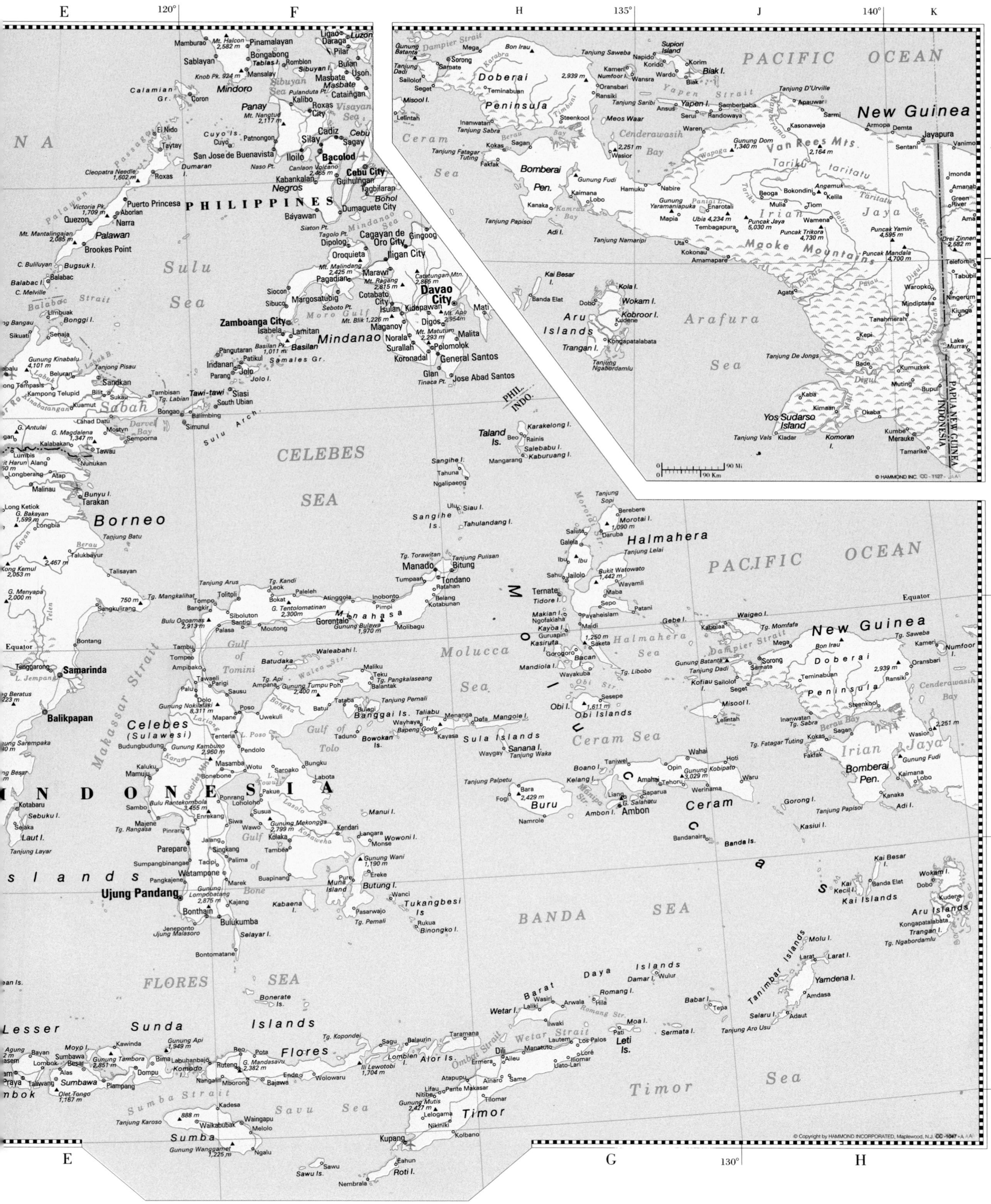

0 90 Mi
0 90 Km

110°
A
120°
B
130°
C
140°
D
150°
E
160°
F
170°
G
180°
48
70
2
3
4
5
6
7
8
20°
10°
0°
10°
20°
30°
CHINA
Changsha
Nanchang
Jingdezhen
Ningbo
Kuocang Shan 1,375 m
Xiangtan
Hengyang
Zhuzhou
Huanggang Shan 2,158 m
Wenzhou
Ji'an
Guilin
Dayun Shan 1,849 m
Ganzhou
Fuzhou
Tonggu Zhang 1,528 m
Xiamen
Chaozhou
Guangzhou
Shantou
Macao
MACAO (PORT.)
Victoria
HONG KONG (U.K.)
Kaohsiung
Tainan
Taichung
Taipei
TAIWAN
Taiwan Str.
EAST CHINA SEA
RYUKYU IS.
Ishigaki
Sakishima Is.
Okinawa Is.
Naha
Naze
Amami Is.
JAPAN
Daito Is.
Tokara Is.
Kyūshū
Ōsumi Is.
Tori-Shima (JAPAN)
Ogasawara
BONIN IS. (JAPAN)
Mukoshima Is.
Chichishima Is.
Hahashima Is.
Ritaiō
VOLCANO IS. (JAPAN)
Iwo Jima
Minamiiō
Tropic of Cancer
Minami-Tori-Shima (JAPAN)
Bashi Channel
Itbayat I.
Batan Is.
Luzon Strait
Calayan I.
Babuyan Is.
SOUTH CHINA SEA
Okino-Tori-Shima (JAPAN)
Laoag
Vigan
Luzon
Baguio
Dagupan City
Mt. Pinatubo 1,759 m
Cabanatuan City
Manila
Quezon City
Batangas
Lucena
Naga City
Catanduanes
Legaspi
Mindoro
PHILIPPINE SEA
PHILIPPINES
Panay
Iloilo City
Masbate
Samar
Tacloban
Leyte
Bacolod
Palawan
Negros
Cebu City
Bohol
Quezon
Butuan
Sulu Sea
Balabac Str.
Cagayan de Oro City
Kudat
Zamboanga City
Basilan
Moro Gulf
Davao City
Mindanao
General Santos
Sandakan
MALAYSIA
SABAH
Sulu Archipelago
Tawau
CELEBES SEA
Talaud Is.
Sangihe Is.
Tarakan
Borneo
Kendari
Manado
Morotai
Halmahera
Ternate
Gorontalo
Gulf of Tomini
Waigeo
Dampier Str.
Equator
Manokwari
Schouten Is.
Samarinda
Molucca Sea
Obi
Sorong
Yapen
Cenderawasih Bay
Palu
Makassar Strait
Sula Is.
Misool
Ceram Sea
Berau Bay
Celebes
Ceram
Fakfak
Jayapura
Gulf of Bone
Buru
Ambon
Maoke Mts.
Puncak Jaya 5,030 m
New
Ujung Pandang
Muna
Butung
INDONESIA
Kabaena
BANDA SEA
Kai Is.
Aru Is.
Salayar
FLORES SEA
Wetar
Tanimbar Is.
Kolepom
Flores
Alor
Dili
Babar Is.
Leti Is.
Sumbawa
Ruteng
Savu Sea
Timor
ARAFURA SEA
Sumba
Kupang
Timor Sea
Melville I.
Darwin
INDIAN OCEAN
Bonaparte Arch.
Pine Creek
Katherine
Gulf of Carpentaria
Wyndham
Daly Waters
Kimberley Plateau
Halls Creek
Broome
Tennant Creek
Camooweal
Great Sandy Desert
Port Hedland
Marble Bar
Roebourne
Fortescue
Onslow
Exmouth
Mt. Bruce 1,235 m
Tropic of Capricorn
Gibson Desert
AUSTRALIA
Alice Springs
Uluru (Ayers Rock) 867 m
Musgrave Ras.
Carnarvon
L. Carnegie
Wiluna
Meekatharra
Murchison
Oodnadatta
L. Eyre
Great Victoria Desert
Coober Pedy
Marree
Leonora
Northampton
Geraldton
Barlee
Kalgoorlie
Boulder
Nullarbor Plain
Merredin
Northam
Norseman
Perth
Great Australian Bight
Woomera
Torrens
Broken Hill
Port Augusta
Whyalla
Port Pirie
Streaky Bay
Spencer Gulf
Port Lincoln
Adelaide
Murray Bridge
Murray
Mildura
Darling
Lachlan
Cootamundra
Wagga Wagga
Albury
Mt. Kosciusko 2,228 m
Canberra
Wollongong
Sydney
Lithgow
Newcastle
Orange
Dubbo
Cobar
Bourke
Tamworth
Armidale
Moree
Port Macquarie
Grafton
Lismore
Gold Coast
Brisbane
Toowoomba
Saint George
Cunnamulla
Roma
Gympie
Charleville
Warrego
Birdsville
Diamantina
Thomson
Bundaberg
Rockhampton
Emerald
Barcaldine
Longreach
Clermont
Boulia
Mackay
Great Dividing Range
Cloncurry
Hughenden
Bowen
Townsville
Normanton
Flinders
Gilbert
Cairns
Cooktown
Cape York Peninsula
Coen
C. York
Torres Strait
Great Barrier Reef
CORAL SEA ISLANDS TERRITORY (AUSTL.)
CORAL SEA
Vanimo
Aitape
Wewak
Sepik
Mt. Wilhelm 4,509 m
Mt. Hagen
Goroka
Kundiawa
Madang
Karkar I.
Ramu
L. Murray
Fly
Lae
Bulolo
Wau
PAPUA NEW GUINEA
Daru
Merauke
Gulf of Papua
Port Moresby
Popondetta
D'Entrecasteaux Is.
Esa'ala
Alotau
Milne Bay
Normanby
Samarai
Louisiade Arch.
Tagula
Rossel I.
Woodlark I.
Trobriand Is.
Solomon Sea
Umboi
Kimbe
New Britain
Rabaul
Pomio
New Ireland
Namatanai
Kavieng
New Hanover
Lorengau
Manus
Admiralty Islands
Ninigo Is.
Mussau
St. Matthias Group
BISMARCK ARCHIPELAGO
Bismarck Sea
Lyra Reef
Nuguria Is.
Nissan I.
Buka
Tulin Is.
Bougainville
Kieta
Tauu Is.
Nukumanu Atoll
Ontong Java
Arawa
Shortland I.
Choiseul
Gizo
New Georgia Is.
Kia
Santa Isabel
Buala
Auki
Malaita
Honiara
Guadalcanal
Pocklington Reef
SOLOMON ISLANDS
Kirakira
San Cristobal
Rennell I.
SANTA CRUZ IS.
Reef Is.
Lata
Ndende
Duff Is.
Utupua
Vanikoro
Torres Is.
VANUATU
Banks Is.
Espiritu Santo
Tabwemasana 1,879 m
Luganville
Oba
Maewo
Pentecost
Ambrym
Malekula
Epi
Norsup
Shepherd Is.
NEW HEBRIDES
Vila
Efate
Erromango
Tanna
Isangel
Aneityum
NEW CALEDONIA (FR.)
Chesterfield Is.
Bellona Reefs
Mont Panié 1,628 m
Koumac
Hienghène
Koné
Bourail
Thio
New Caledonia
Nouméa
Humboldt 1,618 m
Ile des Pins
LOYALTY IS.
Wé
Farallon de Pajaros
Maug Is.
Asuncion
Agrihan
Pagan
Alamagan
Guguan
Sarigan
Farallon de Medinilla
Anathan
NORTHERN MARIANAS (U.S.)
Saipan
Capitol Hill
Aguijan
Tinian
Rota
Agaña
Guam (U.S.)
Micronesia
Ulithi
Colonia
Yap Is.
Ngulu
Sorol
Faraulep
West Fayu
Pikelot
Namonuito
Kavangel Is.
Babelthuap
Koror
PALAU (U.S.)
Sonsorol Is.
Olimarao
Woleai
Ifalik
Elato
Lamotrek
Pulap
Puluwat
Moen
Truk Is.
Hall Is.
Eauripik
Oroluk
CAROLINE ISLANDS
Etal
Lukunor
Satawan
Senyavin Is.
Kolonia
Ant
Pohnpei
Mokil
Ngatik
Pingelap
Lelu
Kosrae
Nukuoro
FEDERATED STATES OF MICRONESIA
Kapingamarangi
NORTH PACIFIC
Wake I. (U.S.)
Enewetak
Ujelang
Bikini
Rongerik
Rongelap
Bikar
Utirik
Ailuk
Wotho
Kwajalein
RALIK CHAIN
RATAK CHAIN
MARSHALL ISLANDS
Wotje
Ujae
Lae
Erikub
Maloelap
Namu
Aur
Ailinglapalap
Majuro
Arno
Jaluit
Mili
Namorik
Ebon
Butaritari
Makin
Abaiang
Tarawa
Bairiki
Birkenebeu
Maiana
Abemama
Kuria
Aranuka
Banaba
Tabiang
GILBERT ISLANDS
Nonouti
Utiroa
Tabiteuea
Beru
Nikunau
Onotoa
Tamana
Arorae
NAURU
Melanesia
Nanumea
Lolua
Niutau
Nanumanga
Nui
Vaitupu
Nukufetau
Funafuti
Fongafale
TUVALU
Nukulaelae
Niulakita
Polynesia
Ahau
Rotuma I.
WALLIS & FUTUNA (FR.)
FIJI
Vanua Levu
Lambasa
Yasawa Group
Savusavu
Lautoka
Nadi
Viti Levu
Suva
Vunisea
Kadavu
Koro Sea
Moala Group
International Date Line
SOUTH PACIFIC
Kingston
Norfolk I. (AUSTL.)
Macauley I.
Curtis I.
KERMADEC IS. (N.Z.)
Lord Howe I. (AUSTL.)
TASMAN SEA
Three Kings Is.
North Cape
Whangarei
NEW ZEALAND
Auckland
Manukau
Tauranga
Hamilton
Rotorua
North
Longitude East of Greenwich

Central Pacific Ocean

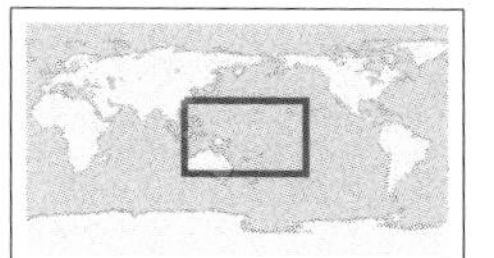

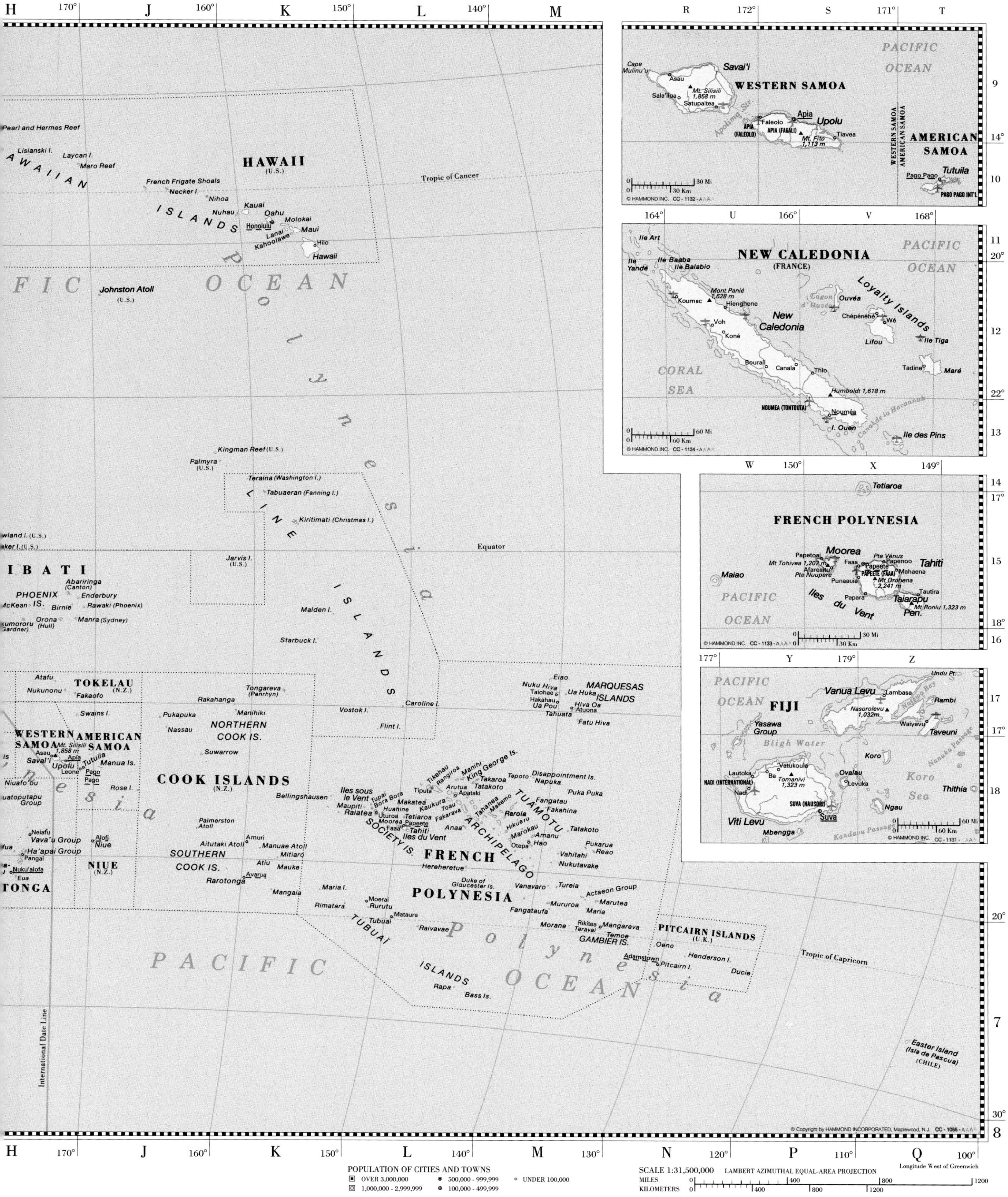

WESTERN SAMOA

AMERICAN SAMOA

NEW CALEDONIA (FRANCE)

FRENCH POLYNESIA

FIJI

POPULATION OF CITIES AND TOWNS

- OVER 3,000,000
- 1,000,000 - 2,999,999
- 500,000 - 999,999
- 100,000 - 499,999
- UNDER 100,000

SCALE 1:31,500,000 LAMBERT AZIMUTHAL EQUAL-AREA PROJECTION

MILES 0 400 800 1200

KILOMETERS 0 400 800 1200

Longitude West of Greenwich

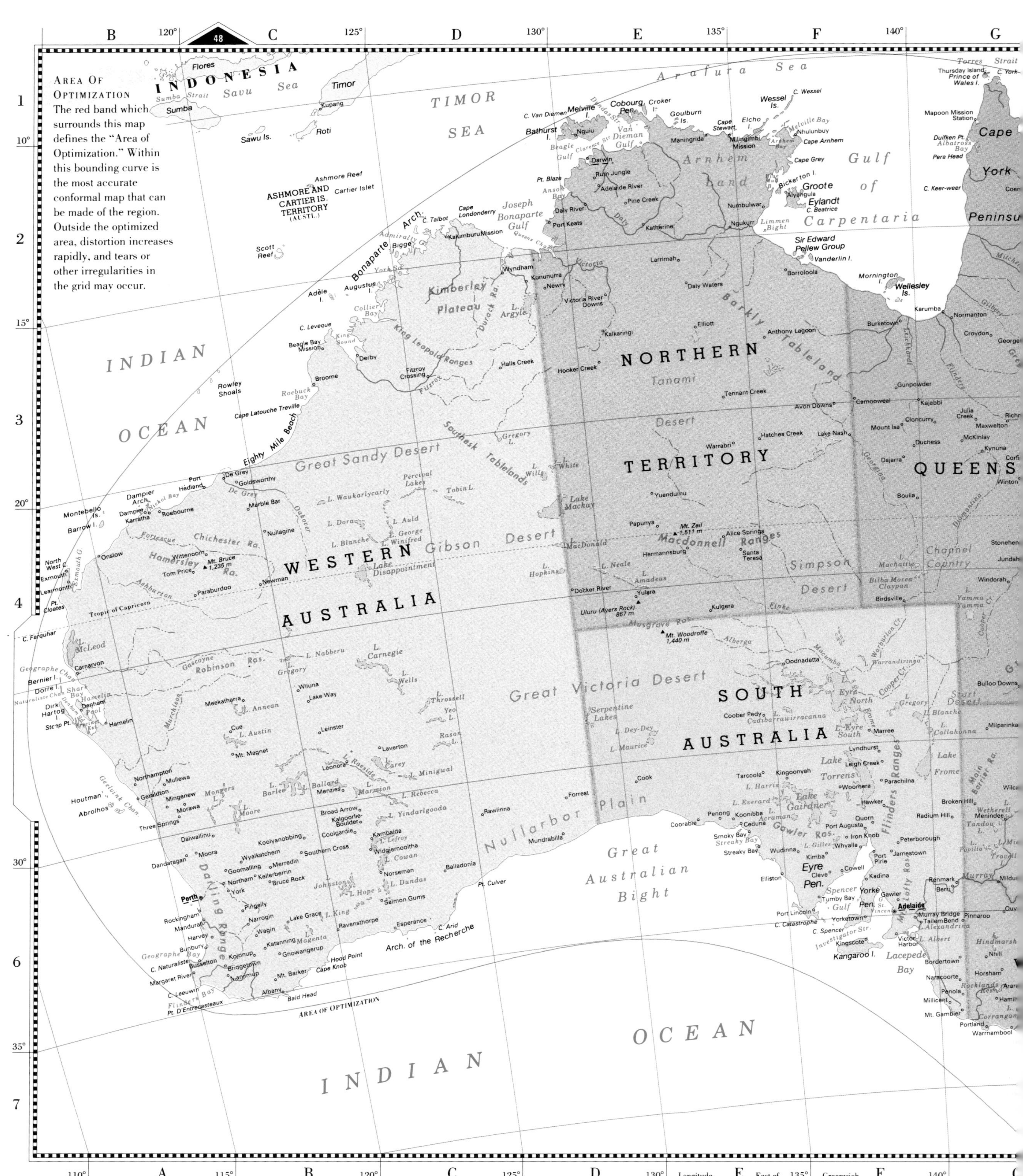

48
AREA OF OPTIMIZATION
The red band which surrounds this map defines the "Area of Optimization." Within this bounding curve is the most accurate conformal map that can be made of the region. Outside the optimized area, distortion increases rapidly, and tears or other irregularities in the grid may occur.
INDONESIA
Flores
Sumba
Savu Sea
Timor
Kupang
Roti
Sawu Is.
TIMOR SEA
Ashmore Reef
Cartier Islet
ASHMORE AND CARTIER IS. TERRITORY (AUSTL.)
Scott Reef
Arafura Sea
Torres Strait
Thursday Island
Prince of Wales I.
C. York
Cape York Peninsula
Gulf of Carpentaria
C. Van Diemen
Melville I.
Bathurst I.
Cobourg Pen.
Croker I.
Van Dieman Gulf
Darwin
Rum Jungle
Adelaide River
Pine Creek
Katherine
Daly River
Port Keats
Arnhem Land
Goulburn Is.
Maningrida
Cape Stewart
Milingimbi Mission
Elcho I.
Wessel Is.
C. Wessel
Melville Bay
Nhulunbuy
Cape Arnhem
Cape Grey
Groote Eylandt
Numbulwar
Ngukurr
Limmen Bight
Sir Edward Pellew Group
Vanderlin I.
Borroloola
Mornington I.
Wellesley Is.
Karumba
Normanton
Croydon
Burketown
Mapoon Mission Station
Duifken Pt.
Albatross Bay
Pera Head
C. Keer-weer
Joseph Bonaparte Gulf
C. Londonderry
C. Talbot
Kalumburu Mission
Bonaparte Arch.
Admiralty G.
Wyndham
Kununurra
Newry
Victoria River Downs
Kimberley Plateau
Durack Ra.
L. Argyle
King Leopold Ranges
Derby
Fitzroy Crossing
Halls Creek
Broome
Roebuck Bay
Beagle Bay Mission
C. Leveque
Adèle I.
Augustus I.
Collier Bay
King Sound
Larrimah
Daly Waters
Elliott
Kalkaringi
Hooker Creek
Anthony Lagoon
Barkly Tableland
NORTHERN TERRITORY
Tanami Desert
Tennant Creek
Avon Downs
Camooweal
Gunpowder
Kajabbi
Cloncurry
Julia Creek
Richmond
Mount Isa
Duchess
McKinlay
Kynuna
Dajarra
Boulia
Winton
QUEENSLAND
Hatches Creek
Lake Nash
Warrabri
Yuendumu
Papunya
Mt. Zeil 1,511 m
Alice Springs
Santa Teresa
Hermannsburg
Macdonnell Ranges
Simpson Desert
L. Neale
L. Amadeus
Docker River
Yulara
Uluru (Ayers Rock) 867 m
Kulgera
Musgrave Ras.
Mt. Woodroffe 1,440 m
INDIAN OCEAN
Rowley Shoals
Cape Latouche Treville
Eighty Mile Beach
Great Sandy Desert
Port Hedland
De Grey
Goldsworthy
Dampier Arch.
Dampier
Karratha
Roebourne
Montebello Is.
Barrow I.
Marble Bar
Nullagine
Chichester Ra.
Hamersley Ra.
Mt. Bruce 1,235 m
Wittenoom
Tom Price
Onslow
North West C.
Exmouth
Learmonth
Pt. Cloates
Paraburdoo
Newman
Tropic of Capricorn
WESTERN AUSTRALIA
Gibson Desert
Lake Disappointment
L. Mackay
L. White
L. Hopkins
C. Farquhar
L. McLeod
Carnarvon
Gascoyne
Robinson Ras.
Bernier I.
Dorre I.
Shark Bay
Denham
Dirk Hartog I.
Steep Pt.
Hamelin
Meekatharra
Cue
Mt. Magnet
Wiluna
Lake Way
Leinster
Leonora
Laverton
L. Carnegie
L. Wells
L. Throssell
Great Victoria Desert
SOUTH AUSTRALIA
Oodnadatta
Coober Pedy
Lake Eyre North
Lake Eyre South
Marree
Lyndhurst
Leigh Creek
Lake Torrens
Parachilna
Woomera
Kingoonyah
Tarcoola
Lake Gairdner
Flinders Ranges
Lake Frome
Cook
Forrest
Nullarbor Plain
Rawlinna
Mundrabilla
Great Australian Bight
Coorabie
Penong
Koonibba
Ceduna
Smoky Bay
Streaky Bay
Wudinna
Gawler Ras.
Port Augusta
Iron Knob
Whyalla
Quorn
Hawker
Port Pirie
Peterborough
Jamestown
Kimba
Eyre Pen.
Cleve
Cowell
Elliston
Port Lincoln
Spencer Gulf
Yorke Pen.
Kadina
Adelaide
Gawler
Murray Bridge
Tailem Bend
L. Alexandrina
Victor Harbor
Kangaroo I.
Lacepede Bay
Bordertown
Naracoorte
Penola
Millicent
Mt. Gambier
Portland
Warrnambool
Birdsville
Windorah
Bulloo Downs
Broken Hill
Menindee
Renmark
Berri
Pinnaroo
Geraldton
Northampton
Mullewa
Houtman Abrolhos
Three Springs
Dalwallinu
Moora
Dandaragan
Perth
Rockingham
Mandurah
Harvey
Bunbury
Busselton
C. Naturaliste
Margaret River
C. Leeuwin
Bridgetown
Manjimup
Albany
Mt. Barker
Katanning
Narrogin
Wagin
Kalgoorlie-Boulder
Coolgardie
Kambalda
Norseman
Southern Cross
Merredin
Menzies
Ravensthorpe
Esperance
Arch. of the Recherche
Hood Point
Cape Knob
Bald Head
Pt. D'Entrecasteaux
Balladonia
Pt. Culver
AREA OF OPTIMIZATION
INDIAN OCEAN
Longitude East of Greenwich

Australia; New Zealand

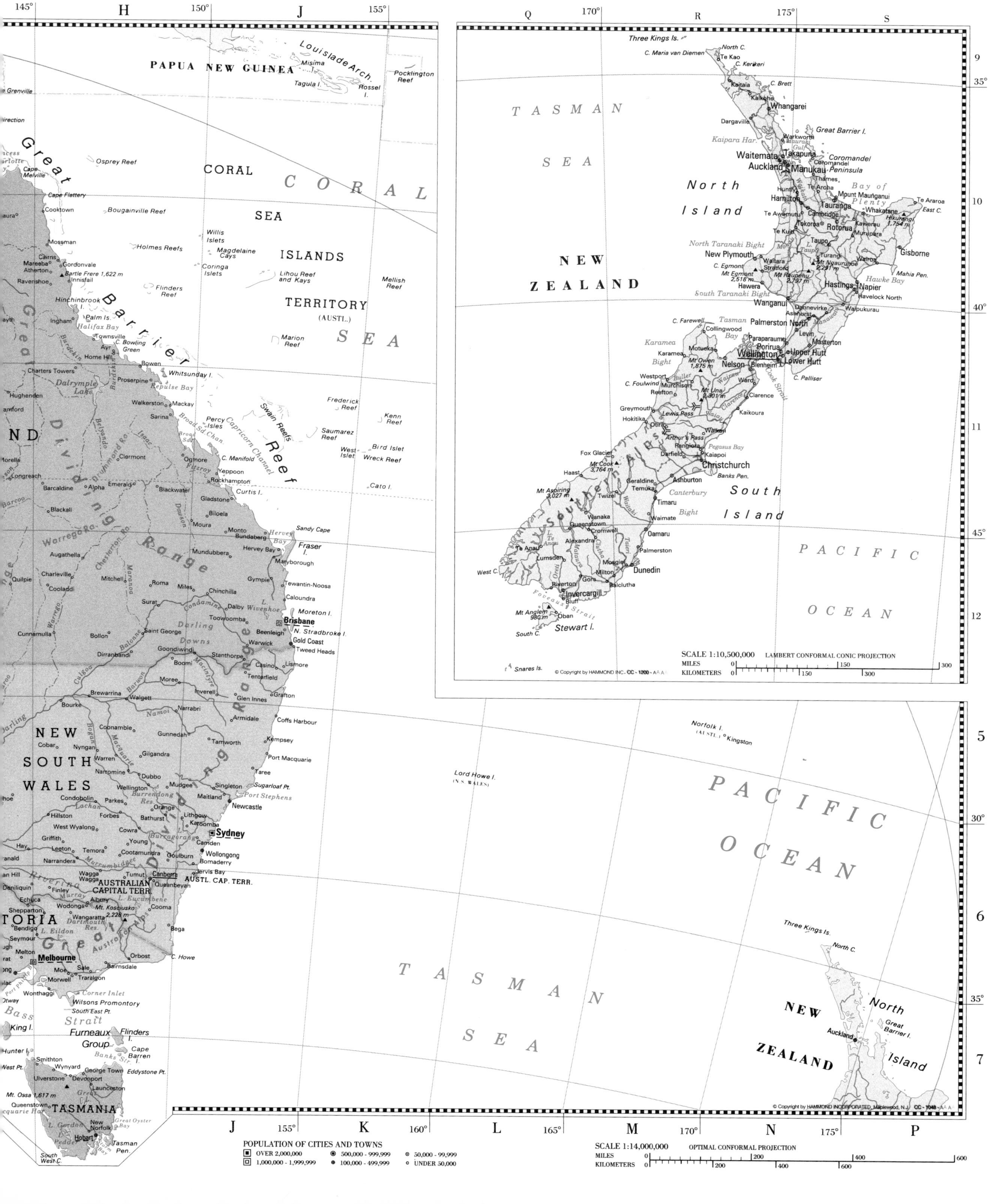

SCALE 1:10,500,000 LAMBERT CONFORMAL CONIC PROJECTION

MILES 0 150 300

KILOMETERS 0 150 300

POPULATION OF CITIES AND TOWNS

- ■ OVER 2,000,000
- ▣ 1,000,000 - 1,999,999
- ◉ 500,000 - 999,999
- ● 100,000 - 499,999
- ◎ 50,000 - 99,999
- ○ UNDER 50,000

SCALE 1:14,000,000 OPTIMAL CONFORMAL PROJECTION

MILES 0 200 400 600

KILOMETERS 0 200 400 600

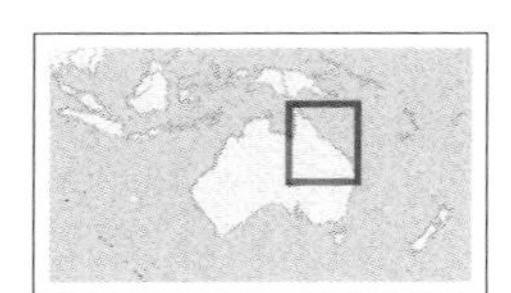

Northeastern Australia

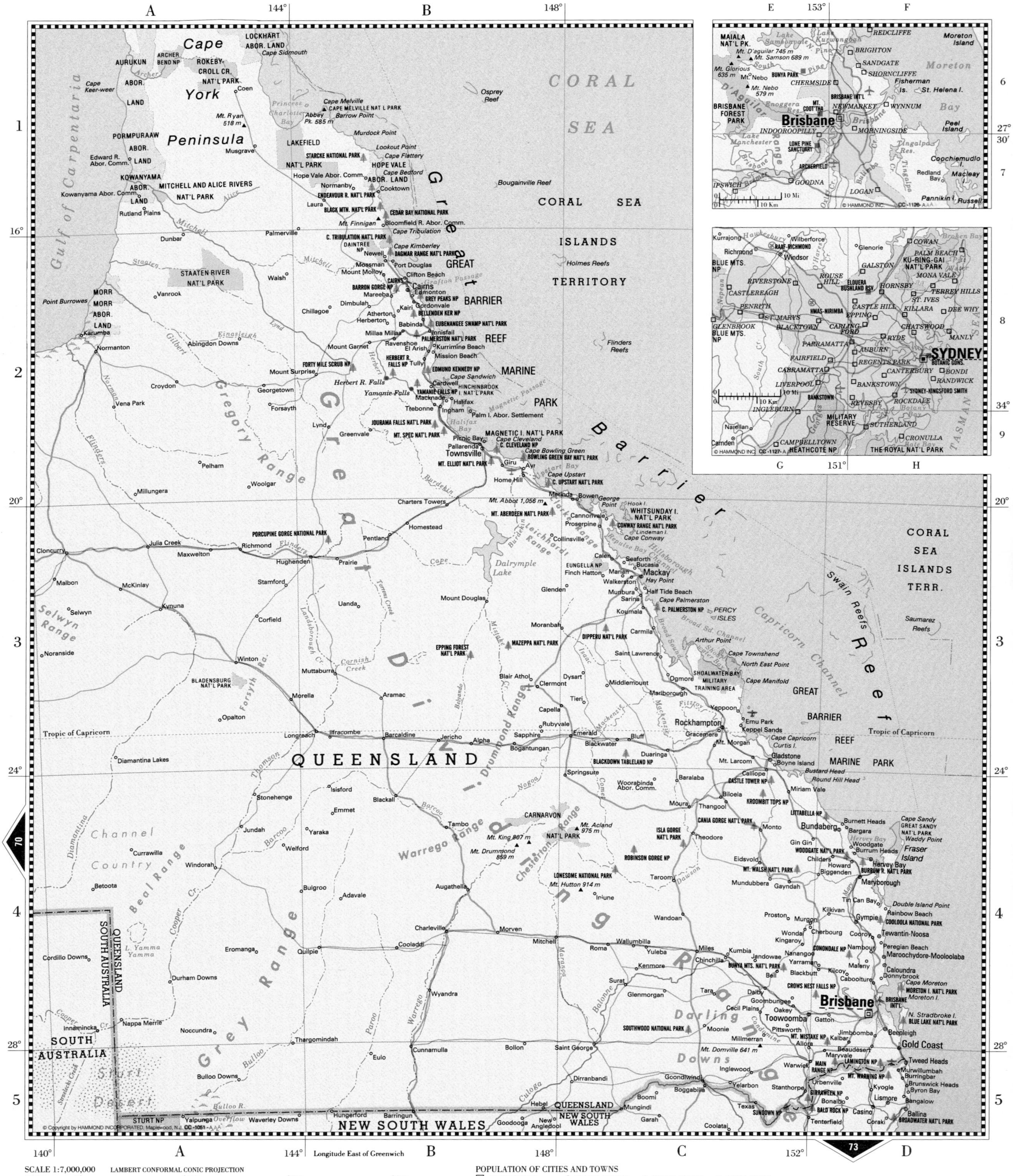

70

73

Longitude East of Greenwich

SCALE 1:7,000,000 LAMBERT CONFORMAL CONIC PROJECTION

MILES 0 100 200 300

KILOMETERS 0 100 200 300

POPULATION OF CITIES AND TOWNS

- ▣ OVER 2,000,000
- ◉ 500,000 - 999,999
- ● 100,000 - 249,999
- ◦ 10,000 - 29,999
- ▢ 1,000,000 - 1,999,999
- ◎ 250,000 - 499,999
- ◦ 30,000 - 99,999
- ◦ UNDER 10,000

Southeastern Australia

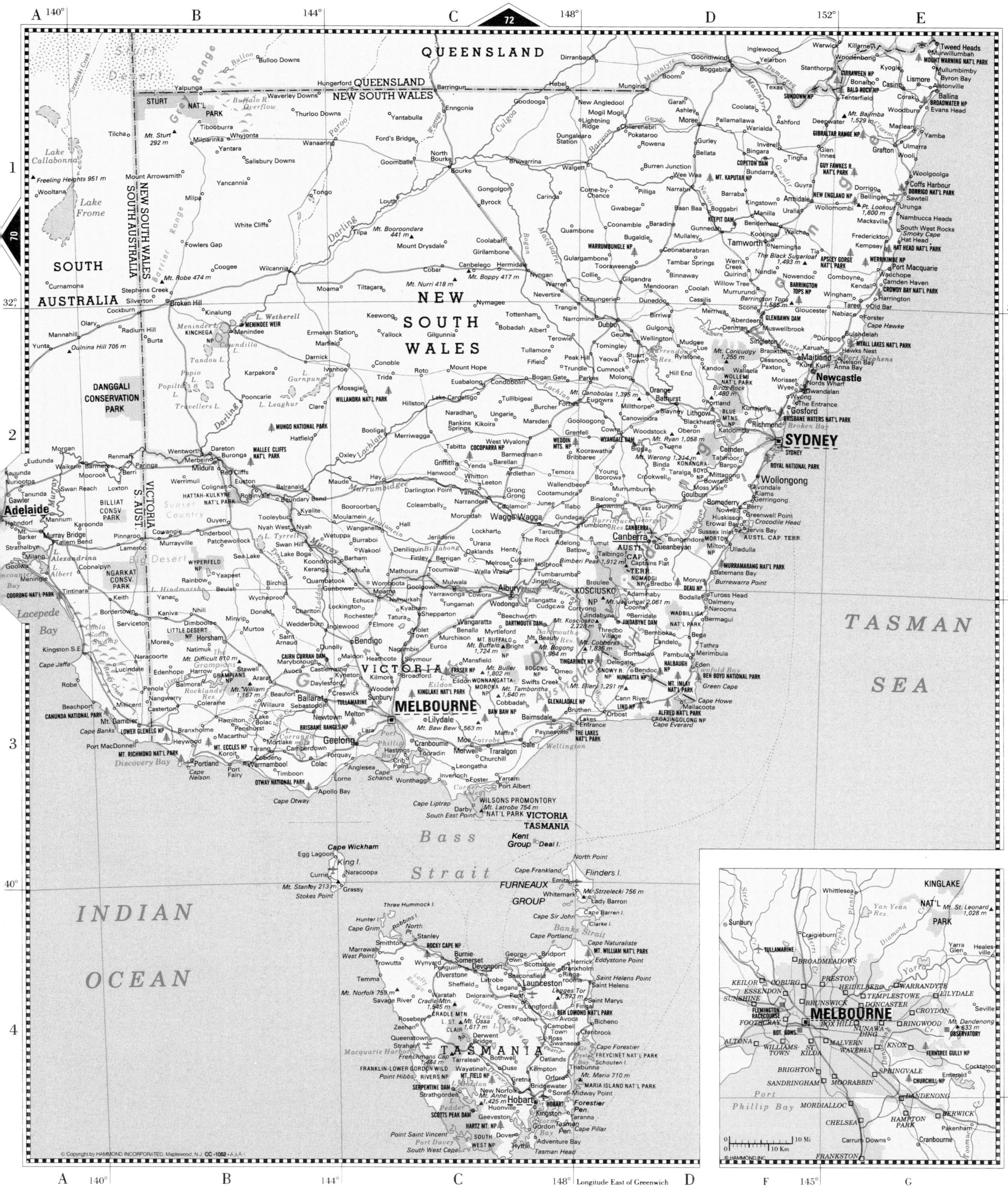

A 140° B 144° C 72 148° D 152° E

QUEENSLAND

NEW SOUTH WALES

SOUTH AUSTRALIA

VICTORIA

TASMANIA

TASMAN SEA

INDIAN OCEAN

Bass Strait

A 140° B 144° C 148° Longitude East of Greenwich D F 145° G

POPULATION OF CITIES AND TOWNS

■ OVER 2,000,000	◉ 500,000 - 999,999	● 100,000 - 249,999	⊙ 10,000 - 29,999
□ 1,000,000 - 1,999,999	◎ 250,000 - 499,999	⊚ 30,000 - 99,999	○ UNDER 10,000

SCALE 1:7,000,000 LAMBERT CONFORMAL CONIC PROJECTION

MILES 0 100 200 300

KILOMETERS 0 100 200 300

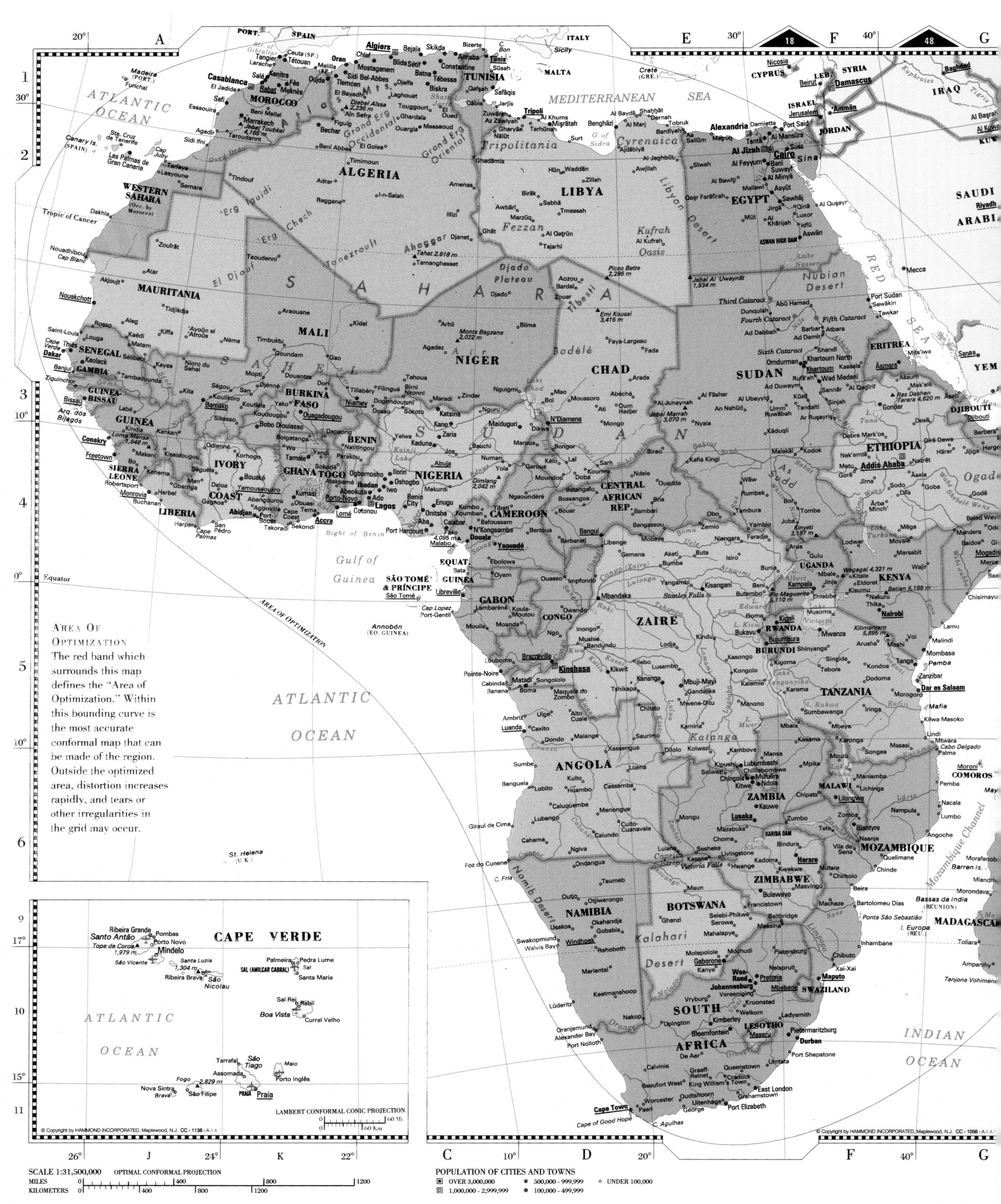

AREA OF OPTIMIZATION
The red band which surrounds this map defines the "Area of Optimization." Within this bounding curve is the most accurate conformal map that can be made of the region. Outside the optimized area, distortion increases rapidly, and tears or other irregularities in the grid may occur.
AREA OF OPTIMIZATION
ATLANTIC OCEAN
MEDITERRANEAN SEA
RED SEA
INDIAN OCEAN
Gulf of Guinea
Mozambique Channel
MOROCCO
ALGERIA
TUNISIA
LIBYA
EGYPT
WESTERN SAHARA
MAURITANIA
MALI
NIGER
CHAD
SUDAN
ERITREA
DJIBOUTI
ETHIOPIA
SENEGAL
GAMBIA
GUINEA-BISSAU
GUINEA
SIERRA LEONE
LIBERIA
IVORY COAST
BURKINA FASO
GHANA
TOGO
BENIN
NIGERIA
CAMEROON
CENTRAL AFRICAN REP.
EQUAT. GUINEA
SÃO TOMÉ & PRÍNCIPE
GABON
CONGO
ZAIRE
UGANDA
KENYA
RWANDA
BURUNDI
TANZANIA
ANGOLA
ZAMBIA
MALAWI
MOZAMBIQUE
ZIMBABWE
NAMIBIA
BOTSWANA
SOUTH AFRICA
LESOTHO
SWAZILAND
COMOROS
MADAGASCAR
SAUDI ARABIA
SYRIA
IRAQ
JORDAN
ISRAEL
CYPRUS
SPAIN
PORT.
ITALY
MALTA
S A H A R A
Tropic of Cancer
Equator
CAPE VERDE
ATLANTIC OCEAN
LAMBERT CONFORMAL CONIC PROJECTION
© Copyright by HAMMOND INCORPORATED, Maplewood, N.J. CC - 1136 - AAA
© Copyright by HAMMOND INCORPORATED, Maplewood, N.J. CC - 1056 - AAA
SCALE 1:31,500,000 OPTIMAL CONFORMAL PROJECTION
MILES 0 400 800 1200
KILOMETERS 0 400 800 1200
POPULATION OF CITIES AND TOWNS
OVER 3,000,000
1,000,000 - 2,999,999
500,000 - 999,999
100,000 - 499,999
UNDER 100,000

Africa

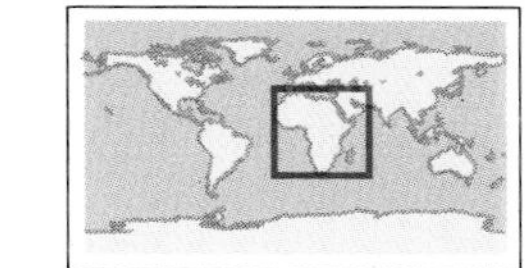

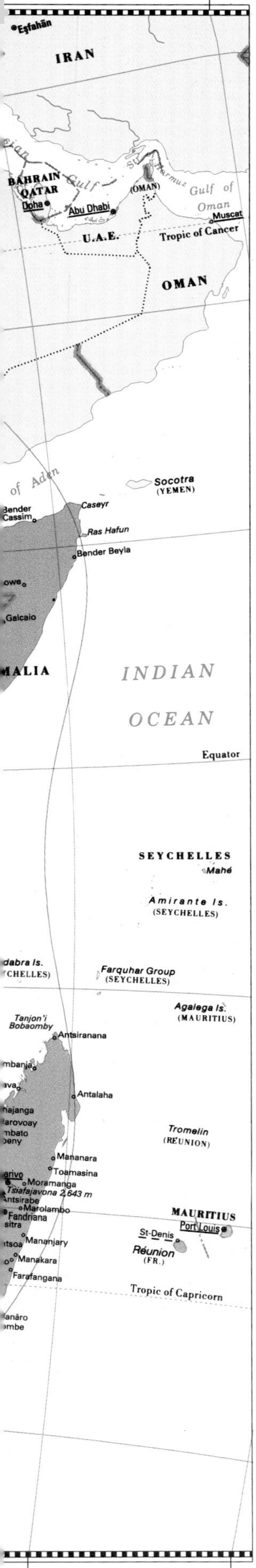

H 60°

IRAN
BAHRAIN
QATAR
Doha
Abu Dhabi
U.A.E.
(OMAN)
Gulf of Oman
Muscat
Tropic of Cancer
OMAN
Socotra (YEMEN)
Caseyr
Ras Hafun
Bender Beyla
MALIA
INDIAN OCEAN
Equator
SEYCHELLES
Mahé
Amirante Is. (SEYCHELLES)
Farquhar Group (SEYCHELLES)
Agalega Is. (MAURITIUS)
Antsiranana
Antalaha
Tromelin (RÉUNION)
Mananara
Toamasina
Moramanga
MAURITIUS
Port Louis
St-Denis
Réunion (FR.)
Manakara
Farafangana
Tropic of Capricorn
50° H 60°

8° L 6° M 4° N 2° P

0 30 Mi
0 30 Km

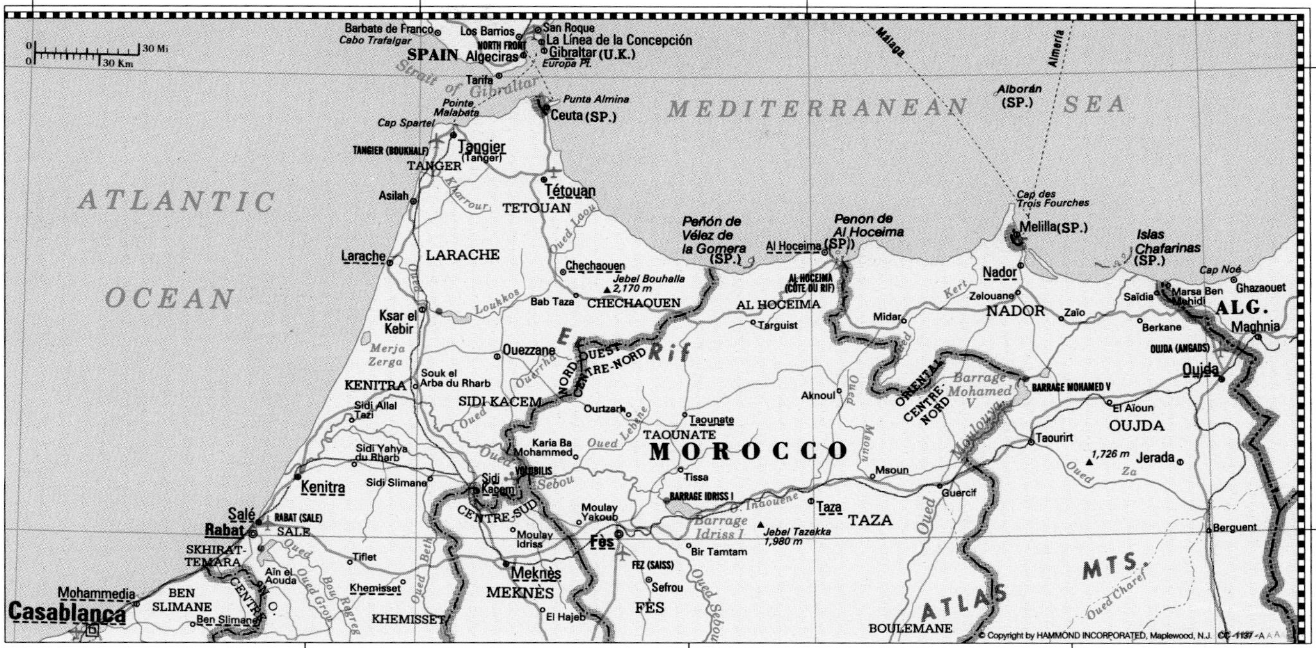

SPAIN
Barbate de Franco
Cabo Trafalgar
Los Barrios
San Roque
La Línea de la Concepción
Gibraltar (U.K.)
Europa Pt.
Algeciras
NORTH FRONT
Tarifa
Strait of Gibraltar
Punta Almina
Ceuta (SP.)
Pointe Malabata
Cap Spartel
TANGIER (BOUKHALF)
Tangier (Tanger)
TANGER
Tétouan
TETOUAN
Asilah
MEDITERRANEAN SEA
Alborán (SP.)
Málaga
Almería
ATLANTIC OCEAN
Peñón de Vélez de la Gomera (SP.)
Penon de Al Hoceima (SP.)
Al Hoceima
Cap des Trois Fourches
Melilla (SP.)
Islas Chafarinas (SP.)
Cap Noé
Larache
LARACHE
Chechaouen
Jebel Bouhalla 2,170 m
Bab Taza
CHECHAOUEN
AL HOCEIMA
Targuist
Nador
NADOR
Zeghanghane
Zelouane
Zaïo
Berkane
Saïdia
Marsa Ben Mehidi
Ghazaouet
ALG.
Maghnia
Ksar el Kebir
Ouezzane
Er Rif
NORD-OUEST
CENTRE-NORD
Merja Zerga
KENITRA
Souk el Arba du Rharb
SIDI KACEM
Sidi Allal Tazi
Ourtzarh
Taounate
TAOUNATE
Aknoul
ORIENTAL
CENTRE-NORD
Barrage Mohamed V
BARRAGE MOHAMED V
El Aïoun
OUJDA
Oujda
OUJDA (ANGADS)
Taourirt
Jerada
1,726 m
MOROCCO
Karia Ba Mohammed
Sidi Yahya du Rharb
Sidi Slimane
Sidi Kacem
Kenitra
Salé
RABAT (SALE)
SALE
Rabat
SKHIRAT-TEMARA
Tiflet
Khemisset
KHEMISSET
Moulay Yakoub
Barrage Idriss I
BARRAGE IDRISS I
Jebel Tazekka 1,980 m
Taza
TAZA
Msoun
Guercif
Berguent
Moulay Idriss
Fès
FEZ (SAISS)
Sefrou
FÈS
Meknès
MEKNÈS
El Hajeb
Bir Tamtam
Tissa
Aïn el Aouda
Mohammedia
BEN SLIMANE
Ben Slimane
Casablanca
CENTRE
CENTRE-SUD
ATLAS MTS
BOULEMANE
Oued Charef
© Copyright by HAMMOND INCORPORATED, Maplewood, N.J.

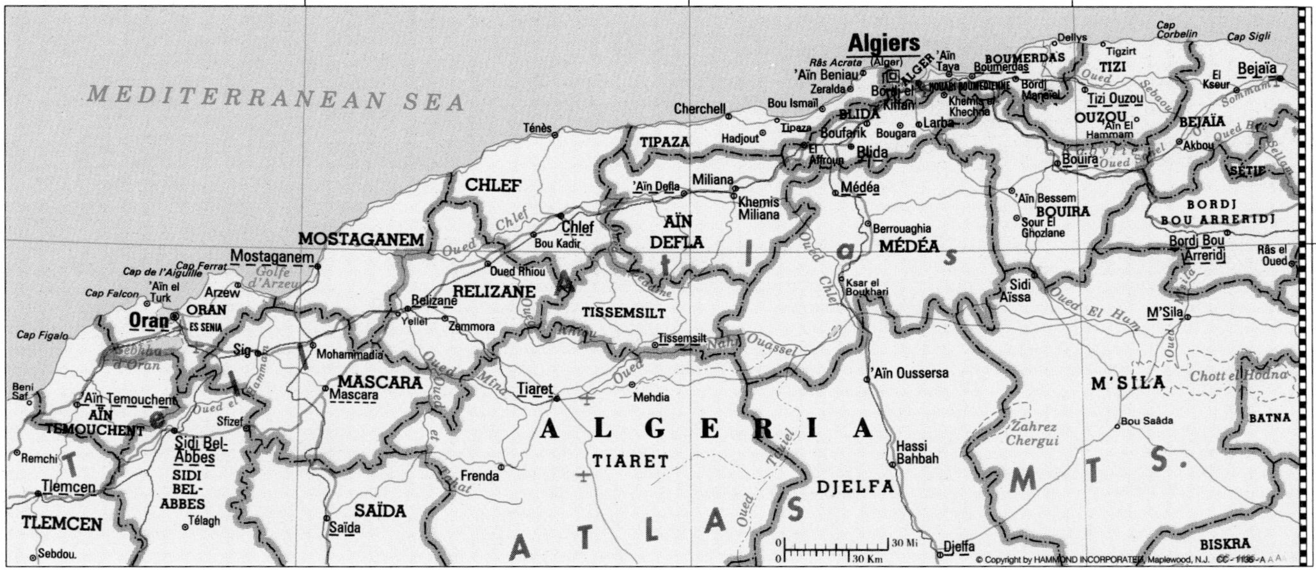

12 36° 13 34° 14

Q 0° R 2° S 4° T

Algiers (Alger)
Râs Acrata
'Aïn Beniau
Zeralda
ALGER
'Aïn Taya
BOUMERDAS
Boumerdas
Dellys
Tigzirt
Cap Corbelin
Cap Sigli
TIZI OUZOU
Tizi Ouzou
Béjaïa
BEJAÏA
El Kseur
Akbou
SETIF
MEDITERRANEAN SEA
Cherchell
Bou Ismaïl
BLIDA
Blida
Boufarik
Bougara
Larba
Ténès
TIPAZA
Hadjout
Tipaza
El Affroun
Médéa
MÉDÉA
Bouira
BOUIRA
'Aïn Bessem
Sour El Ghozlane
BORDJ BOU ARRERIDJ
Bordj Bou Arreridj
Râs el Oued
CHLEF
Chlef
'Aïn Defla
AÏN DEFLA
Miliana
Khemis Miliana
Bou Kadir
Berrouaghia
MOSTAGANEM
Mostaganem
Oued Rhiou
Cap Ferrat
Cap de l'Aiguille
Arzew
Golfe d'Arzew
Cap Falcon
'Aïn el Turk
ORAN
Oran
ES SENIA
Cap Figalo
Sebkha d'Oran
Relizane
RELIZANE
Yellel
Zemmora
TISSEMSILT
Tissemsilt
Ksar el Boukhari
Sidi Aïssa
M'Sila
M'SILA
Chott el Hodna
Sig
Mohammadia
MASCARA
Mascara
Tiaret
Mehdia
'Aïn Oussersa
Beni Saf
'Aïn Temouchent
AÏN TEMOUCHENT
Sfizef
Sidi Bel-Abbes
SIDI BEL-ABBES
Remchi
Tlemcen
TLEMCEN
Télagh
ALGERIA
TIARET
Frenda
DJELFA
Hassi Bahbah
Zahrez Chergui
Bou Saâda
BATNA
SAÏDA
Saïda
Sebdou
TELL ATLAS
SAHARAN ATLAS MTS.
Djelfa
BISKRA
0 30 Mi
0 30 Km
© Copyright by HAMMOND INCORPORATED, Maplewood, N.J.

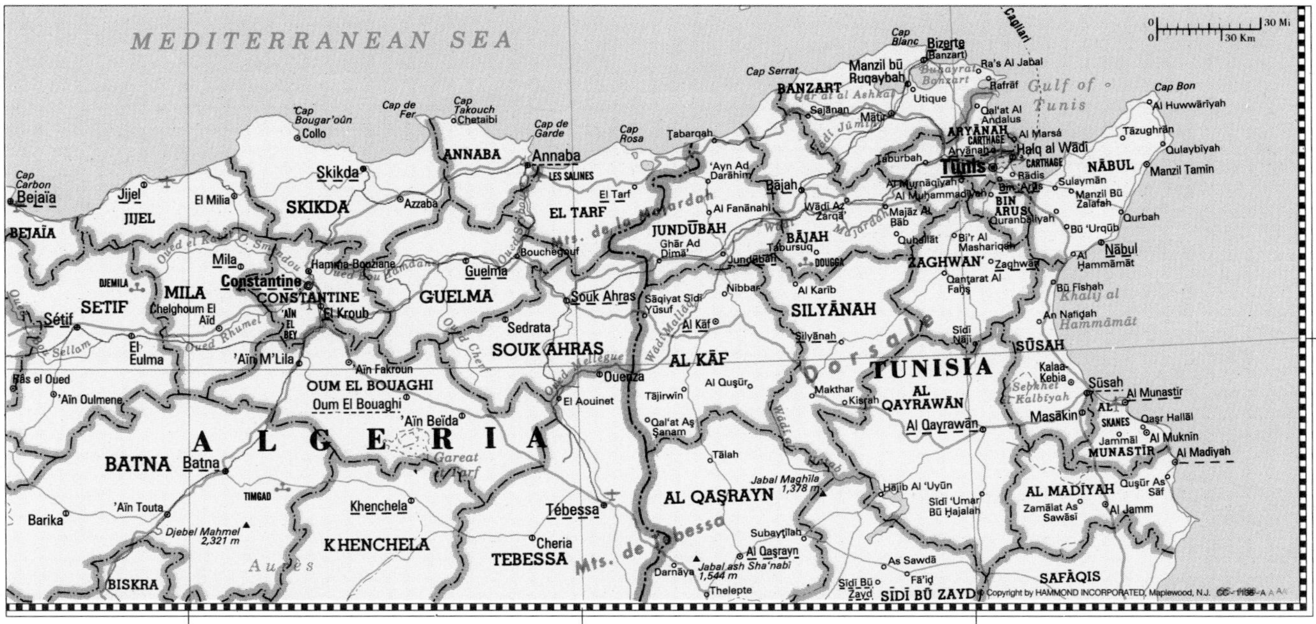

15 36° 16

MEDITERRANEAN SEA
0 30 Mi
0 30 Km
Cagliari
Cap Blanc
Bizerta (Banzart)
Ra's Al Jabal
Manzil Bū Ruqaybah
Cap Serrat
BANZART
Buhayrat Banzart
Utique
Rafrāf
Gulf of Tunis
Cap Bon
Al Huwwārīyah
Qal'at Al Andalus
Al Marsá
CARTHAGE
ARYĀNAH
Aryānah
Halq al Wādī
Tunis
Rādis
Tāzughrān
Qulaybīyah
NĀBUL
Manzil Tamīn
Sulaymān
Manzil Bū Zalafah
Qurbah
Nābul
Al Hammāmāt
Khalīj al Hammāmāt
Cap Bougar'oûn
Collo
Cap de Fer
Cap Takouch
Chetaïbi
Cap de Garde
Cap Rosa
ANNABA
Annaba
LES SALINES
Tabarqah
'Ayn Ad Darāhim
Bājah
Sejnane
Mātir
Tuburbah
Al Murnāqīyah
Al Muhammadīyah
BIN 'ARUS
Majāz Al Bāb
Bir Al Mashariqah
ZAGHWĀN'
Zaghwān
Qantarat Al Fahs
Bū Fīshah
An Nafidah
Cap Carbon
Béjaïa
BEJAÏA
Jijel
JIJEL
El Milia
Skikda
SKIKDA
Azzaba
EL TARF
El Tarf
JUNDŪBAH
Jundūbah
Ghār Ad Dimā'
Mts. de la Medjerda
BĀJAH
Tabursuq
Wādī Majardah
Mila
MILA
Constantine
CONSTANTINE
Hamma-Bouziane
Guelma
GUELMA
Bouchegouf
Souk Ahras
SOUK AHRAS
Sedrata
Sāqiyat Sīdī Yūsuf
Al Kāf
AL KĀF
Nibbar
Al Karīb
SILYĀNAH
Silyānah
Sīdī Bū 'Alī
SŪSAH
Sūsah
Kalaa Kebira
Sebkhet Kalbīyah
Al Munastīr
MUNASTĪR
Qasr Hallāl
Al Muknīn
Jammāl
Al Mahdīyah
AL MAHDĪYAH
Qusūr As Sāf
Al Jamm
SETIF
Sétif
El Eulma
Chelghoum El Aïd
'Aïn M'Lila
Aïn el Bey
El Khroub
'Aïn Fakroun
OUM EL BOUAGHI
Oum El Bouaghi
Ouenza
El Aouinet
'Aïn Beïda
Râs el Oued
'Aïn Oulmene
Tājirwīn
Al Qusūr
Makthar
Kisrah
TUNISIA
AL QAYRAWĀN
Al Qayrawān
Masākin
Dorsale
ALGERIA
Qal'at As Sanam
Tālah
BATNA
Batna
Garaet et Tarf
Jabal Maghīlah 1,378 m
Hājib Al 'Uyūn
Sīdī 'Umar Bū Hajalah
AL QASRAYN
'Aïn Touta
TIMGAD
Djebel Mahmel 2,321 m
Khenchela
KHENCHELA
Tébessa
TEBESSA
Cheria
Mts. de Tebessa
Barika
Aurès
BISKRA
Subaytilah
Al Qasrayn
Jabal ash Sha'nabī 1,544 m
Darnāya
Thelepte
As Sawdā
Fā'id
Sīdī Bū Zayd
SĪDĪ BŪ ZAYD
SAFĀQIS
Zamālat As Sawāsī
© Copyright by HAMMOND INCORPORATED, Maplewood, N.J.

17 36° 18

U 6° V 8° W 10° X

A
B
C
D
E
F
G
H
1
2
3
4
5
6
7
8
30°
25°
20°
15°
10°
5°
0°
Longitude
West of
Greenwich
Longitude
East of
Greenwich
ATLANTIC OCEAN
Mediterranean Sea
Canary Is. (SP.)
Madeira (PORT.)
MOROCCO
ALGERIA
TUNISIA
WESTERN SAHARA (occ. by Morocco)
MAURITANIA
MALI
NIGER
SENEGAL
GAMBIA
GUINEA-BISSAU
GUINEA
SIERRA LEONE
LIBERIA
IVORY COAST (CÔTE D'IVOIRE)
BURKINA FASO
GHANA
TOGO
BENIN
NIGERIA
CAMEROON
EQUATORIAL GUINEA
SÃO TOMÉ AND PRÍNCIPE
GABON
CONGO
SPAIN
MALTA
Casablanca
Rabat
Algiers
Tunis
Tripoli
Dakar
Nouakchott
Banjul
Bissau
Conakry
Freetown
Monrovia
Bamako
Ouagadougou
Niamey
Abidjan
Accra
Lomé
Porto-Novo
Lagos
Malabo
Yaoundé
Libreville
São Tomé
N'Djamena
Grand Erg Occidental
Grand Erg Oriental
Atlas Saharien
Haut Atlas
Anti-Atlas
Moyen Atlas
Plateau du Tademaït
Erg Iguidi
Erg Chech
Tanezrouft
Ahaggar
Adrar des Iforas
Aïr
Ténéré
Plateau du Djado
Fezzan
El Djouf
Tropic of Cancer
Lake Chad
Gulf of Guinea
Bight of Benin
Bight of Biafra
Equator
Gold Coast
Ivory Coast
Grain Coast
SAHARA

Northern Africa

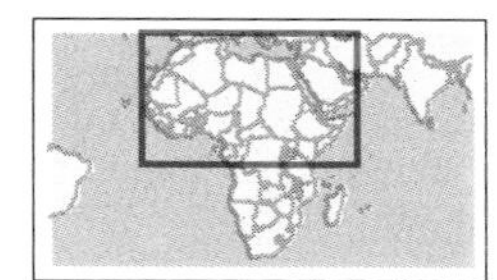

POPULATION OF CITIES AND TOWNS

▣ OVER 2,000,000	◉ 500,000 - 999,999	◎ 50,000 - 99,999
◻ 1,000,000 - 1,999,999	● 100,000 - 499,999	○ UNDER 50,000

SCALE 1:17,500,000 POLYCONIC PROJECTION

MILES 0 250 500 750

KILOMETERS 0 250 500 750

76
A
16°
B
12°
C
8°
D
4°
1
2
4
5
20°
16°
8°
MAURITANIA
ADRAR
INCHIRI
DAKHLET NOUADHIBOU
PN DU BANC D'ARGUIN
Nouakchott
TRARZA
BRAKNA
TAGANT
HODH ECH CHARGUI
HODH EL GHARBI
ASSABA
GORGOL
GUIDIMAKA
SAINT-LOUIS
Saint-Louis
LOUGA
DIOURBEL
Dakar
Thiès
SENEGAL
KAOLACK
Kaolack
TAMBACOUNDA
Tambacounda
GAMBIA
Banjul
KOLDA
Ziguinchor
GUINEA-BISSAU
Bissau
Bijagos
BOKÉ
LABE
KINDIA
Conakry
CONAKRY
FARANAH
GUINEA
KANKAN
Kankan
NZÉRÉKORÉ
SIERRA LEONE
Freetown
NORTHERN
EASTERN
SOUTHERN
WESTERN AREA
LIBERIA
Monrovia
LOFA
BONG
NIMBA
GRAND BASSA
SINO
GRAND GEDEH
MARYLAND
MONTSERRADO
GRAND CAPE MOUNT
KAYES
Kayes
PN DE LA BOUCLE DU BAOLÉ
PN DU NIOKOLO-KOBA
BAMAKO
Bamako
SÉGOU
Ségou
SIKASSO
Sikasso
MOPTI
Mopti
KOSSI
HOUET
Bobo Dioulasso
KÉNÉDOUGOU
COMOÉ
PARC NATIONAL DE LA COMOÉ
IVORY COAST (CÔTE D'IVOIRE)
Bouaké
Yamoussoukro
Abidjan
PN DE TAÏ
PN DU MONT SANGBÉ
PN DE LA MARAOUÉ
ATLANTIC OCEAN
Grain Coast
Ivory Coast
S A
Longitude West of Greenwich
© Copyright by HAMMOND INCORPORATED, Maplewood, N.J.
SCALE 1:7,000,000
POLYCONIC PROJECTION
MILES 0 100 200 300
KILOMETERS 0 100 200 300

West Africa

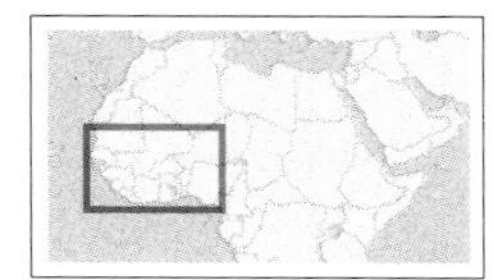

0° Longitude East of Greenwich

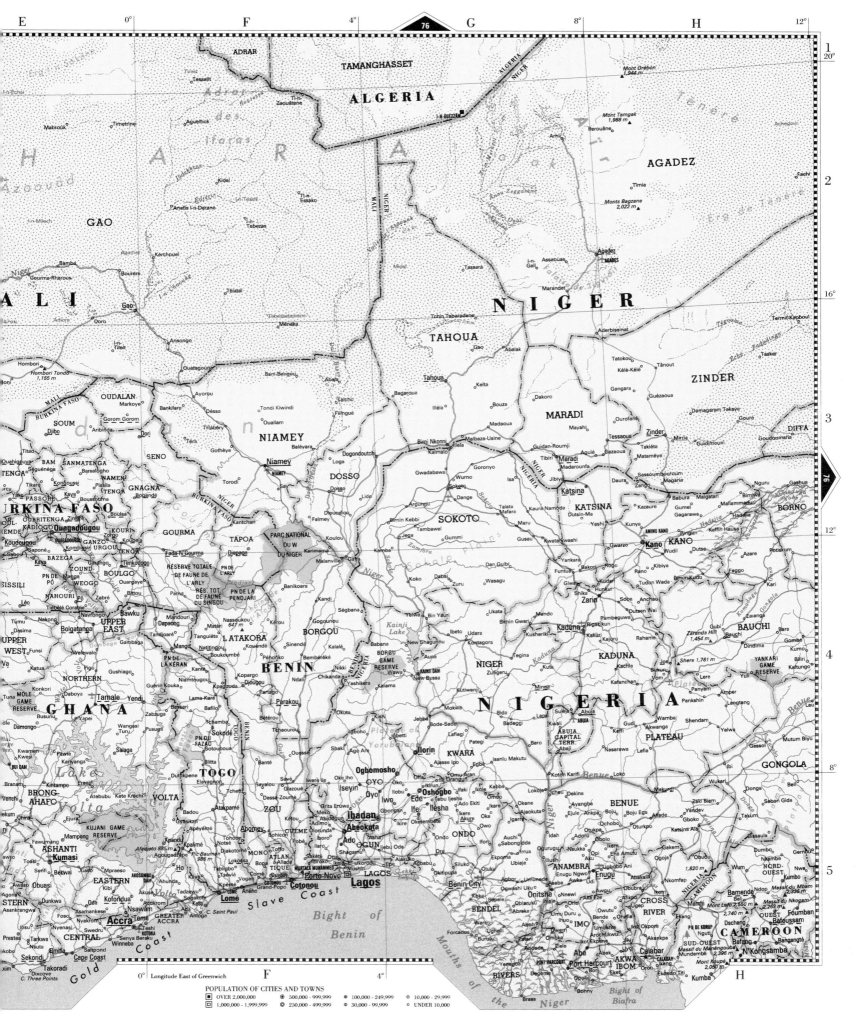

POPULATION OF CITIES AND TOWNS

OVER 2,000,000	100,000 - 249,999
1,000,000 - 1,999,999	30,000 - 99,999
500,000 - 999,999	10,000 - 29,999
250,000 - 499,999	UNDER 10,000

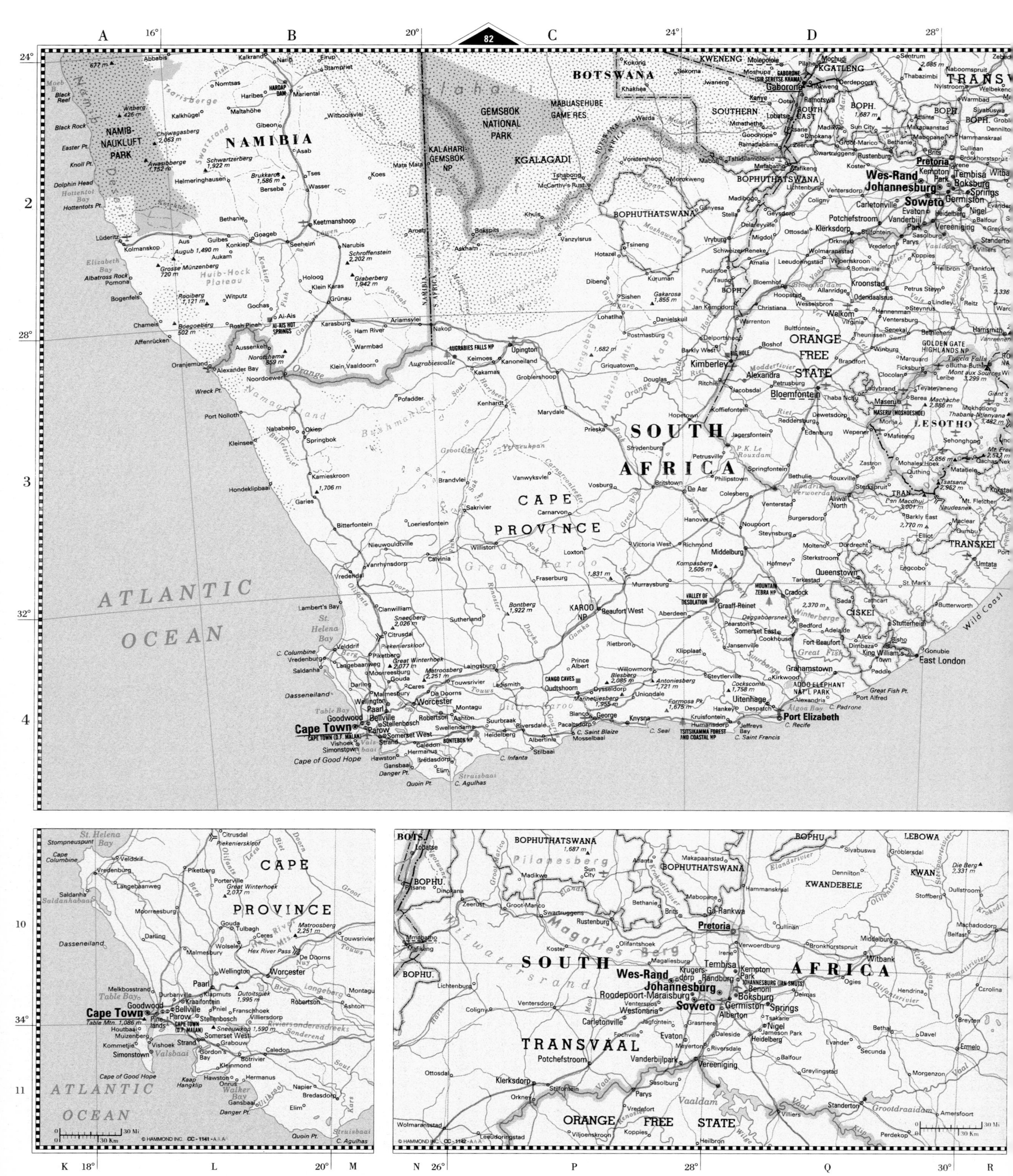

82
NAMIBIA
BOTSWANA
GEMSBOK NATIONAL PARK
KALAHARI-GEMSBOK NP
MABUASEHUBE GAME RES
KGALAGADI
KWENENG
KGATLENG
SOUTHERN
SOUTH EAST
BOPHUTHATSWANA
NAMIB-NAUKLUFT PARK
SOUTH AFRICA
CAPE PROVINCE
ORANGE FREE STATE
LESOTHO
TRANSKEI
CISKEI
ATLANTIC OCEAN
Cape Town
Port Elizabeth
East London
Kimberley
Bloemfontein
Pretoria
Wes-Rand
Johannesburg
Soweto
Gaborone
Upington
Keetmanshoop
Lüderitz
Worcester
Paarl
Cape of Good Hope
C. Agulhas
VALLEY OF DESOLATION
MOUNTAIN ZEBRA NP
KAROO NP
ADDO ELEPHANT NAT'L PARK
TSITSIKAMMA FOREST AND COASTAL NP
BONTEBOK NP
AUGRABIES FALLS NP
CANGO CAVES
GOLDEN GATE HIGHLANDS NP
TRANSVAAL
KWANDEBELE
LEBOWA
KWAN.
Magaliesberg
Witwatersrand
Vaal
Vaaldam
© HAMMOND INC.

South Africa

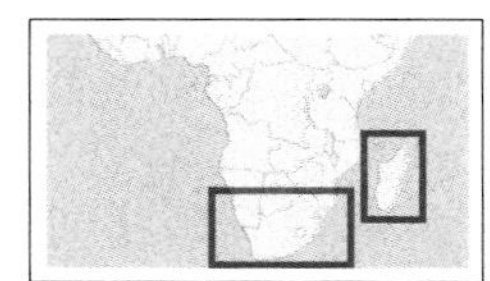

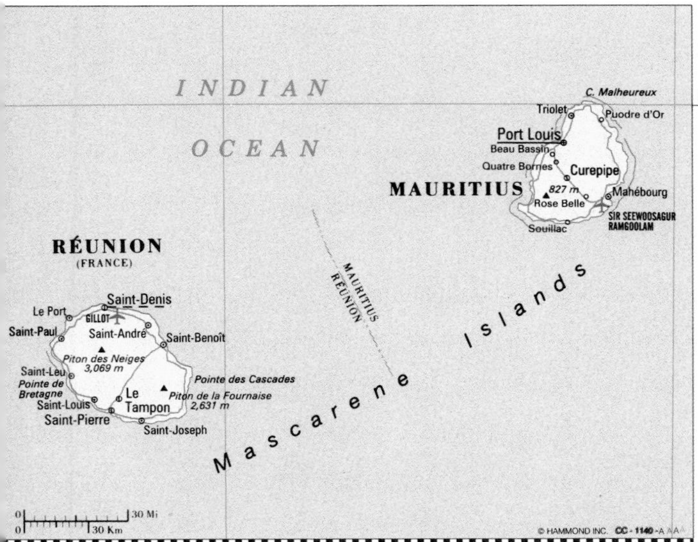

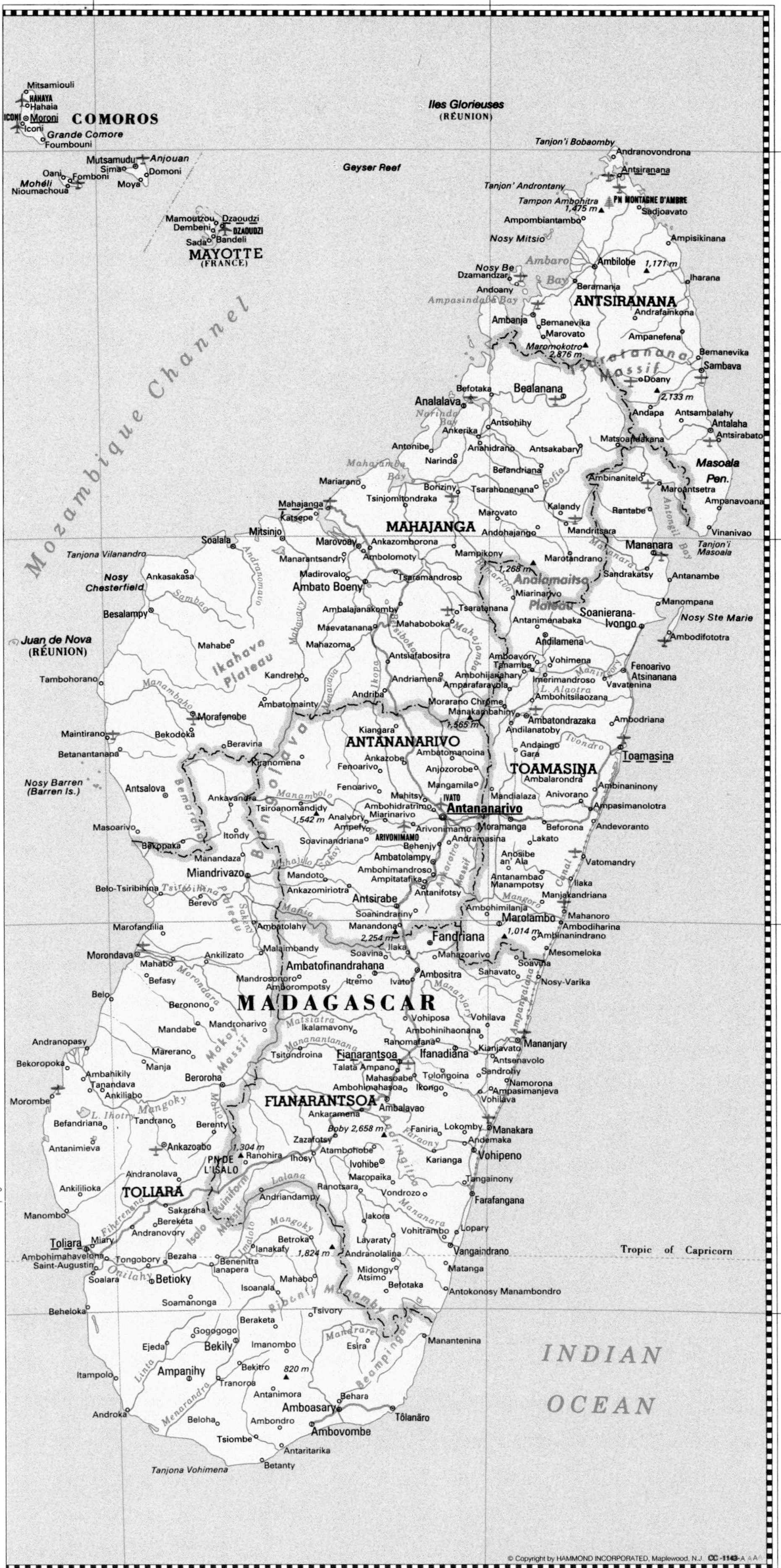

MOZAMBIQUE

SWAZILAND

NATAL

INDIAN OCEAN

Mozambique Channel

COMOROS

MAYOTTE (FRANCE)

MADAGASCAR

MAURITIUS

RÉUNION (FRANCE)

Mascarene Islands

POPULATION OF CITIES AND TOWNS

- OVER 2,000,000
- 1,000,000 - 1,999,999
- 500,000 - 999,999
- 250,000 - 499,999
- 100,000 - 249,999
- 30,000 - 99,999
- 10,000 - 29,999
- UNDER 10,000

SCALE 1:7,000,000 LAMBERT CONFORMAL CONIC PROJECTION

MILES 0 100 200 300

KILOMETERS 0 100 200 300

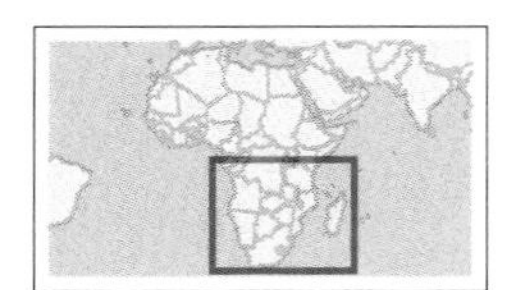

Southern Africa

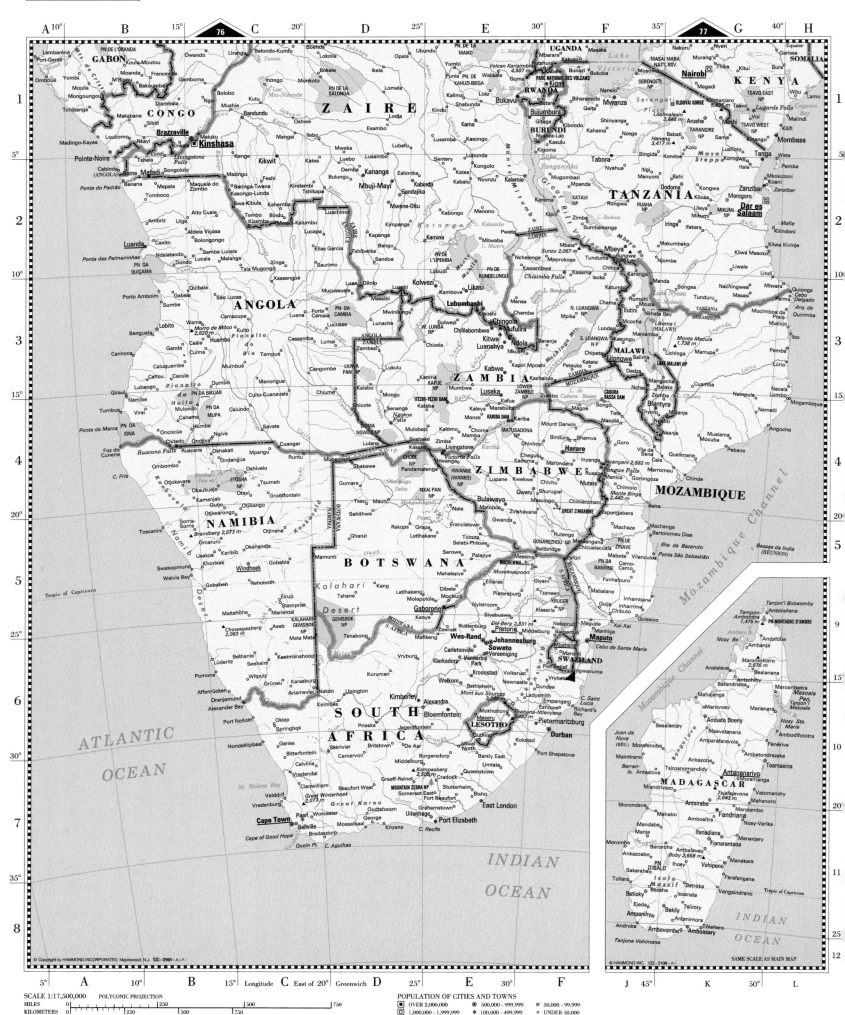

SCALE 1:17,500,000 POLYCONIC PROJECTION

MILES 0 250 500 750

KILOMETERS 0 250 500 750

POPULATION OF CITIES AND TOWNS

- OVER 2,000,000
- 1,000,000 - 1,999,999
- 500,000 - 999,999
- 100,000 - 499,999
- 50,000 - 99,999
- UNDER 50,000

SAME SCALE AS MAIN MAP

Antarctica

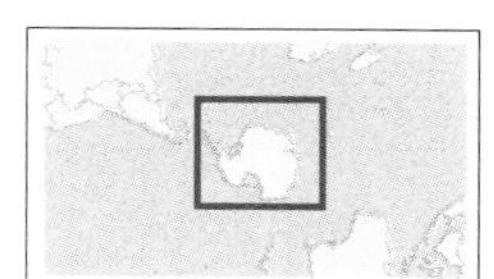

X 30° Y 15° Z 0° A 15° B 30° C

South Sandwich Is. (U.K.)
Bird I.
South Georgia (U.K.)
ATLANTIC OCEAN
Scotia Sea
Antarctic Circle
INDIAN OCEAN
South Orkney Is. (U.K.)
ORCADAS (ARG.)
SIGNY (U.K.)
Drake Passage
SANAE III (S. AFRICA)
GEORG VON NEUMAYER (GERMANY)
DAKSHIN GANGOTRI (INDIA)
NOVOLAZAREVSKAYA (RUSSIA)
Princess Astrid Coast
Fimbul Ice Shelf
C. Norvegia
Princess Martha Coast
New Schwabenland
Riiser-Larsen Ice Shelf
Queen Maud Land
Riiser-Larsen Peninsula
Princess Ragnhild Coast
Lützow-Holm Bay
SYOWA (JAPAN)
Casey Bay
White I.
Amundsen Bay
C. Ann
Prince Harold Coast
Mt. Fukushima 2,360 m
MOLODEZHNAYA (RUSSIA)
Prince Olav Coast
MIZUHO (JAPAN)
2,532 m
South Shetland Is. (U.K.)
Elephant I.
Joinville I.
BELLINGSHAUSEN (RUSSIA)
ARCTOWSKI (POLAND)
TTE. MARSH (CHILE)
JUBANY (ARG.)
ESPERANZA (ARG.)
GEN. B. O'HIGGINS (CHILE)
VICECOMODORO MARAMBIO (ARG.)
CAP. ARTURO PRAT (CHILE)
Weddell Sea
Lyddan I.
Caird Coast
3,212 m
HALLEY (U.K.)
NEW HALLEY (U.K.)
TENIENTE MATIENZO (ARG.)
PRIMAVERA (ARG.)
Antarctic
Palmer Arch.
ALMIRANTE BROWN (ARG.)
PALMER (U.S.)
COMANDANTE FERRAZ (BRAZIL)
FARADAY (U.K.)
C. Alexander
Graham Land
Larsen Ice Shelf
Biscoe Is.
C. Agassiz
Hearst I.
Peninsula
Adelaide I.
ROTHERA (U.K.)
GEN. SAN MARTÍN (ARG.)
Marguerite Bay
Kemp Pen.
Mt. Jackson 4,190 m
Palmer Land
Lassiter Coast
Smith Pen.
DRUZHNAYA II (RUSSIA)
FILCHNER (GERMANY)
GEN. BELGRANO II (ARG.)
GEN. BELGRANO III (ARG.)
Filchner Ice Shelf
Coats Land
Luitpold Coast
2,311 m
3,498 m
3,318 m
Enderby Land
C. Boothby
Edward VIII Bay
Mawson Coast
MAWSON (AUSTL.)
Mac. Robertson Land
Mt. Macey 1,960 m
80°
2,512 m
3,624 m
Fisher Glacier
C. Darnley
SOYUZ (RUSSIA)
Amery Ice Shelf
Mackenzie Bay
Prydz Bay
Lambert Glacier
George VI Sound
Alexander I.
C. Vostok
Wilkins Sound
FOSSIL BLUFF (U.K.)
Orville Coast
Ronne Ice Shelf
694 m
SOBRAL (ARG.)
Charcot I.
C. Byrd
Latady I.
Berlioz Pt.
English Coast
Ronne Entr.
Spaatz I.
Smyley I.
Dufek Massive
Pensacola Mts.
2,628 m
3,718 m
Ingrid Christianson Coast
DAVIS (AUSTL.)
2,190 m
POLE OF INACCESSIBILITY
American Highland
West Ice Shelf
Leopold and Astrid Coast
Bryan Coast
SIPLE (U.S.)
Ellsworth
Bellingshausen Sea
Vinson Massif 4,897 m
1,369 m
Ellsworth Mts.
Transantarctic
South Polar Plateau
3,106 m
SOUTH POLE
2,800 m
AMUNDSEN-SCOTT (U.S.)
3,832 m
3,650 m
3,100 m
Wilhelm II Coast
Davis Sea
Peter I Island (NORWAY)
Farwell I.
Eights Coast
Land
Abbot Ice Shelf
1,745 m
3,269 m
MIRNYY (RUSSIA)
Queen Mary Coast
Thurston I.
Walgreen Coast
900 m
Marie
C. Flying Fish
Burke I.
Pine I. Bay
Thwaites Iceberg Tongue
984 m
Horlick Ice Stream
Queen Maud Mts.
2,801 m
2,896 m
VOSTOK (RUSSIA)
3,497 m
Masson I.
Shackleton Ice Shelf
Denman Glacier
Mill I.
Bowman I.
Knox Coast
1,266 m
BYRD (U.S.)
Byrd
Gould Coast
Beardmore Glacier
Blizzard Pk. 3,373 m
Mt. Kirkpatrick 4,528 m
Shackleton Coast
2,593 m
Nimrod Glacier
Martin Pen.
Amundsen Sea
Bakutis Coast
Getz Ice Shelf
Carney I.
Rockefeller Plateau
Mt. Sidley 4,181 m
1,245 m
Siple Coast
Ross Ice Shelf
2,407 m
2,854 m
DOME C (U.S.)
Wilkes Land
2,192 m
Vincennes Bay
CASEY (AUSTL.)
Budd Coast
C. Poinsett
Totten Glacier
Mt. Siple 3,100 m
Siple I.
C. Dart
Hobbs Coast
RUSSKAYA (RUSSIA)
Land
Sanders Coast
Roosevelt Island
80°
Byrd Glacier
Hillary Coast
Mountains
Edward VII Pen.
Sulzberger Ice Shelf
Sulzberger Bay
C. Colbeck
MCMURDO (U.S.)
SCOTT (N.Z.)
VANDA (N.Z.)
2,479 m
Shapeless Mtn. 2,739 m
C. Crozier
Ross I.
Mt. Erebus 3,794 m
Scott Coast
Victoria Land
Sabrina Coast
Moscow U. Ice Shelf
Banzare Coast
Voyeykov Ice Shelf
2,498 m
Ross Sea
Franklin I.
Mt. New Zealand 2,888 m
2,220 m
Frost Glacier
C. Goodenough
Porpoise Bay
Clarie Coast
Coulman I.
C. Hallett
Borchgrevnik Coast
LILLIE MARLEEN HÜTTE (GERMANY)
Ninnis Glacier
Mertz Glacier
Adélie Coast
Dibble Iceberg Tongue
DUMONT D'URVILLE (FRANCE)
George V Coast
C. Adare
Mt. Blowaway 1,342 m
LENINGRADSKAYA (RUSSIA)
Cook Ice Shelf
C. Hudson
SOUTH MAGNETIC POLE
70°
Balleny Is.
Antarctic Circle
PACIFIC OCEAN
INDIAN OCEAN
60°
45° 60° 75° 90° 105° 120° 135°
W V U T S R
D E F G H J

Q Longitude West 150° of Greenwich P 165° N 180° M 165° L 150° Longitude East of Greenwich K

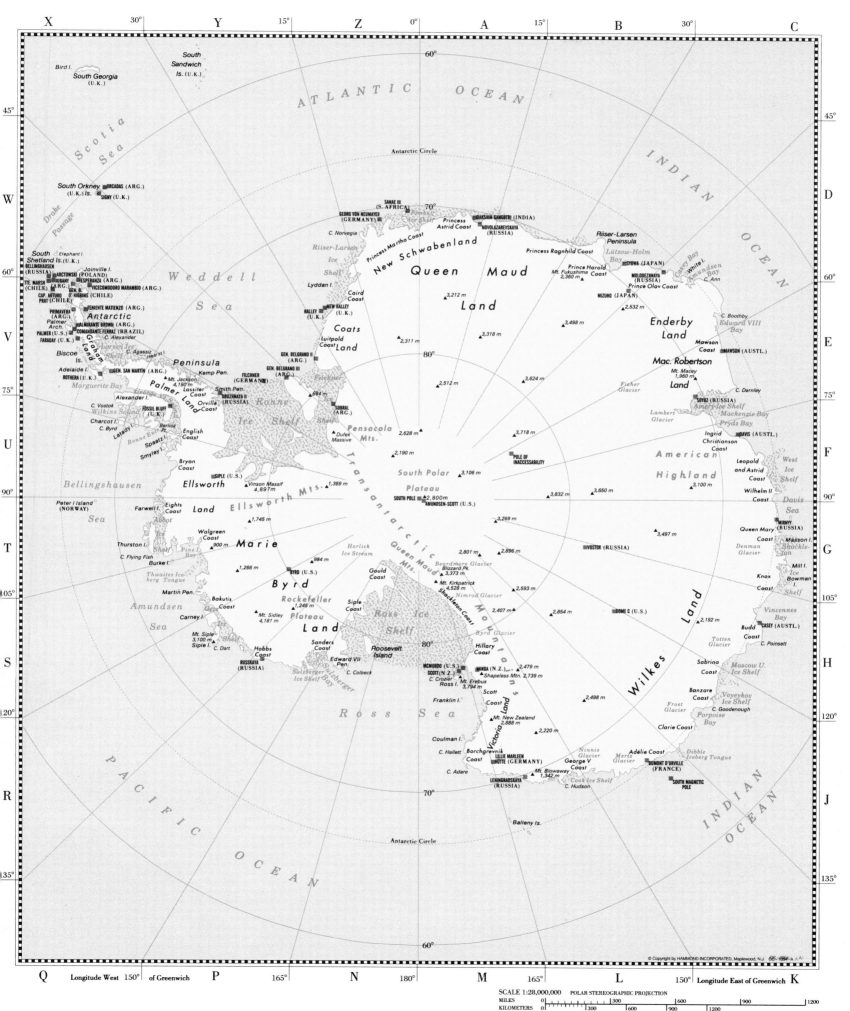

SCALE 1:28,000,000 POLAR STEREOGRAPHIC PROJECTION
MILES 0 300 600 900 1200
KILOMETERS 0 300 600 900 1200

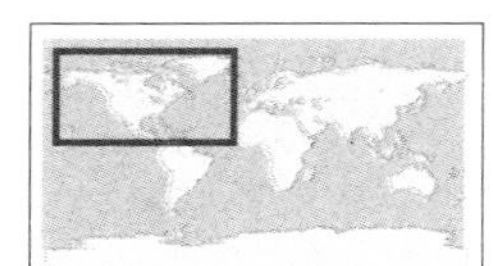

North America

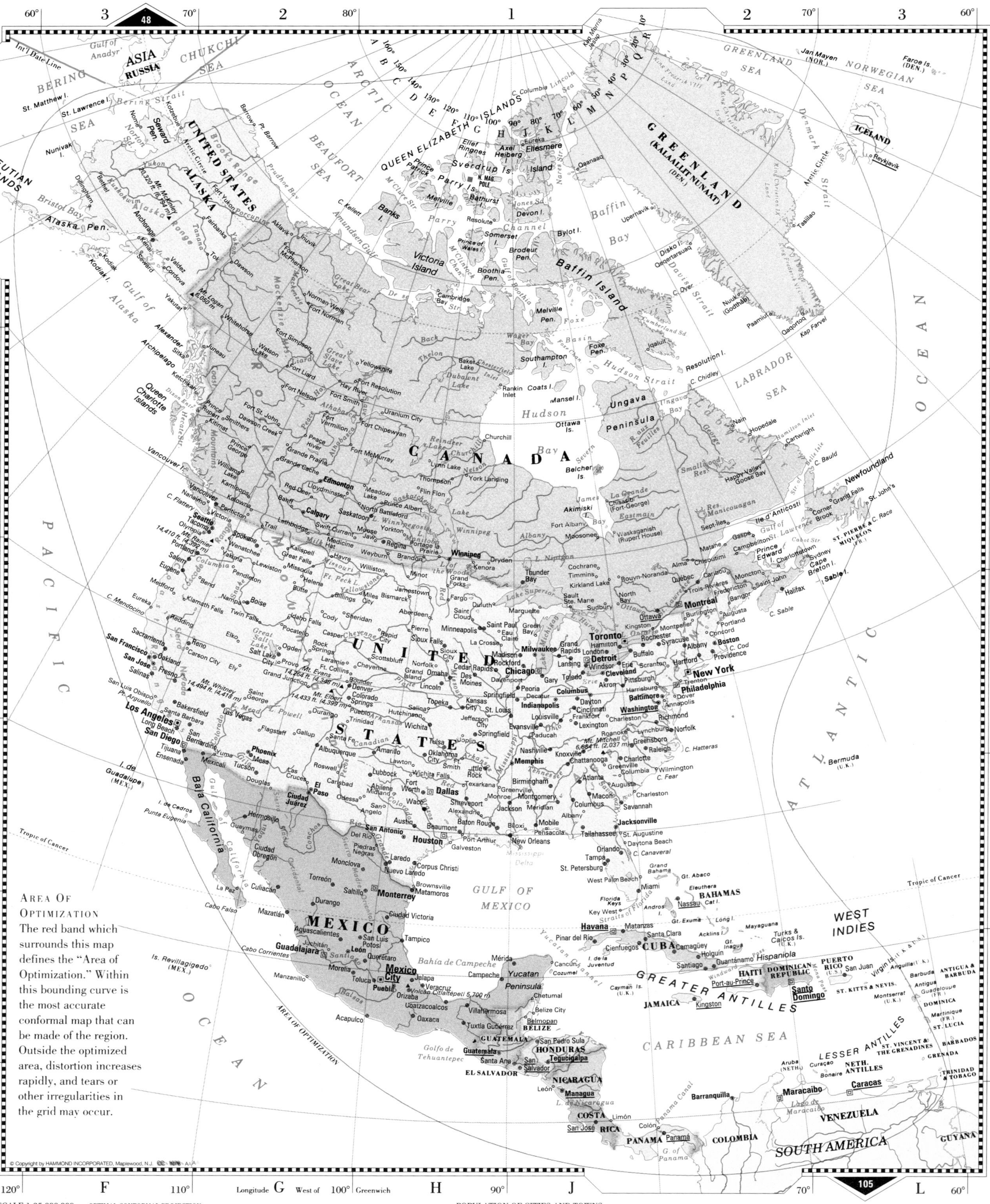

AREA OF OPTIMIZATION

The red band which surrounds this map defines the "Area of Optimization." Within this bounding curve is the most accurate conformal map that can be made of the region. Outside the optimized area, distortion increases rapidly, and tears or other irregularities in the grid may occur.

SCALE 1:35,000,000 OPTIMAL CONFORMAL PROJECTION

MILES 0 500 1000 1500

KILOMETERS 0 500 1000 1500

POPULATION OF CITIES AND TOWNS

- OVER 3,000,000
- 1,000,000 - 2,999,999
- 500,000 - 999,999
- 100,000 - 499,999
- UNDER 100,000

Alaska

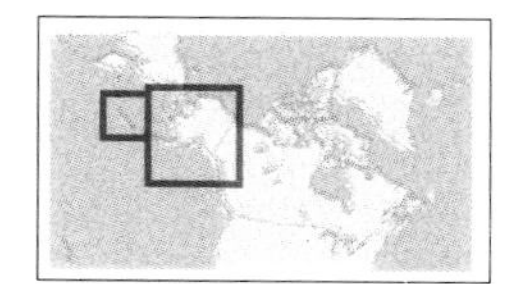

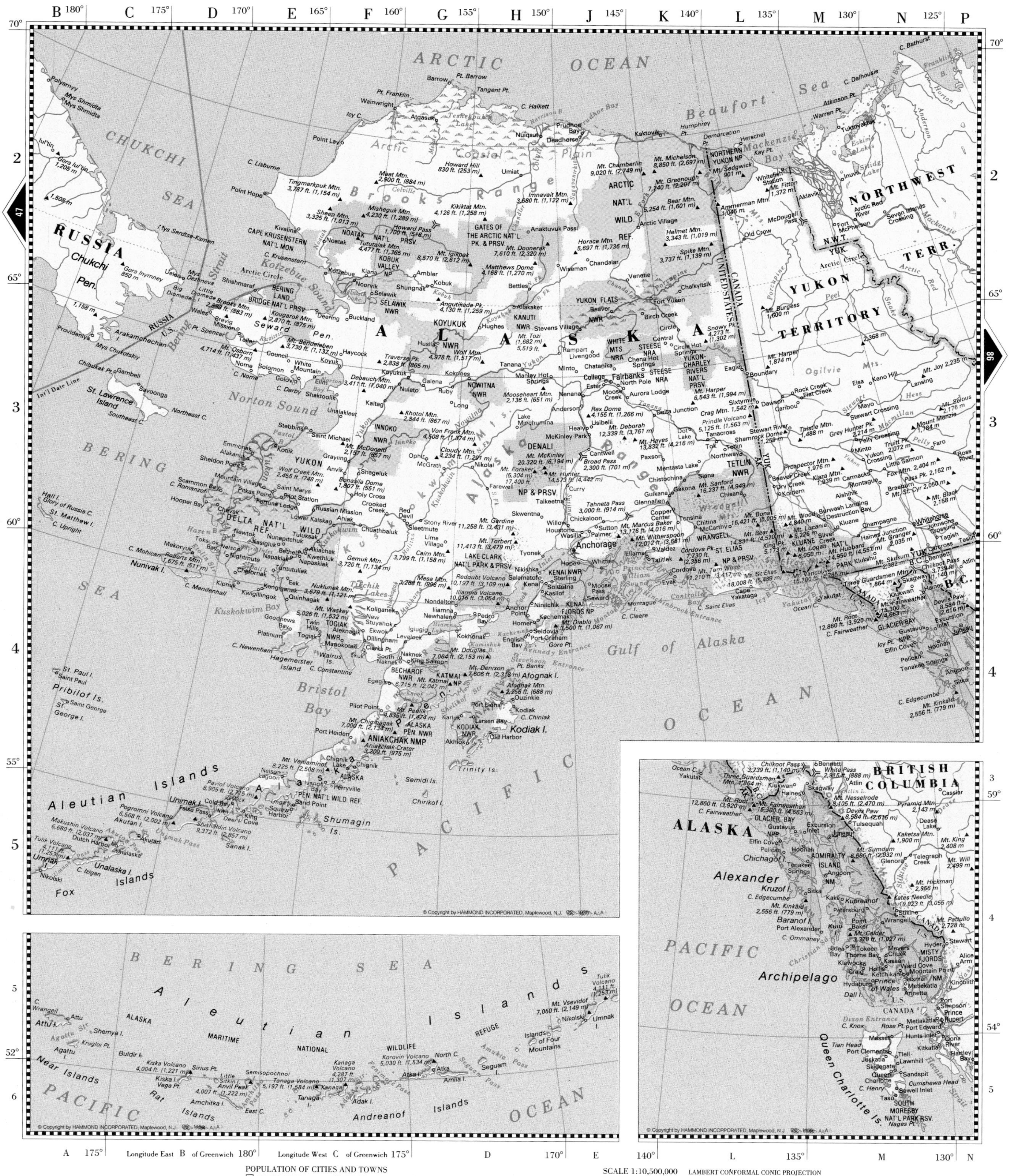

ARCTIC OCEAN

ALASKA

BERING SEA

Gulf of Alaska

PACIFIC OCEAN

Longitude East of Greenwich 180° Longitude West of Greenwich

POPULATION OF CITIES AND TOWNS

- OVER 2,000,000
- 1,000,000 - 1,999,999
- 500,000 - 999,999
- 250,000 - 499,999
- 100,000 - 249,999
- 30,000 - 99,999
- 10,000 - 29,999
- UNDER 10,000

SCALE 1:10,500,000 LAMBERT CONFORMAL CONIC PROJECTION

MILES 0 150 300 450

KILOMETERS 0 150 300 450

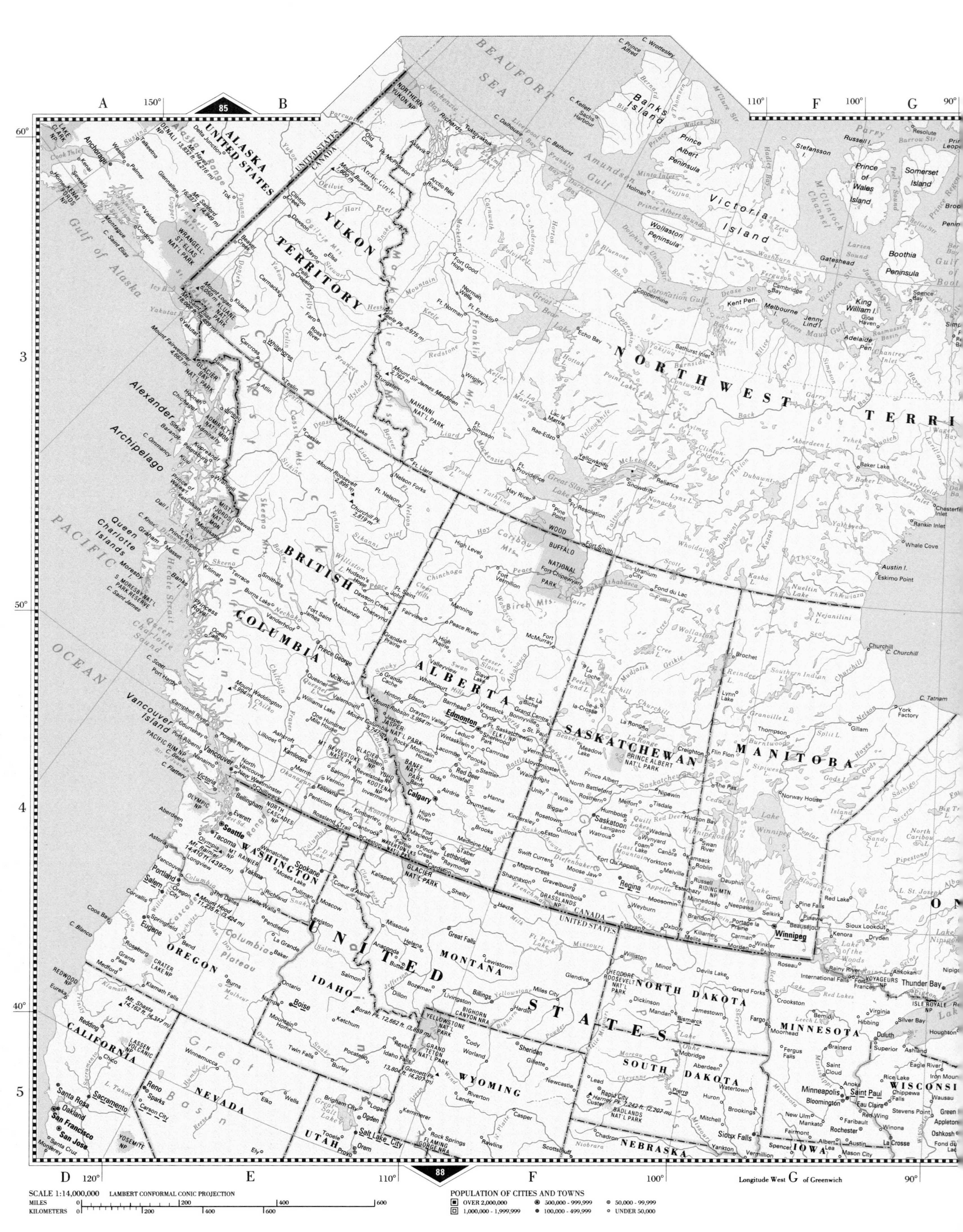

85
A
150°
B
110°
F
100°
G
90°
60°
3
4
5
50°
40°
BEAUFORT SEA
Banks Island
Victoria Island
Prince Albert Peninsula
Wollaston Peninsula
Prince of Wales Island
Somerset Island
Boothia Peninsula
King William I.
Amundsen Gulf
Coronation Gulf
Queen Maud Gulf
M'Clintock Channel
Great Bear Lake
Great Slave Lake
Lake Athabasca
Lake Winnipeg
ALASKA
UNITED STATES
UNITED STATES
CANADA
YUKON TERRITORY
NORTHWEST TERRI
BRITISH COLUMBIA
ALBERTA
SASKATCHEWAN
MANITOBA
UNITED STATES
WASHINGTON
OREGON
IDAHO
MONTANA
WYOMING
NORTH DAKOTA
SOUTH DAKOTA
NEBRASKA
MINNESOTA
IOWA
WISCONSI
CALIFORNIA
NEVADA
UTAH
Gulf of Alaska
Alexander Archipelago
Queen Charlotte Islands
Vancouver Island
PACIFIC OCEAN
Anchorage
Whitehorse
Dawson
Yellowknife
Edmonton
Calgary
Vancouver
Victoria
Seattle
Tacoma
Portland
Salem
Spokane
Boise
Regina
Saskatoon
Winnipeg
Helena
Bismarck
Pierre
Salt Lake City
Sacramento
San Francisco
Oakland
San Jose
Carson City
Minneapolis
Saint Paul
Thunder Bay
WOOD BUFFALO NATIONAL PARK
PRINCE ALBERT NAT'L PARK
GLACIER NAT'L PARK
YELLOWSTONE NAT'L PARK
GRAND TETON NAT'L PARK
Mt. Rainier 14,410 ft. (4392 m)
Mt. Shasta 14,162 ft. (4,317 m)
Mount Robson 3,954 m
Mount Logan 6,050 m
D
120°
E
110°
88
F
100°
Longitude West G of Greenwich
90°
SCALE 1:14,000,000 LAMBERT CONFORMAL CONIC PROJECTION
MILES 0 200 400 600
KILOMETERS 0 200 400 600
POPULATION OF CITIES AND TOWNS
OVER 2,000,000
1,000,000 - 1,999,999
500,000 - 999,999
100,000 - 499,999
50,000 - 99,999
UNDER 50,000

Canada

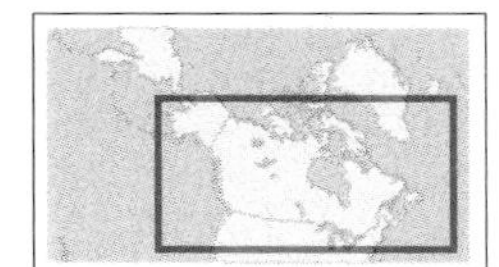

Map continued at right

H 80° J 70° K 60° L 50°

140° Q 120° R 100° S 80° T 60°

ARCTIC OCEAN
Queen Elizabeth Islands
Sverdrup Islands
Parry Islands
Ellesmere Island
Axel Heiberg Island
Devon Island
Melville Island
Banks Island
Baffin Bay
NORTH MAGNETIC POLE
GREENLAND (KALAALLIT NUNAAT) (DEN.)

Map continued at left

Baffin Island
Baffin Bay
Davis Strait
Foxe Basin
Hudson Strait
Hudson Bay
Ungava Peninsula
Ungava Bay
LABRADOR SEA
NEWFOUNDLAND
Newfoundland
QUÉBEC
James Bay
Gulf of St. Lawrence
Cabot Strait
NEW BRUNSWICK
NOVA SCOTIA
PRINCE EDWARD ISLAND
ST. PIERRE & MIQUELON (FR.)
MAINE
NEW YORK
VT.
N.H.
MASS.
ONTARIO
MICHIGAN
Gulf of Maine
ATLANTIC OCEAN
Lake Huron
Lake Ontario
Lake Erie
Montréal
Québec
Ottawa
Toronto
Boston
St. John's
Halifax

H J 70° K 60° L

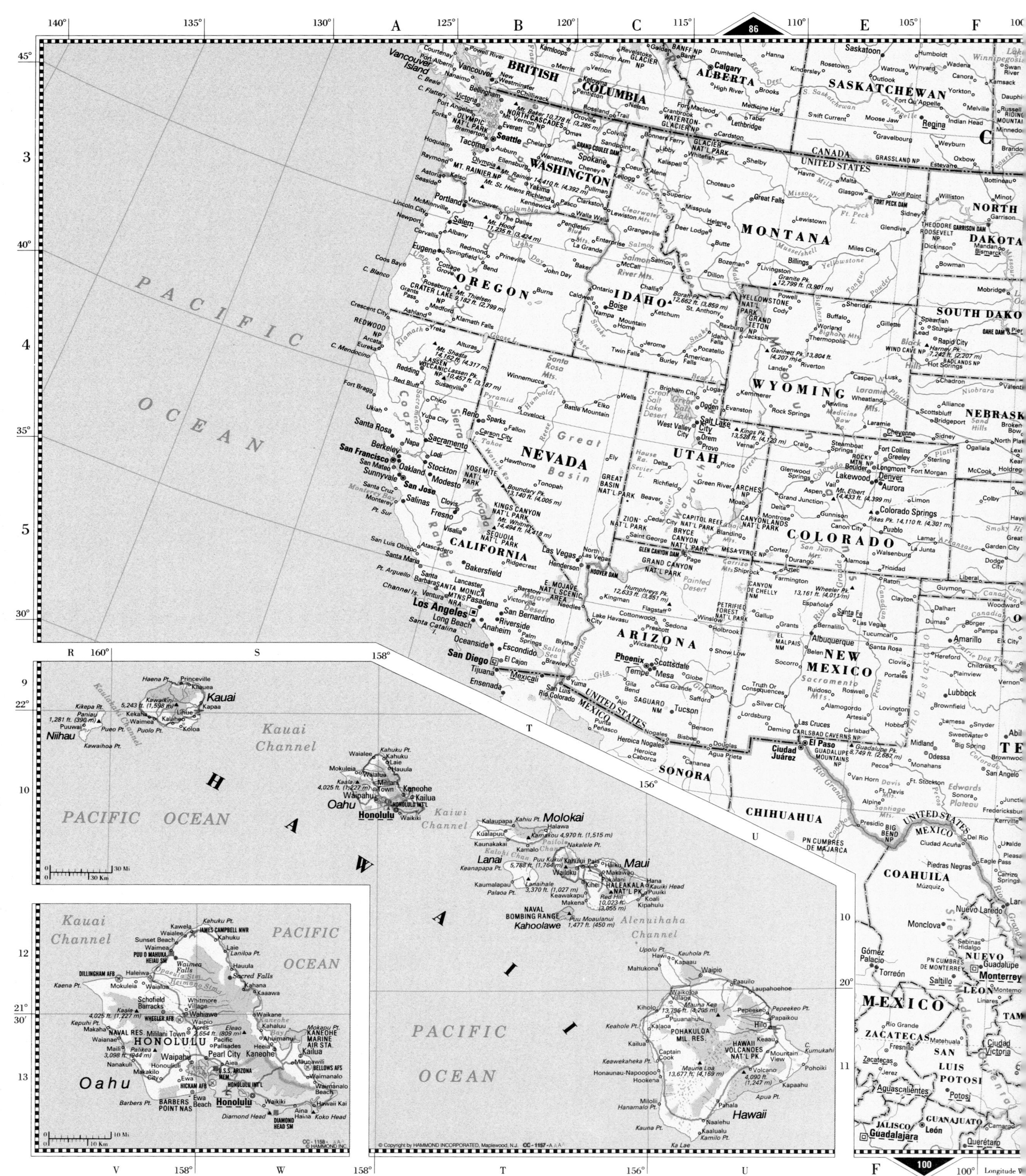

86
100
140° 135° 130° 125° 120° 115° 110° 105° 100°
A B C D E F
45° 40° 35° 30°
3 4 5
PACIFIC OCEAN
BRITISH COLUMBIA
ALBERTA
SASKATCHEWAN
CANADA
UNITED STATES
WASHINGTON
OREGON
IDAHO
MONTANA
NORTH DAKOTA
SOUTH DAKOTA
WYOMING
NEBRASKA
NEVADA
UTAH
COLORADO
CALIFORNIA
ARIZONA
NEW MEXICO
SONORA
CHIHUAHUA
COAHUILA
NUEVO LEON
ZACATECAS
SAN LUIS POTOSI
JALISCO
GUANAJUATO
MEXICO
Vancouver Island
Vancouver
Victoria
Calgary
Seattle
Tacoma
Olympia
Spokane
Portland
Salem
Eugene
Boise
Helena
Great Falls
Billings
Salt Lake City
Ogden
Provo
Reno
Carson City
Sacramento
San Francisco
Oakland
San Jose
Fresno
Las Vegas
Bakersfield
Los Angeles
Long Beach
San Diego
Tijuana
Mexicali
Phoenix
Tucson
Denver
Colorado Springs
Pueblo
Albuquerque
Santa Fe
El Paso
Ciudad Juárez
Lubbock
Amarillo
Cheyenne
Regina
Saskatoon
Monterrey
Saltillo
Torreón
Guadalajara
León
Great Salt Lake
Great Basin
Mojave Desert
Painted Desert
Rio Grande
GRAND CANYON NAT'L PARK
YELLOWSTONE NAT'L PARK
GRAND TETON NP
YOSEMITE NAT'L PARK
SEQUOIA NAT'L PARK
KINGS CANYON NAT'L PARK
CRATER LAKE NP
REDWOOD NP
BIG BEND NP
Mt. Whitney 14,494 ft. (4,418 m)
Mt. Rainier 14,410 ft. (4,392 m)
Mt. Elbert 14,433 ft. (4,399 m)
HAWAII
Kauai
Niihau
Oahu
Honolulu
Molokai
Lanai
Maui
Kahoolawe
Hawaii
Hilo
Kauai Channel
Kaiwi Channel
Alenuihaha Channel
Mauna Kea 13,796 ft. (4,205 m)
Mauna Loa 13,677 ft. (4,169 m)
HALEAKALA NAT'L PK.
HAWAII VOLCANOES NAT'L PK.
R S T U V W
160° 158° 156°
9 10 11 12 13
22° 20° 21° 30′
HONOLULU
Pearl City
Kaneohe
Kailua
Waikiki
Diamond Head
Pearl Harbor
0 30 Mi
0 30 Km
0 10 Mi
0 10 Km
© Copyright by HAMMOND INCORPORATED, Maplewood, N.J.
Longitude W

United States

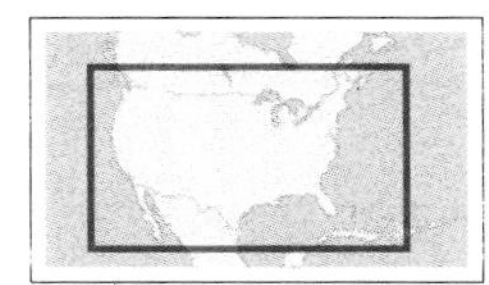

87

101

GULF OF MEXICO

ATLANTIC OCEAN

CARIBBEAN SEA

POPULATION OF CITIES AND TOWNS

- ■ OVER 2,000,000
- ▣ 1,000,000 - 1,999,999
- ◉ 500,000 - 999,999
- ● 100,000 - 499,999
- ◎ 50,000 - 99,999
- ○ UNDER 50,000

SCALE 1:14,000,000 LAMBERT CONFORMAL CONIC PROJECTION

MILES 0 200 400 600

KILOMETERS 0 200 400 600

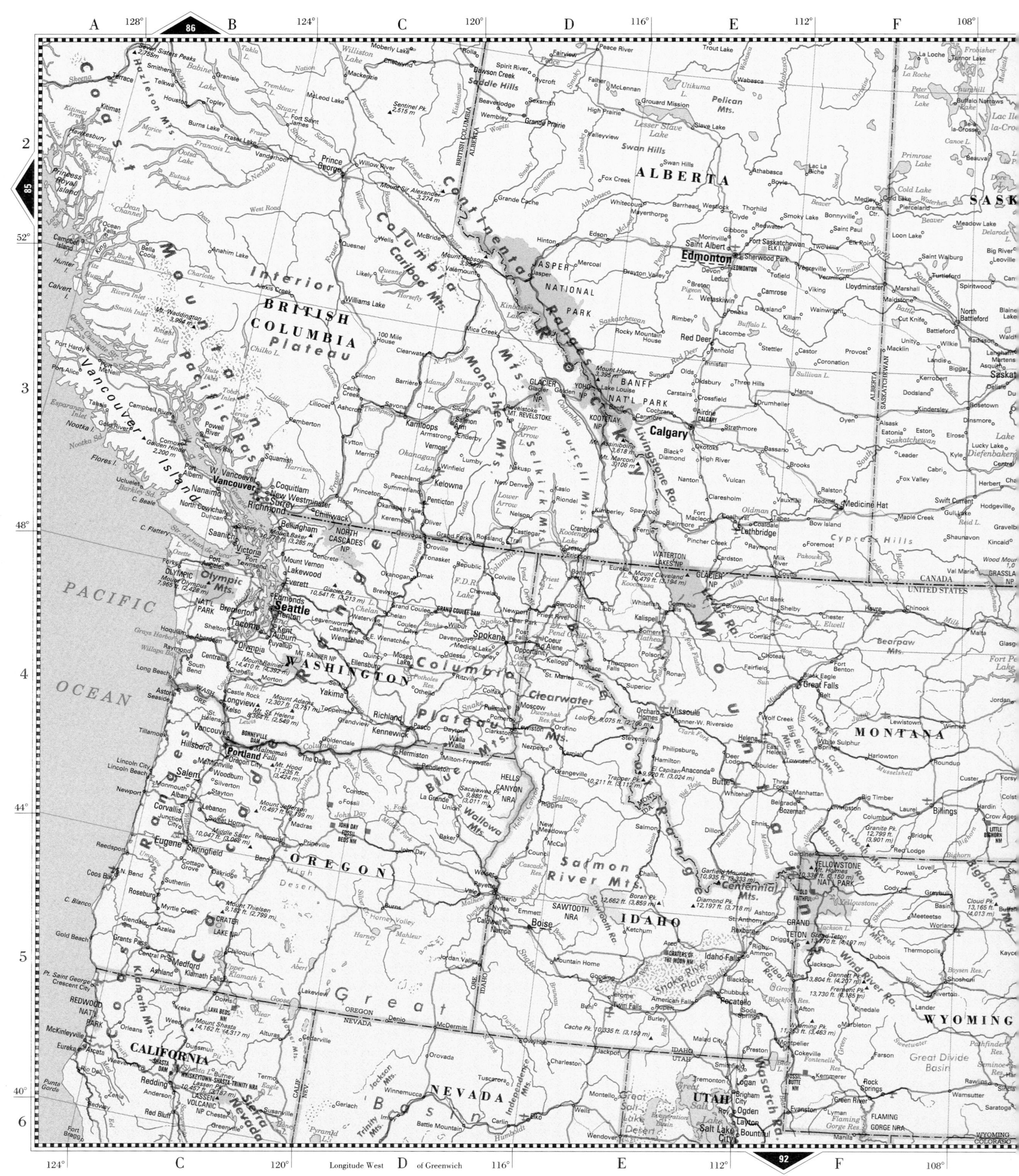

A
128°
86
B
124°
C
120°
D
116°
E
112°
F
108°
2
85
52°
3
48°
4
44°
5
40°
6
124°
C
120°
Longitude West
D
of Greenwich
116°
E
112°
92
F
108°
ALBERTA
BRITISH COLUMBIA
SASK
WASHINGTON
OREGON
IDAHO
MONTANA
WYOMING
NEVADA
UTAH
CALIFORNIA
CANADA
UNITED STATES
PACIFIC
OCEAN
Coast Mountains
Interior Plateau
Continental Ranges
Rocky Mountains
Columbia Mts.
Cariboo Mts.
Monashee Mts.
Selkirk Mts.
Purcell Mts.
Livingstone Ra.
Cascade Range
Coast Ranges
Klamath Mts.
Olympic Mts.
Blue Mts.
Wallowa Mts.
Columbia Plateau
Clearwater Mts.
Bitterroot Range
Salmon River Mts.
Sawtooth Ra.
Centennial Mts.
Lewis Ra.
Wind River Ra.
Bighorn Mts.
Wasatch Ra.
Great Basin
Great Divide Basin
Snake River Plain
Vancouver Island
Swan Hills
Pelican Mts.
Saddle Hills
Cypress Hills
Bearpaw Mts.
Edmonton
Calgary
Vancouver
Victoria
Seattle
Tacoma
Olympia
Spokane
Portland
Salem
Eugene
Boise
Missoula
Great Falls
Helena
Butte
Billings
Pocatello
Idaho Falls
Ogden
Salt Lake City
Kamloops
Kelowna
Prince George
Lethbridge
Medicine Hat
Red Deer
Grande Prairie
Yakima
Richland
Kennewick
Pasco
Walla Walla
Lewiston
Moscow
Pendleton
The Dalles
Bend
Medford
Klamath Falls
Redding
Eureka
Twin Falls
Logan
Elko
Winnemucca
Kalispell
Bozeman
JASPER NATIONAL PARK
BANFF NAT'L PARK
GLACIER NP
YELLOWSTONE NAT'L PARK
NORTH CASCADES NP
OLYMPIC NAT'L PARK
MT. RAINIER NP
CRATER LAKE NP
REDWOOD NAT'L PARK
LASSEN VOLCANIC NP
HELLS CANYON NRA
SAWTOOTH NRA
FLAMING GORGE NRA
Mount Robson 3,954 m
Mount Rainier 14,410 ft. (4,392 m)
Mount Hood 11,235 ft. (3,424 m)
Mount Shasta 14,162 ft. (4,317 m)
Mt. St. Helens 8,365 ft. (2,549 m)
Mount Adams 12,307 ft. (3,751 m)
Borah Pk. 12,662 ft. (3,859 m)
Gannett Pk. 13,804 ft. (4,207 m)
Grand Teton 13,770 ft. (4,197 m)
Great Salt Lake
Lake Koocanusa
Flathead L.
Yellowstone L.

Southwestern Canada, Northwestern United States

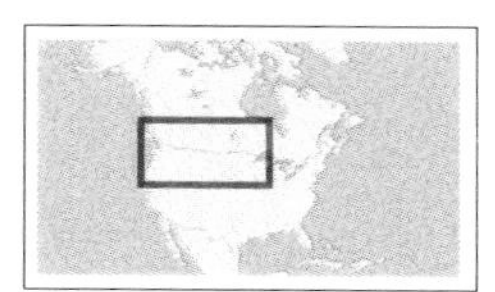

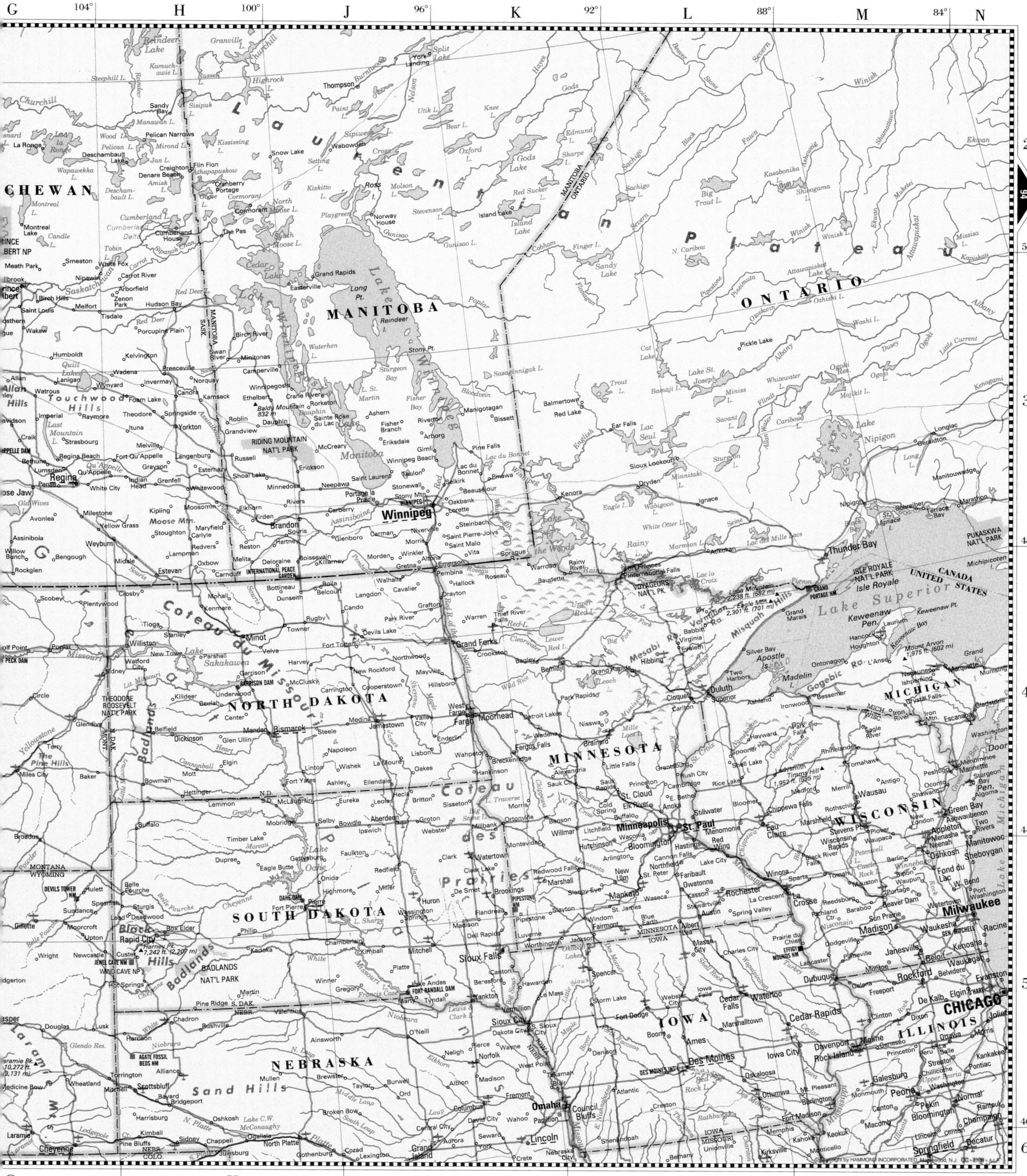

G 104° H 100° J 96° K 92° L 88° M 84° N

POPULATION OF CITIES AND TOWNS

- ■ OVER 2,000,000
- ▣ 1,000,000 - 1,999,999
- ◉ 500,000 - 999,999
- ◎ 250,000 - 499,999
- ● 100,000 - 249,999
- ⊕ 30,000 - 99,999
- ◦ 10,000 - 29,999
- ○ UNDER 10,000

SCALE 1:7,000,000 LAMBERT CONFORMAL CONIC PROJECTION

MILES 0 100 200 300

KILOMETERS 0 100 200 300

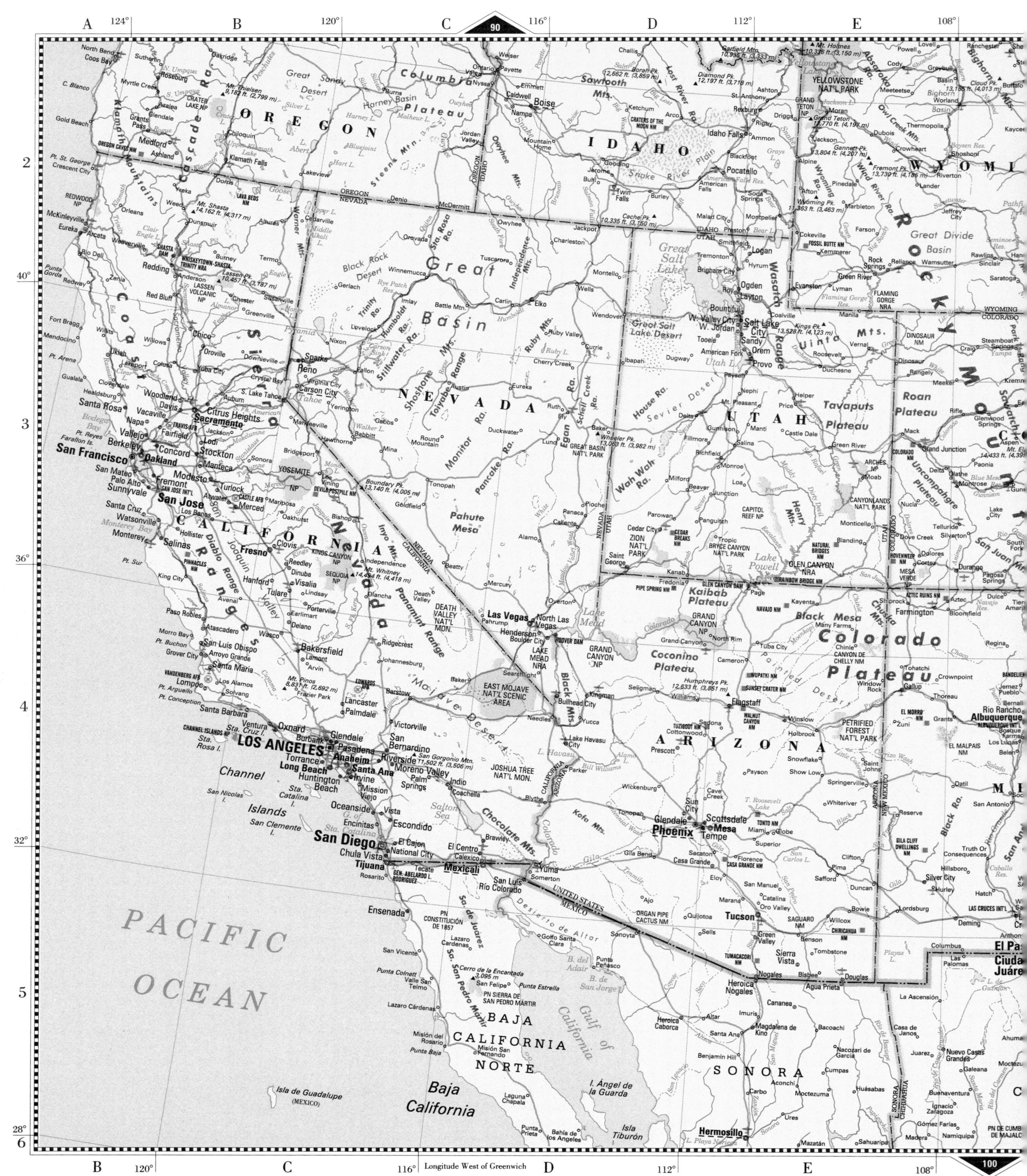

A
124°
B
120°
C
90
116°
D
112°
E
108°
2
3
4
5
6
40°
36°
32°
28°
OREGON
IDAHO
WYOMING
NEVADA
UTAH
CALIFORNIA
ARIZONA
BAJA CALIFORNIA NORTE
SONORA
PACIFIC OCEAN
Columbia Plateau
Harney Basin
Great Sandy Desert
Sawtooth Mts.
Snake River Plain
Great Basin
Great Salt Lake
Great Salt Lake Desert
Black Rock Desert
Great Divide Basin
Rocky Mountains
Wasatch Range
Uinta Mts.
Tavaputs Plateau
Roan Plateau
Colorado Plateau
Kaibab Plateau
Coconino Plateau
Mojave Desert
Sierra Nevada
Coast Ranges
Cascade Ra.
Klamath Mountains
Channel Islands
Gulf of California
Baja California
Desierto de Altar
YELLOWSTONE NAT'L PARK
GRAND TETON NP
CRATER LAKE NP
LASSEN VOLCANIC NP
YOSEMITE NP
KINGS CANYON NP
SEQUOIA NP
DEATH VALLEY NAT'L MON.
JOSHUA TREE NAT'L MON.
EAST MOJAVE NAT'L SCENIC AREA
GRAND CANYON NP
ZION NAT'L PARK
BRYCE CANYON NAT'L PARK
CAPITOL REEF NP
CANYONLANDS NAT'L PARK
ARCHES NP
GREAT BASIN NAT'L PARK
PETRIFIED FOREST NAT'L PARK
ORGAN PIPE CACTUS NM
GLEN CANYON NRA
LAKE MEAD NRA
Boise
Salt Lake City
Sacramento
San Francisco
Oakland
San Jose
Fresno
Reno
Carson City
Las Vegas
LOS ANGELES
San Diego
Tijuana
Mexicali
Phoenix
Tucson
Flagstaff
Albuquerque
Hermosillo
Ensenada
Nogales
Yuma
Provo
Ogden
Pocatello
Idaho Falls
Medford
Redding
Eureka
Santa Barbara
Bakersfield
Lake Powell
Lake Mead
UNITED STATES
MEXICO
B
120°
C
116°
Longitude West of Greenwich
D
112°
E
108°
100

Southwestern United States

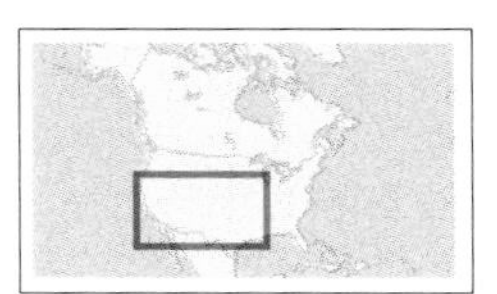

POPULATION OF CITIES AND TOWNS

OVER 2,000,000	500,000 - 999,999	100,000 - 249,999	10,000 - 29,999
1,000,000 - 1,999,999	250,000 - 499,999	30,000 - 99,999	UNDER 10,000

SCALE 1:7,000,000 LAMBERT CONFORMAL CONIC PROJECTION

MILES 0 100 200 300

KILOMETERS 0 100 200 300

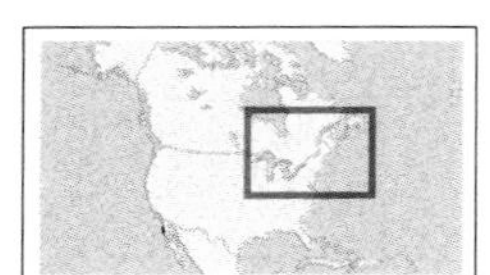

Southeastern Canada, Northeastern United States

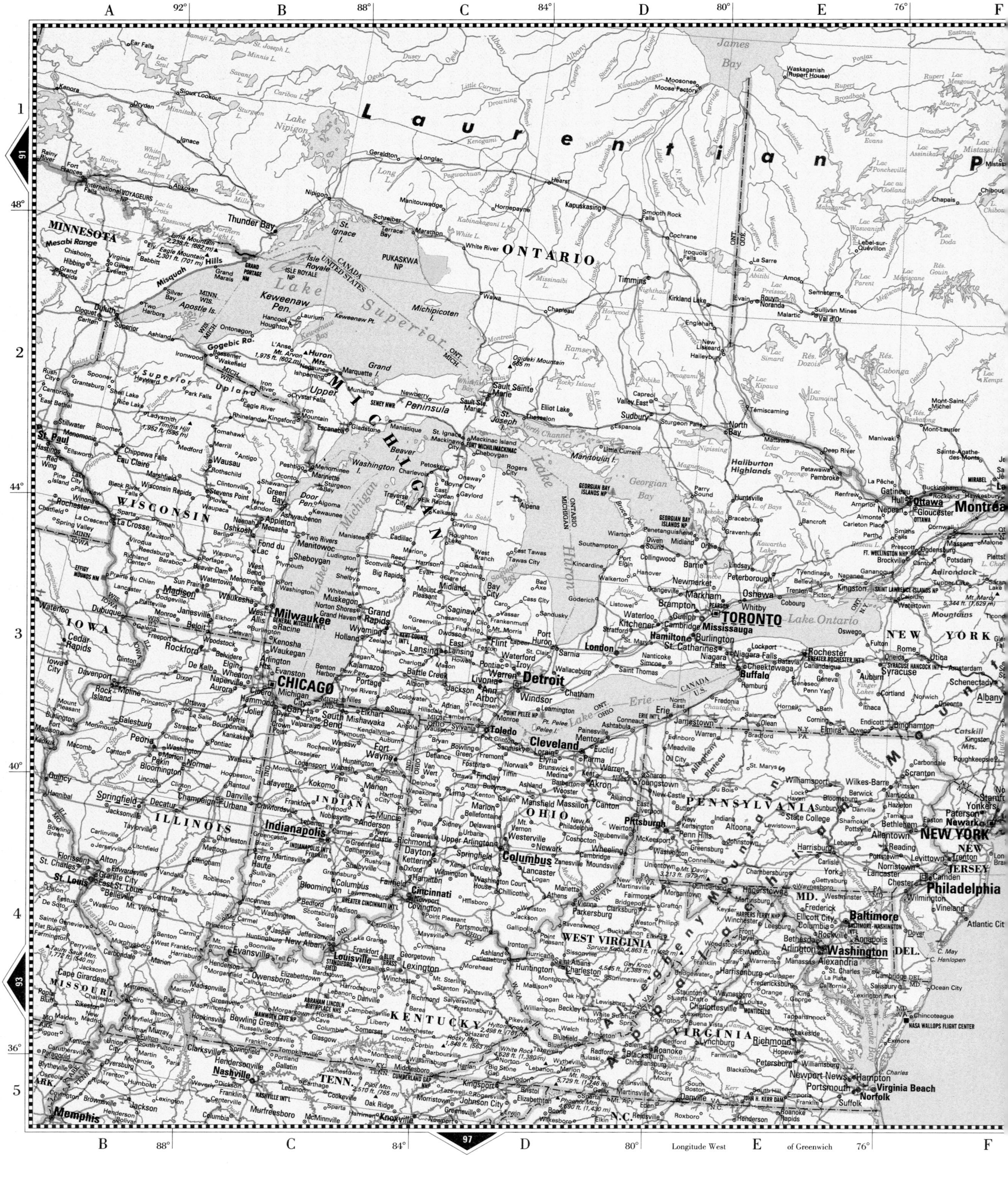

91

93

97

Longitude West of Greenwich

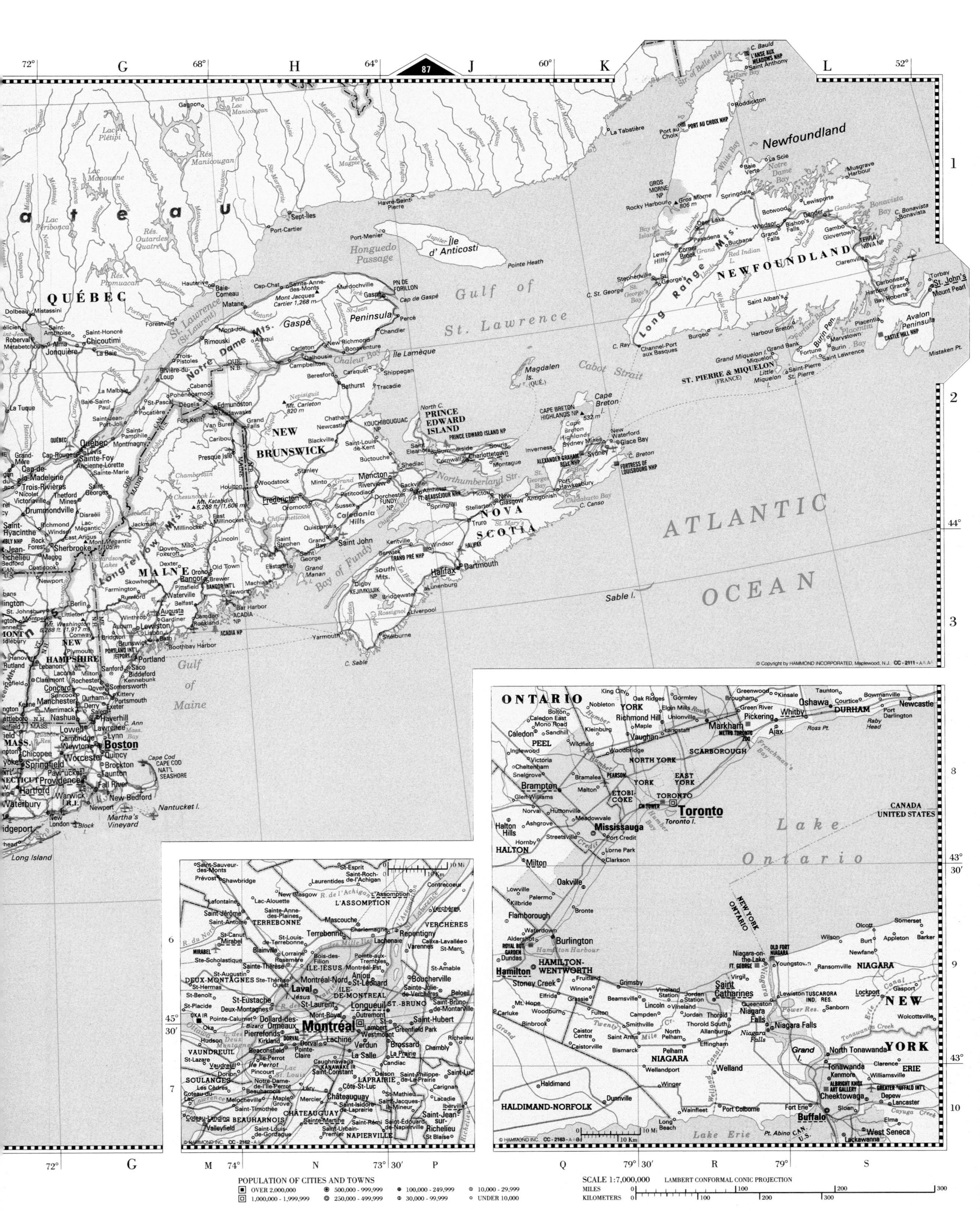

87
72° G 68° H 64° J 60° K L 52°
QUÉBEC
Gulf of St. Lawrence
Newfoundland
NEWFOUNDLAND
Long Range Mts.
Île d' Anticosti
Honguedo Passage
Gaspé Peninsula
Notre Dame Mts.
Magdalen Is. (QUÉ.)
Cabot Strait
ST. PIERRE & MIQUELON (FRANCE)
PRINCE EDWARD ISLAND
NEW BRUNSWICK
NOVA SCOTIA
Northumberland Str.
Bay of Fundy
ATLANTIC OCEAN
Sable I.
Cape Breton I.
MAINE
Gulf of Maine
NEW HAMPSHIRE
MASS.
Boston
Cape Cod
Nantucket I.
Martha's Vineyard
Long Island
St. John's
Halifax
Saint John
Fredericton
Charlottetown
Sydney
Québec
Montréal
Toronto
Mississauga
Hamilton
Burlington
Oakville
Brampton
Oshawa
Buffalo
Niagara Falls
St. Catharines
ONTARIO
Lake Ontario
Lake Erie
NEW YORK
CANADA
UNITED STATES
NIAGARA
HALDIMAND-NORFOLK
HAMILTON-WENTWORTH
HALTON
PEEL
YORK
DURHAM
L'ASSOMPTION
TERREBONNE
DEUX-MONTAGNES
VAUDREUIL
SOULANGES
BEAUHARNOIS
CHÂTEAUGUAY
NAPIERVILLE
LAPRAIRIE
VERCHÈRES
© Copyright by HAMMOND INCORPORATED, Maplewood, N.J. CC-2111
© HAMMOND INC. CC-2162
© HAMMOND INC. CC-2163
72° G M 74° N 73° 30' P Q 79° 30' R 79° S
POPULATION OF CITIES AND TOWNS
OVER 2,000,000
1,000,000 - 1,999,999
500,000 - 999,999
250,000 - 499,999
100,000 - 249,999
30,000 - 99,999
10,000 - 29,999
UNDER 10,000
SCALE 1:7,000,000
LAMBERT CONFORMAL CONIC PROJECTION
MILES 0 100 200 300
KILOMETERS 0 100 200 300

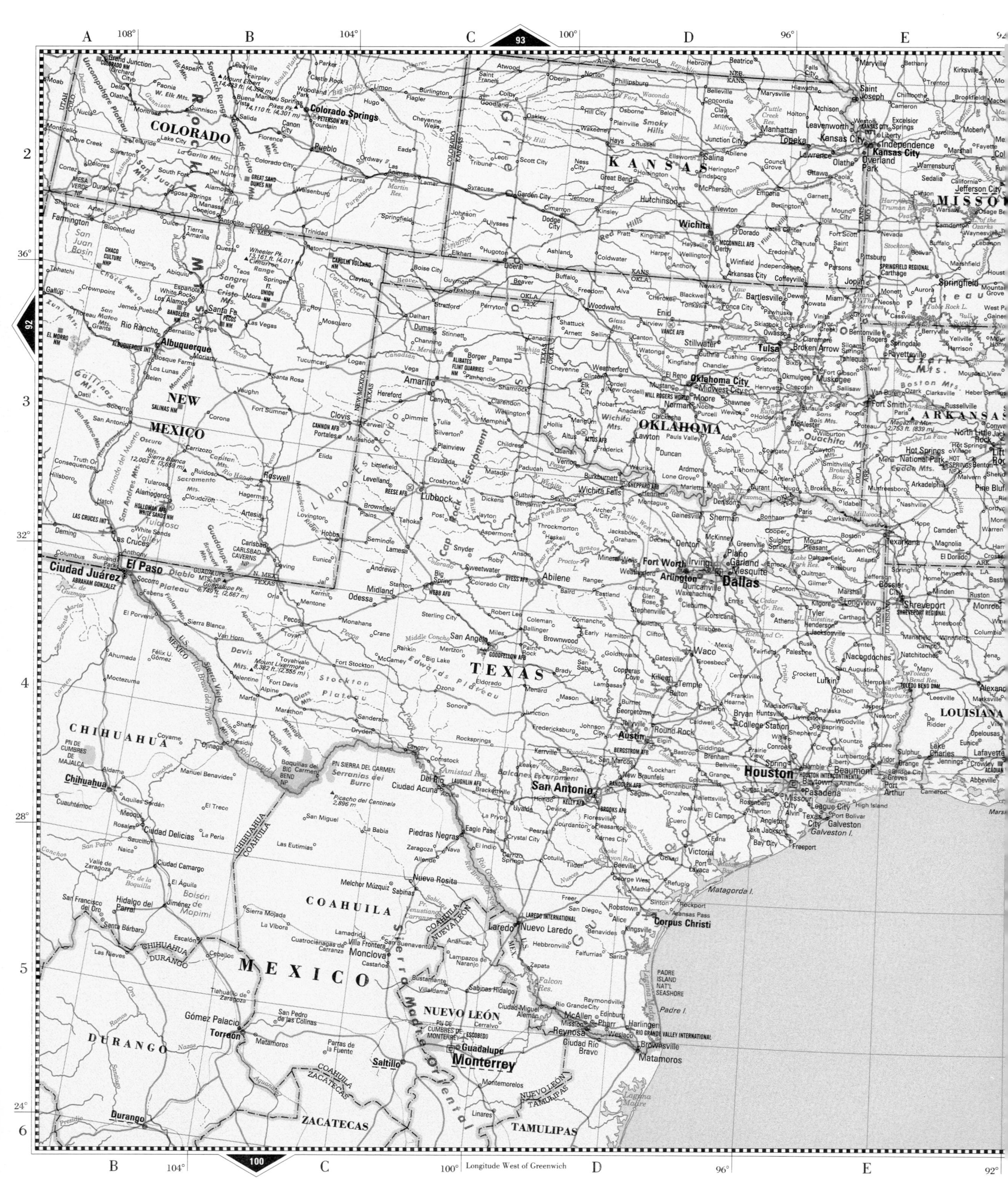

B
104°
100
C
100°
Longitude West of Greenwich
D
96°
E
92°

Southeastern United States

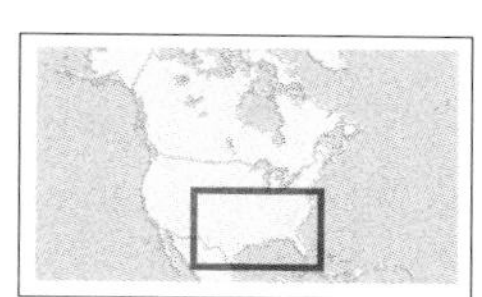

ILLINOIS INDIANA OHIO WEST VIRGINIA VIRGINIA KENTUCKY TENNESSEE NORTH CAROLINA SOUTH CAROLINA MISSISSIPPI ALABAMA GEORGIA FLORIDA BAHAMAS

ATLANTIC OCEAN

GULF OF MEXICO

POPULATION OF CITIES AND TOWNS

▣ OVER 2,000,000	◉ 500,000 - 999,999	⊕ 100,000 - 249,999	⊙ 10,000 - 29,999
◻ 1,000,000 - 1,999,999	◎ 250,000 - 499,999	⊖ 30,000 - 99,999	○ UNDER 10,000

SCALE 1:7,000,000 LAMBERT CONFORMAL CONIC PROJECTION

MILES 0 100 200 300

KILOMETERS 0 100 200 300

Los Angeles, New York, Philadelphia, Washington

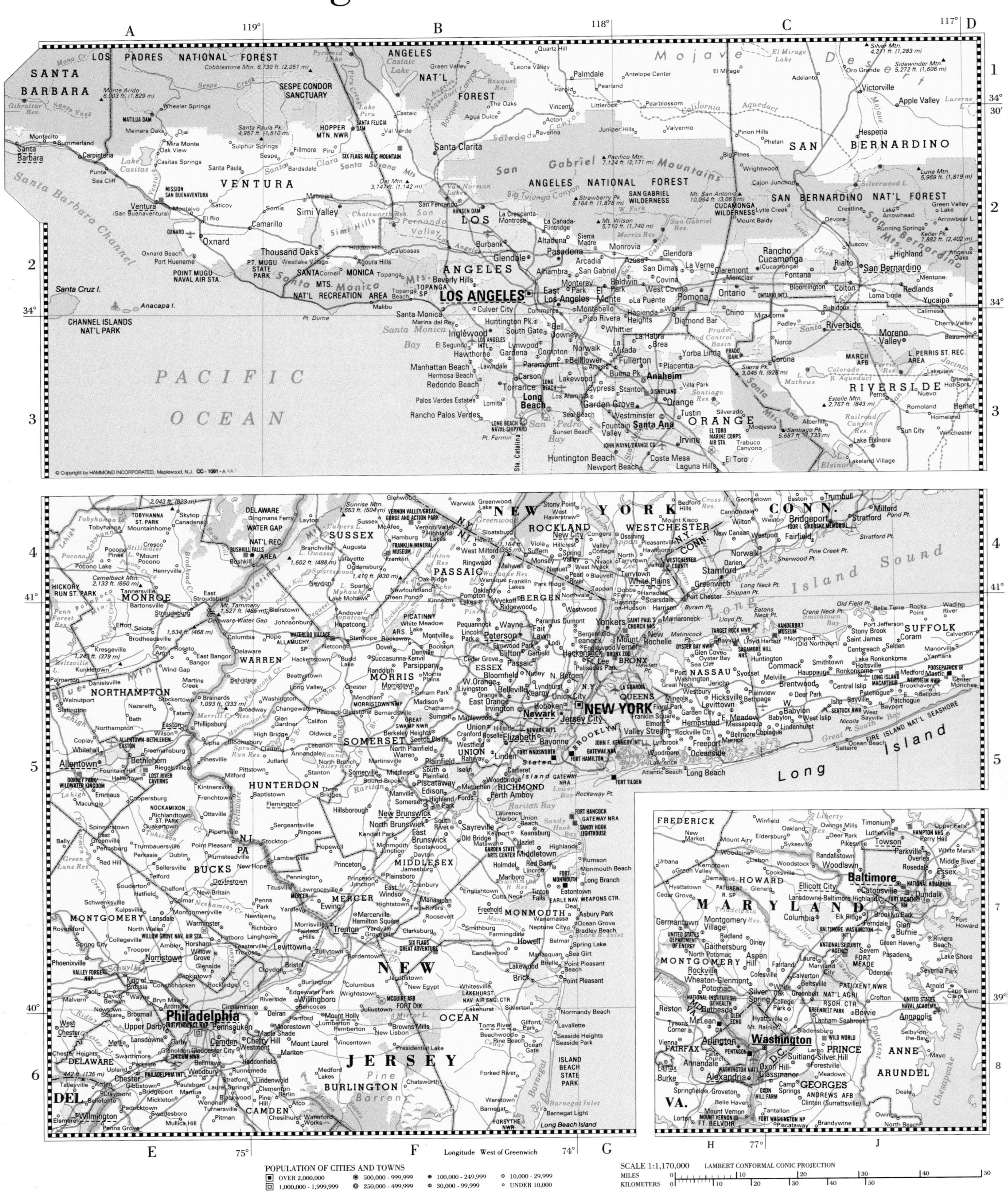

Seattle, San Francisco, Detroit, Chicago

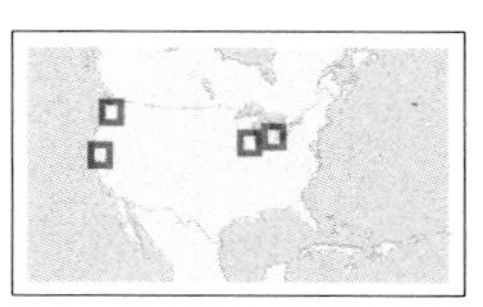

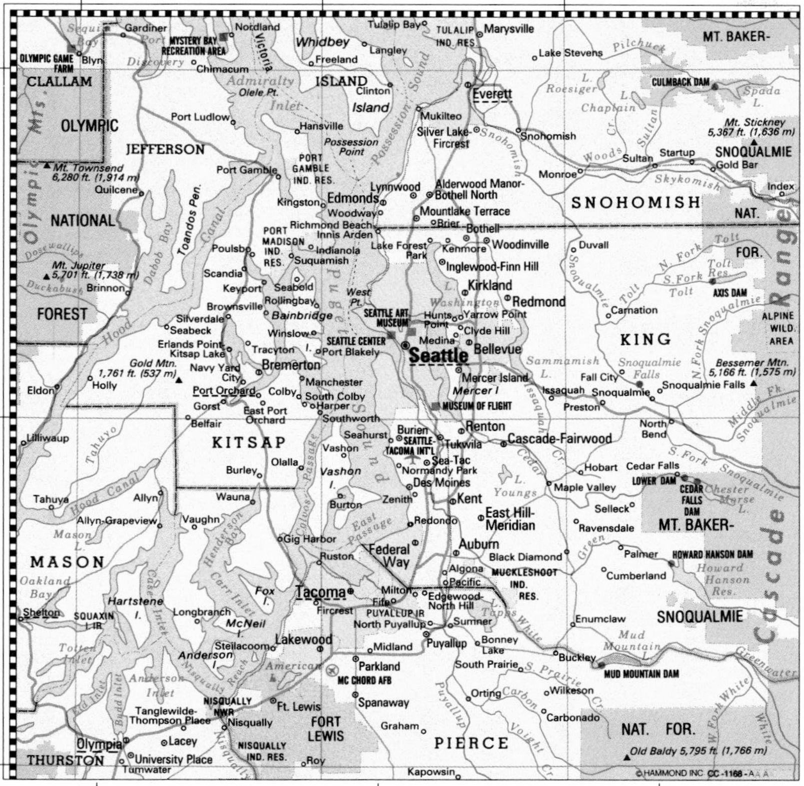

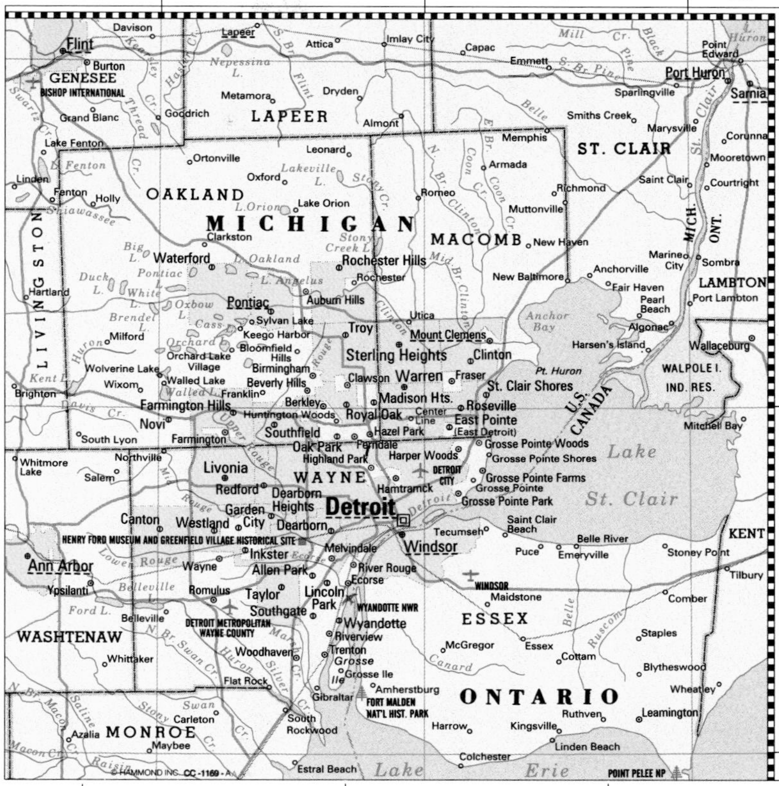

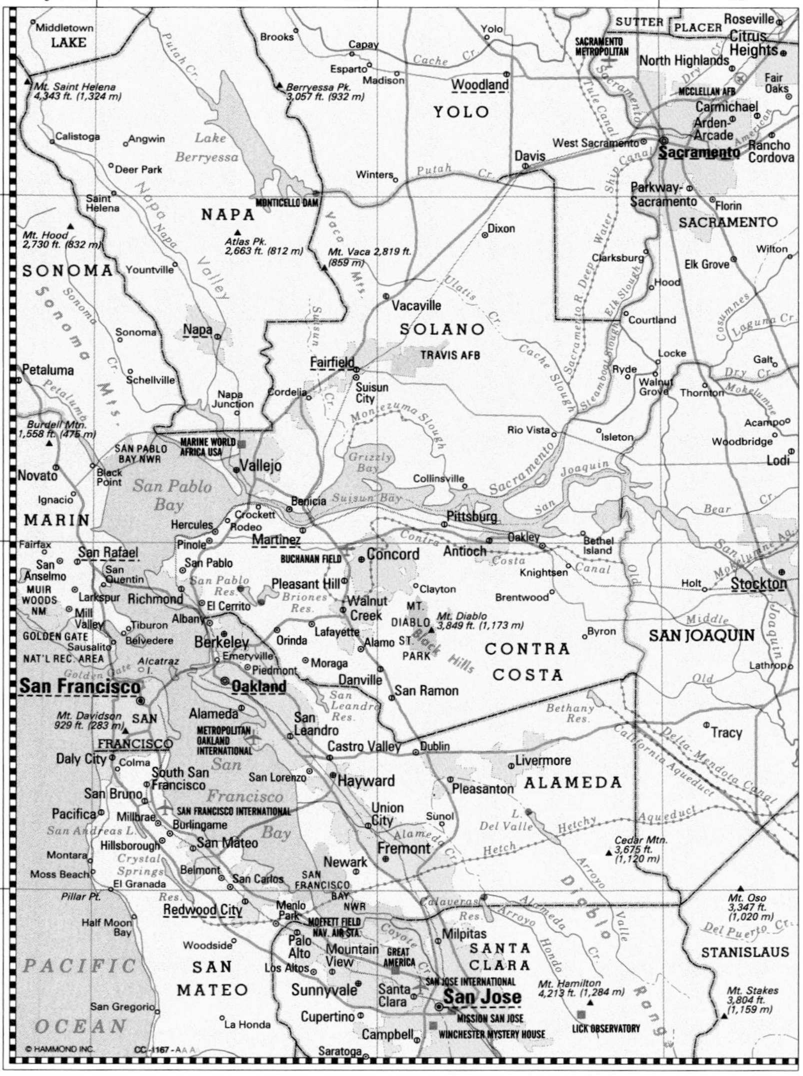

Longitude West of Greenwich

© HAMMOND INC. CC-1168

© HAMMOND INC. CC-1169

© HAMMOND INC. CC-1167

© HAMMOND INC. CC-1170

SCALE 1:1,170,000 LAMBERT CONFORMAL CONIC PROJECTION

MILES 0 10 20 30 40 50

KILOMETERS 0 10 20 30 40 50

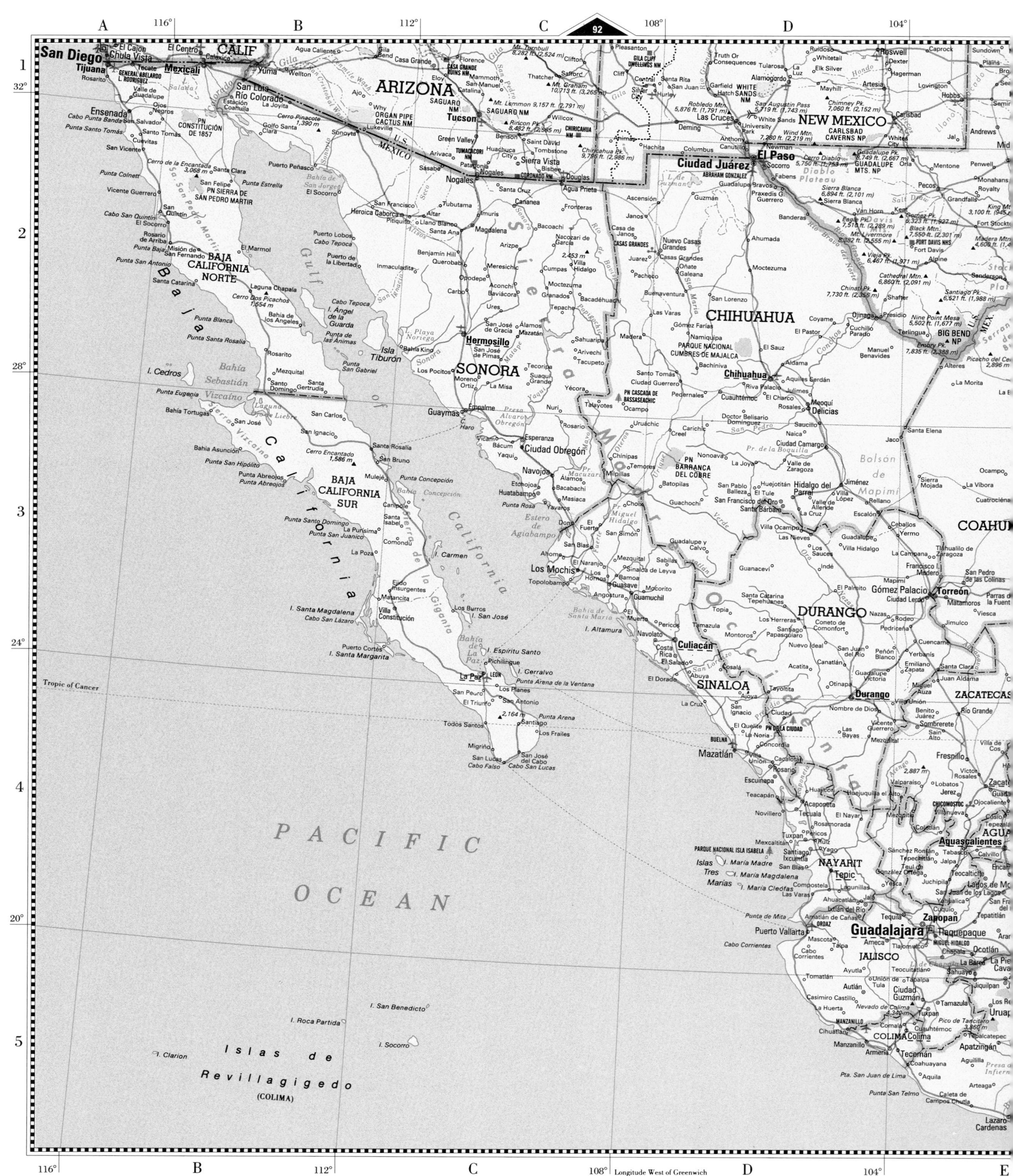

A
116°
B
112°
C
92
108°
D
104°
1
2
3
4
5
32°
28°
24°
20°
San Diego
El Cajon
Chula Vista
Tijuana
Rosarito
El Centro
CALIF
Calexico
Mexicali
Tecate
Yuma
Wellton
ARIZONA
Tucson
SAGUARO NM
ORGAN PIPE CACTUS NM
Nogales
Douglas
Agua Prieta
Casa Grande
Florence
Eloy
Safford
Sierra Vista
Bisbee
Tombstone
Green Valley
Ajo
Why
Lukeville
Sonoyta
Gila Bend
San Luis Río Colorado
Ensenada
Bahía de los Ángeles
Baja
California
BAJA CALIFORNIA NORTE
BAJA CALIFORNIA SUR
Gulf
of
California
I. Cedros
Bahía Sebastián Vizcaíno
Guerrero Negro
Isla Tiburón
Santa Rosalía
Mulegé
Loreto
Punta Concepción
I. Carmen
Villa Constitución
I. Santa Magdalena
I. Santa Margarita
Puerto Cortés
La Paz
I. Espíritu Santo
I. Cerralvo
Todos Santos
San José del Cabo
Cabo San Lucas
Cabo Falso
Tropic of Cancer
P A C I F I C
O C E A N
I. San Benedicto
I. Roca Partida
I. Socorro
I. Clarion
Islas de
Revillagigedo
(COLIMA)
SONORA
Hermosillo
Guaymas
Empalme
Ciudad Obregón
Navojoa
Huatabampo
Heroica Caborca
Puerto Peñasco
Magdalena
Cananea
Sierra Madre Occidental
Los Mochis
Topolobampo
El Fuerte
Guasave
Guamúchil
SINALOA
Culiacán
Mazatlán
Escuinapa
CHIHUAHUA
Chihuahua
Ciudad Juárez
El Paso
Nuevo Casas Grandes
Delicias
Meoquí
Ciudad Camargo
Hidalgo del Parral
Jiménez
Ojinaga
PN CASCADA DE BASSASEACHIC
PN BARRANCA DEL COBRE
Bolsón de Mapimí
DURANGO
Durango
Torreón
Gómez Palacio
Ciudad Lerdo
ZACATECAS
COAHUILA
NAYARIT
Tepic
Islas Tres Marías
I. María Madre
I. María Magdalena
I. María Cleofas
Puerto Vallarta
Cabo Corrientes
JALISCO
Guadalajara
Zapopan
Tlaquepaque
Aguascalientes
COLIMA
Colima
Manzanillo
Tecomán
Ciudad Guzmán
Apatzingán
Lázaro Cárdenas
NEW MEXICO
Las Cruces
Alamogordo
Deming
Silver City
Roswell
Carlsbad
Hobbs
WHITE SANDS NM
CARLSBAD CAVERNS NP
GUADALUPE MTS. NP
BIG BEND NP
Pecos
Fort Stockton
Alpine
Marfa
Presidio
Van Horn
116°
B
112°
C
108°
Longitude West of Greenwich
D
104°
E

Northern and Central Mexico

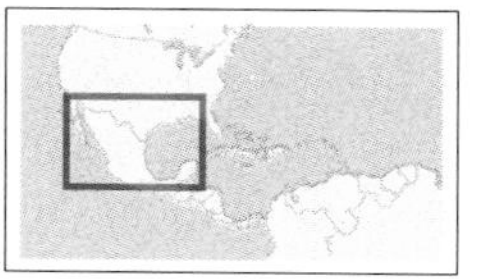

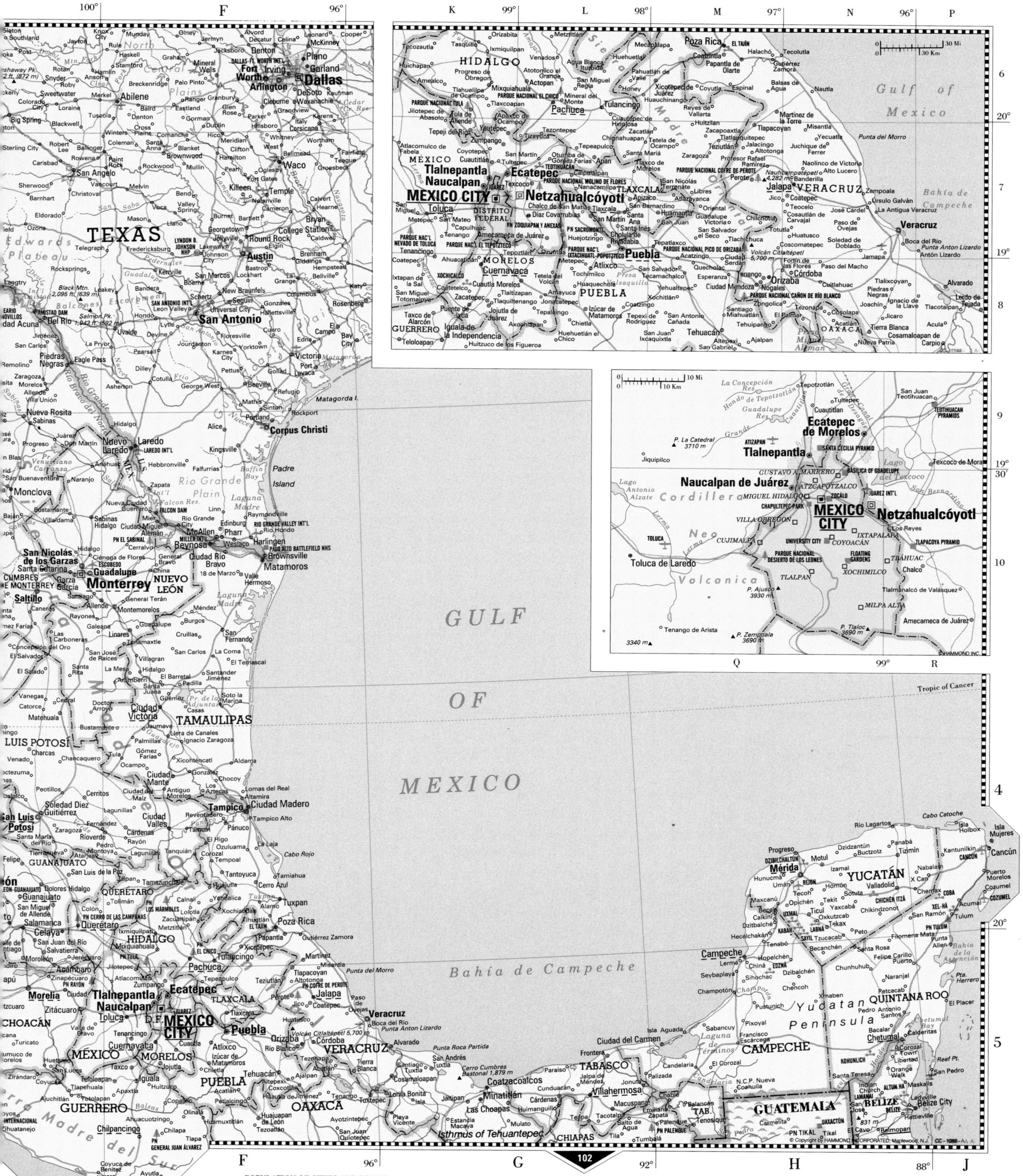

GULF OF MEXICO

Bahía de Campeche

POPULATION OF CITIES AND TOWNS

- OVER 2,000,000
- 1,000,000 - 1,999,999
- 500,000 - 999,999
- 250,000 - 499,999
- 100,000 - 249,999
- 30,000 - 99,999
- 10,000 - 29,999
- UNDER 10,000

SCALE 1:7,000,000 LAMBERT CONFORMAL CONIC PROJECTION

MILES 0 100 200 300

KILOMETERS 0 100 200 300

102

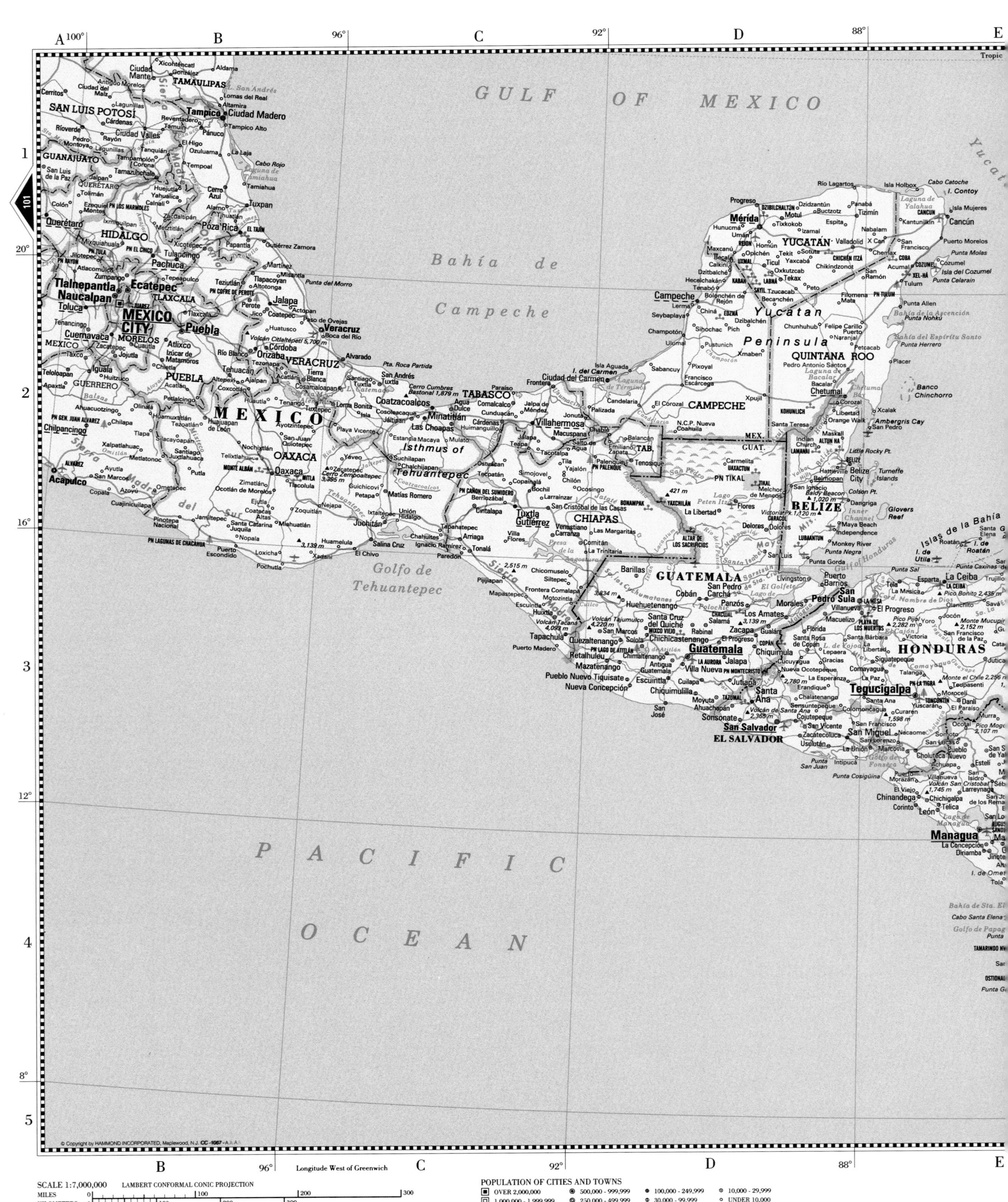

SCALE 1:7,000,000 LAMBERT CONFORMAL CONIC PROJECTION

MILES 0 100 200 300

KILOMETERS 0 100 200 300

POPULATION OF CITIES AND TOWNS

- OVER 2,000,000
- 1,000,000 - 1,999,999
- 500,000 - 999,999
- 250,000 - 499,999
- 100,000 - 249,999
- 30,000 - 99,999
- 10,000 - 29,999
- UNDER 10,000

Southern Mexico, Central America, Western Caribbean

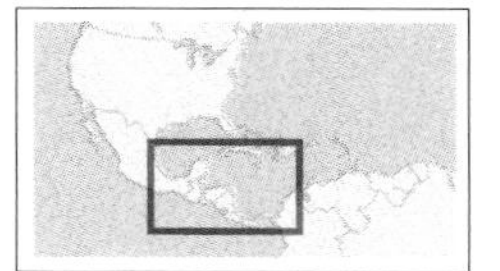

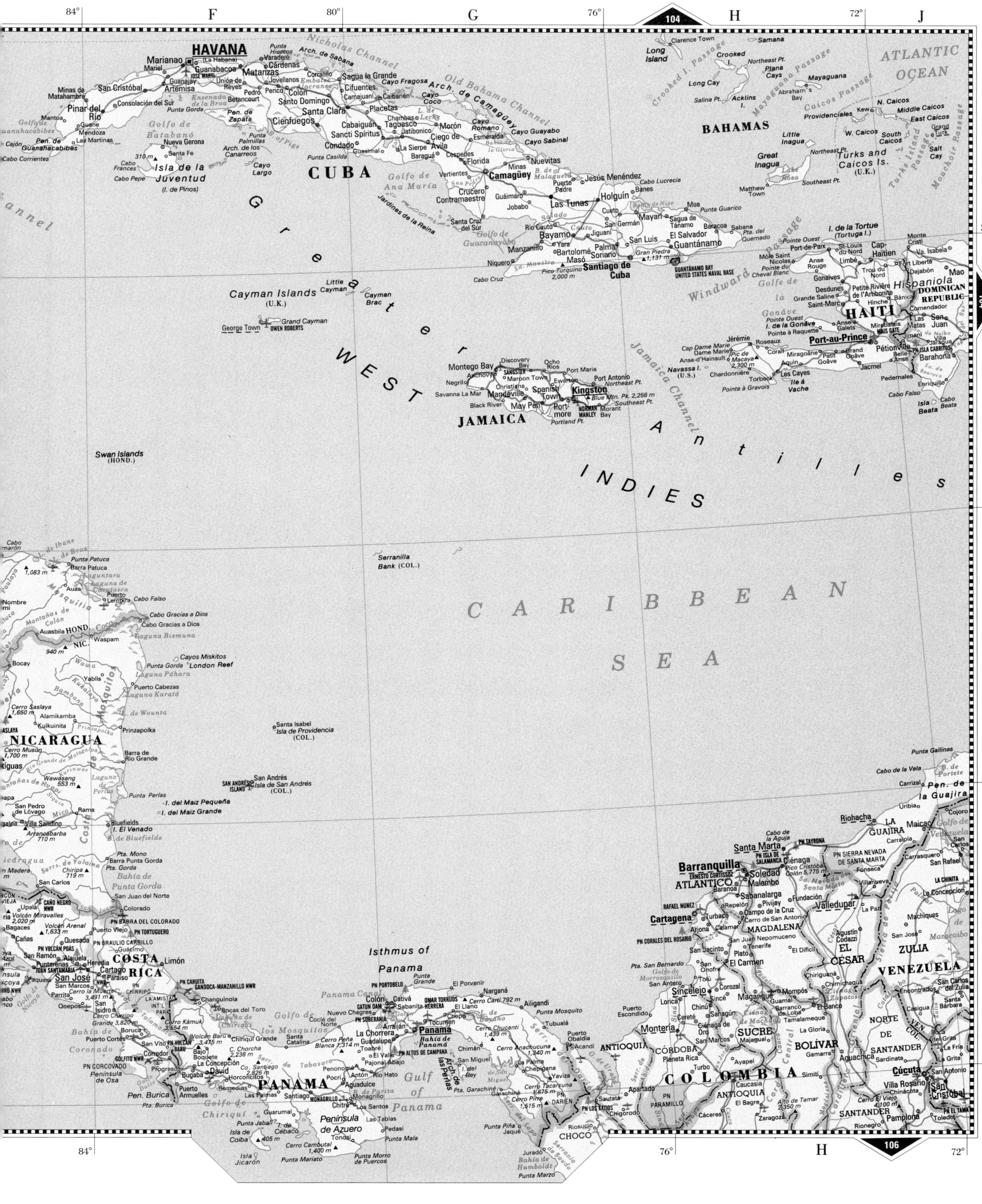

84° F 80° G 76° 104 H 72° J

ATLANTIC OCEAN
BAHAMAS
Long Island
Clarence Town
Samana
Crooked I.
Crooked I. Passage
Northeast Pt.
Plana Cays
Long Cay
Acklins I.
Salina Pt.
Mayaguana Passage
Mayaguana
Abraham's Bay
Caicos Passage
N. Caicos
Middle Caicos
East Caicos
Providenciales
Kew
W. Caicos
South Caicos
Grand Turk
Salt Cay
Turks Island Passage
Mouchoir Passage
Turks and Caicos Is. (U.K.)
Little Inagua
Great Inagua
Lake Rosa
Northeast Pt.
Southeast Pt.
Matthew Town

Nicholas Channel
Old Bahama Channel
HAVANA (La Habana)
JOSÉ MARTÍ
Marianao
Mariel
Guanabacoa
Guanajay
Matanzas
Punta Hicacos
Varadero
Cárdenas
Arch. de Sabana
Corralillo
Sagua la Grande
Cayo Fragosa
Arch. de Camagüey
Cifuentes
Camajuaní
Caibarién
Cayo Coco
Placetas
Unión de Reyes
Jovellanos
Embalse Alacranes
Pedro Betancourt
Perico
Colón
Santo Domingo
Santa Clara
Minas de Matahambre
San Cristóbal
Artemisa
Consolación del Sur
Ensenada de la Broa
Pinar del Río
Punta Gorda
Pen. de Zapata
Cienfuegos
Chambas
Taguasco
Jatibonico
Morón
Cayo Romano
Cayo Guayabo
Cayo Sabinal
Cabaiguán
Sancti Spíritus
Ciego de Ávila
Esmeralda
Bahía de la Gloria
Mantua
Guane
Mendoza
Las Martinas
Golfo de Guanahacabibes
Pen. de Guanahacabibes
Cajón
Cabo Corrientes
Golfo de Batabanó
Nueva Gerona
Santa Fe
Punta Palmillas
Arch. de los Canarreos
Bahía de Pigs
Condado
Guasimal
La Sierpe
Baraguá
Cespedes
Florida
Nuevitas
Minas
Punta Casilda
Cabo Frances
Cabo Pepe
Isla de la Juventud (I. de Pinos)
Cayo Largo
CUBA
Golfo de Ana María
Vertientes
Camagüey
B. de Malagueta
Jesús Menéndez
Cabo Lucrecia
Puerto Padre
Banes
Holguín
Crucero
Contramaestre
Guáimaro
Jobabo
Las Tunas
Jardines de la Reina
Santa Cruz del Sur
Golfo de Guacanayabo
Río Cauto
Cueto
Mayarí
San Germán
Bahía de Nipe
Moa
Punta Guarico
Sagua de Tánamo
Baracoa
Jiguaní
Bayamo
Yara
Manzanillo
Niquero
Bartolomé Masó
Palma Soriano
San Luis
El Salvador
Guantánamo
Sabana
Pta. del Quemado
Sa. Maestra
Pico Turquino 2,000 m
Santiago de Cuba
Gran Piedra 1,131 m
GUANTÁNAMO BAY UNITED STATES NAVAL BASE
Cabo Cruz

I. de la Tortue (Tortuga I.)
Pointe Ouest
Port-de-Paix
Monte Cristi
Môle Saint Nicolas
Pointe du Cheval Blanc
St.-Louis du Nord
Cap-Haïtien
Va. Isabela
Fort Liberté
Dajabón
Mao
Anse Rouge
Limbé
Trou du Nord
Gonaïves
Windward Passage
Golfe de la Gonâve
Desdunes
Petite Rivière de l'Artibonite
Hispaniola
DOMINICAN REPUBLIC
Grande Saline
Saint-Marc
Hinche
Bánica
HAITI
Comendador
I. de la Gonâve
Pointe Ouest
Pointe à Raquette
Anse-à-Galets
Mirebalais
MAÏS GATÉ
Las Matas
San Juan
Jérémie
Roseaux
Port-au-Prince
Jimaní
Pétionville
Villa Jaragua
PN ISLA CABRITOS
Cap Dame Marie
Dame Marie
Anse-d'Hainault
Pic de Macaya 2,300 m
Corail
Miragoâne
Petit Goâve
Grand Goâve
Belle-Anse
Barahona
Sa. de Baoruco
Navassa I. (U.S.)
Chardonnière
Aquin
Les Cayes
Jacmel
Pedernales
Enriquillo
Torbeck
Île à Vache
Pointe à Gravois
Cabo Falso
Isla Beata
Cabo Beata

Great Antilles
WEST INDIES
Jamaica Channel
Cayman Islands (U.K.)
Little Cayman
Cayman Brac
Grand Cayman
George Town
OWEN ROBERTS
Montego Bay
SANGSTER
Discovery Bay
Ocho Rios
Port Maria
Anchovy
Maroon Town
Negril
Christiana
Ewarton
Port Antonio
Northeast Pt.
Savanna La Mar
Mandeville
Spanish Town
Kingston
Blue Mtn. Pk. 2,256 m
Black River
May Pen
Portmore
NORMAN MANLEY
Morant Bay
Southeast Pt.
Portland Pt.
JAMAICA
Swan Islands (HOND.)
Serranilla Bank (COL.)
CARIBBEAN SEA

Cabo Camarón
Punta Patuca
Barra Patuca
Laguna de Caratasca
Puerto Lempira
Cabo Falso
Auas
Montañas de Colón
Cabo Gracias a Dios
Auasbila
HOND.
NIC.
Waspam
Laguna Bismuna
940 m
Cayos Miskitos
Bocay
Punta Gorda
London Reef
Laguna Páhara
Yablis
Puerto Cabezas
Laguna Karatá
Cerro Saslaya 1,650 m
Alamikamba
Kukuinita
R. de Wounta
Prinzapolka
Santa Isabel
Isla de Providencia (COL.)
NICARAGUA
Cerro Musún 1,700 m
Barra de Río Grande
Laguna de Perlas
Wawasang 553 m
San Andrés
SAN ANDRÉS ISLAND
Isla de San Andrés (COL.)
Punta Perlas
I. del Maíz Pequeña
I. del Maíz Grande
San Pedro de Lóvago
Rama
Villa Sandino
Bluefields
I. El Venado
B. de Bluefields
Arrancabarba 710 m
Pta. Mono
Barra Punta Gorda
Pta. Gorda
Chiripa 719 m
Bahía de Punta Gorda
San Carlos
San Juan del Norte
CAÑO NEGRO NWR
Upala
Volcán Miravalles 2,020 m
Bagaces
Volcán Arenal 1,633 m
Colorado
PN BARRA DEL COLORADO
Puerto Viejo
PN TORTUGUERO
Cañas
Quesada
PN BRAULIO CARRILLO
PN VOLCÁN POÁS
Guácimo
San Ramón
Alajuela
Heredia
COSTA RICA
Limón
Puntarenas
JUAN SANTAMARÍA
Cartago
Paraíso
San José
PN CAHUITA
GANDOCA-MANZANILLO NWR
San Marcos
Parrita
Cerro la Muerte 3,491 m
PN CHIRRIPÓ
Changuinola
Quepos
San Isidro
LA AMISTAD INT'L PARK
Bocas del Toro
Cerro Chirripó Grande 3,820 m
Laguna de Chiriquí
Cerro Kámuk 3,554 m
Boruca
Golfo de los Mosquitos
Bahía de Coronado
Puerto Cortés
San Vito
Volcán Barú 3,475 m
Chiriquí Grande
PN CORCOVADO
GOLFITO NWR
Corredor
BARÚ
Bajo Boquete
C. Chorcha 2,238 m
La Concepción
Península de Osa
Golfo Dulce
Progreso
Bugaba
David
Horconcitos
Co. Santiago 2,826 m
Remedios
Pen. Burica
Puerto Armuelles
Pta. Burica
Golfo de Chiriquí
Las Palmas
Santiago
Isla de Coiba
Cébaco
Isla Jicarón
Punta Mariato
PANAMA
Isthmus of Panama
PN PORTOBELO
Punta Grande
El Porvenir
Panama Canal
Colón
Cativá
GATUN DAM
OMAR TORRIJOS
Cerro Cartí 792 m
Narganá
Ailigandí
PN SOBERANÍA
Sabanita
HERRERA
Chepo
El Llano
Punta Mosquito
Nuevo Chagres
Coclé del Norte
Tocumen
L. de Bayano
Tubualá
Arraiján
Panamá
La Chorrera
Cerro Chucanti 1,439 m
Santa Catalina
Cerro Peña Blanca 1,314 m
Bahía de Panamá
Toabré
PN ALTOS DE CAMPANA
Chimán
Cerro Anachucuna 1,340 m
Puerto Obaldía
Acandí
El Valle
Pajonal Abajo
Penonomé
Antón
Río Hato
Arch. de las Perlas
San Miguel
I. del Rey
La Palma
Chepigana
Golfo de San Miguel
Pocrí
Aguadulce
Gulf of Panama
Yaviza
Cerro Tacarcuna 1,875 m
Sautatá
Garachiné
Pta. Garachiné
Cerro Pirre 1,615 m
DARIÉN
Chigorodó
Chitré
MONAGRILLO
Monagrillo
Los Santos
Las Tablas
Península de Azuero
Pedasí
Tonosí
Punta Mala
Cerro Cambutal 1,400 m
Punta Morro de Puercos
Punta Piña
Jaqué
CHOCÓ
Riosucio
Jurado
Bahía de Humboldt
Punta Marzo
Serranía de Baudó
Serranía del Darién
Serranía del Sapo

Punta Gallinas
B. de Portete
Cabo de la Vela
Carrizal
Pen. de la Guajira
Uribia
Cojoro
Riohacha
LA GUAJIRA
Maicao
Golfo de Venezuela
Carraipía
San Carlos
Cabo de la Aguja
Santa Marta
PN TAYRONA
PN SIERRA NEVADA DE SANTA MARTA
Carrasquero
San Rafael
Barranquilla
ERNESTO CORTISSOZ
PN ISLA DE SALAMANCA
Ciénaga
Pico Cristóbal Colón 5,775 m
Fonseca
LA CHINITA
La Concepción
Soledad
Malambo
Villanueva
ATLÁNTICO
Baranoa
Sa. Nevada de Santa Marta
Sabanalarga
Fundación
Valledupar
La Paz
RAFAEL NUÑEZ
Repelón
Pivijay
Machiques
Cartagena
Turbaco
Campo de la Cruz
Cerro de San Antonio
Calamar
MAGDALENA
Arjona
PN CORALES DEL ROSARIO
San Juan Nepomuceno
Tenerife
Agustín Codazzi
San José
ZULIA
El Difícil
San Jacinto
Plato
El Carmen
EL CÉSAR
VENEZUELA
Pta. San Bernardo
Golfo de Morrosquillo
San Onofre
Tolú
Chiriguaná
Chimichagua
San Carlos del Zulia
San Antero
Sincelejo
Corozal
Mompós
Encontrados
Santa Bárbara
Puerto Escondido
Lorica
Chinú
Magangué
Guamal
Barranco de Loba
El Banco
Casigua
Sahagún
Ciénaga de Oro
Tamalameque
Montería
SUCRE
La Gloria
NORTE DE SANTANDER
San Marcos
Majagual
ANTIOQUIA
CÓRDOBA
BOLÍVAR
Planeta Rica
Gamarra
Aguachica
Sardinata
La Fría
La Grita
Ayapel
Turbo
Simití
COLOMBIA
Cúcuta
San Antonio
Apartadó
Caucasia
Villa Rosario
Chinácota
San Cristóbal
PN PARAMILLO
ANTIOQUIA
El Bagre
Alto de Tamar 2,350 m
Cerro El Viejo 4,100 m
PN LOS KATÍOS
Cáceres
Zaragoza
SANTANDER
Pamplona
Toledo
PN EL TAMÁ
Rionegro

1 2 3 4 5
20° 16° 12° 8°

84° 76° H 106 72°

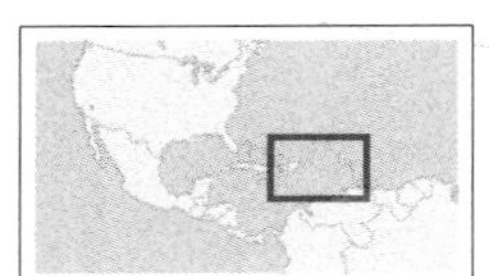

Eastern Caribbean, Bahamas

84° A 97 80° B 76° Longitude West of Greenwich C 72° D

1 GULF OF MEXICO
Lake Okeechobee
Punta Gorda
Moore Haven
West Palm Beach
Cape Coral
Fort Myers
La Belle
FLORIDA
Fort Lauderdale
Naples
C. Romano
The Everglades
Miami
EVERGLADES NAT'L PARK
Highland Pt.
Shark Pt.
Biscayne Bay
Cape Sable
Florida Bay
Key Largo
Dry Tortugas
Key West
Florida Keys
Straits of Florida
U.S. BAHM.
Bimini Is.
Grand Bahama
Great Sale Cay
Settlement Pt.
West End
Freeport
Moore's I.
Hope Town
Marsh Harbour
Great Abaco
Southwest Pt.
N.W. Providence Channel
N.E. Providence Channel
Berry Is.
Spanish Wells
Current
Nicholls Town
Governor's Harbour
Nassau
Eleuthera
New Providence I.
Powell Pt.
Rock Sound
Great Bahama Bank
Andros Town
Tongue of the Ocean
Exuma Sound
Cat I.
The Bight
Hawks Nest Pt.
Andros I.
ATLANTIC OCEAN 1
Cockburn Town
San Salvador (Watling I.)
24°
Southwest Pt.
Great Guana Cay
Rum Cay
Great Exuma
George Town
Tropic of Cancer
Tropic of Cancer
Long I.
Clarence Town

2 Kew North Caicos
Middle Caicos
Turks and Caicos Is. (U.K.)
Caicos Is.
East Caicos
Grand Turk
Turks Is.
Ambergris Cay
Turks Island Passage
ATLANTIC OCEAN
BAHAMAS
Crooked Island Passage
Samana (Atwood Cay)
Crooked I.
Northeast Pt.
Plana Cays
Long Cay (Fortune I.)
Mayaguana Passage
Mayaguana
Abraham's Bay
Salina Pt.
Acklins I.
Caicos Passage 2
North Caicos
Kew
Middle Caicos
Providenciales
East Caicos
Caicos Is.
Cockburn Harbour
Grand Turk
Turks Is.
Little Inagua
BAHM. TURKS
Northeast Pt.
Ambergris Cay
Turks Island Passage
Great Inagua
L. Rosa
Southeast Pt.
Matthew Town
Turks and Caicos Is. (U.K.)

20° Hispaniola
Monte Cristi
Villa Isabela
Cap-Haïtien
Puerto Plata
Fort Liberté
Sosúa
Limbé
Dajabón
DOMINICAN REPUBLIC
Grande Rivière du Nord
Esperanza
Sabaneta
Moca
Santiago
Salcedo
Nagua
PARQUE NACIONAL
C. Samaná
HAITI
PARQUE NACIONAL Po. Duarte 3,175 m
La Vega
San Francisco de Macorís
Samaná
Hinche
Bánica
Juan de Herrera
Jarabacoa
Cotuí
PN LOS HAITISES
Miches
Mirebalais
Comendador
Constanza
Bonao
Monte Plata
Hato Mayor
El Seibo
San Juan
Pétionville
San Cristóbal
Villa Altagracia
San Pedro de Macorís
Higüey
Port-au-Prince
Neiba
Azua
La Romana
PN ISLA CABRITOS
Cabral
Bahía de Ocoa
Baní
Bajos de Haina
Santo Domingo
Barahona
PN DEL ESTE
Pedernales
I. Saona
Enriquillo
C. Beata
I. Beata
Greater Antilles

Mona Passage
I. Mona
PUERTO RICO (U.S.)
San Juan
Isabela
Aguadilla
Arecibo
Carolina
Mayagüez
Utuado
Bayamón
Fajardo
Hormigueros
Caguas
El Yunque 1,065 m
Yauco
Yabucoa
C. Rojo
Ponce
Guayama
U.S. NAV. RES.
Charlotte Amalie
St. Thomas (U.S.)
Virgin Islands
Anegada (U.K.)
Tortola I. (U.K.)
Virgin Gorda (U.K.)
Road Town
St. John (U.S.)
V.I. NP
I. de Vieques (P.R.)
Frederiksted
Christiansted
St. Croix (U.S.)
Anegada Passage

3 The Valley
Anguilla (U.K.)
Marigot
St-Martin (FR.)
Gustavia
St. Maarten (N.A.)
St. Barthélemy (FR.)
Saba (N.A.)
Barbuda
Codrington
Oranjestad
St. Eustatius (N.A.)
ANTIGUA AND BARBUDA
St. Kitts
Basseterre
BRIMSTONE HILL NP
Saint John's
Charlestown
Nevis
Falmouth
Nevis Pk. 1,096 m
Boggy Pk. 402 m
Antigua
ST. KITTS AND NEVIS
Montserrat (U.K.)
Plymouth
Leeward Islands 3
Lesser Antilles
Guadeloupe Passage
Grande-Terre
Port-Louis
Basse-Terre
GUADELOUPE NP
Guadeloupe (FRANCE)
Soufrière 1,484 m
Pointe-à-Pitre
Morne Constant 205 m
16°
Basse-Terre
Marie-Galante
Aves I. (VEN.)
Dominica Passage
Portsmouth
Marigot
DOMINICA
Morne Diablotin 1,447 m
Roseau
Martinique Passage
Mt. Pelée 1,397 m
Saint-Pierre
Sainte-Marie
FORT DESAIX
Fort-de-France
Martinique (FRANCE)
CARIBBEAN SEA
St. Lucia Channel
Castries
Gros Islet
ST. LUCIA 4
4 Mt. Gimie 958 m
Micoud
Vieux Fort
St. Vincent Passage
Soufrière 1,234 m
St. Vincent
BARBADOS
Barrouallie
Georgetown
Mt. Hillaby 336 m
Bathsheba
Kingstown
Bridgetown
ST. VINCENT AND THE GRENADINES
Bequia
Port Elizabeth
Canouan
Windward Islands

Aruba (NETH.)
Oranjestad
Jamanota 188 m
Lesser Antilles
Pta. Gallinas
PN MACUIRA
Sint Nicolaas
St. Christoffel Pk. 372 m
Malmok 240 m
C. San Román
Ascension
Curaçao
Bonaire
El Vínculo
Willemstad
Kralendijk
COLOMBIA 12°
Puerto López
NETH. ANTILLES
Castilletes
Los Taques
Buena Vista
Is. Las Aves
Is. Los Roques
El Roque
I. La Orchila
I. Blanquilla
Carriacou
Sauteurs
Gouyave
Saint George's
Mt. St. Catherine 840 m
GRENADA 12°
Jadacaquiva
Santa Ana
PN MÉDANOS DE CORO
Cojoro
Golfo de Venezuela
Punta Cardón
Puerto Cumarebo
Paraguaipoa
Mitare
Coro
FALCON
Zazárida
Mirimire
San Juan de los Cayos
DEPENDENCIAS FEDERALES
Is. Los Testigos
Dragon's Mouth
Charlotteville
Tobago
576 m
Roxborough
Scarborough

5 San Rafael
ZULIA
Pedregal
San Luis
Cabure
San José de Seque
PN CUEVA DE LA QUEBRADA DEL TORO
Jacura
Agua Larga
Chichiriviche
Isla de Margarita
Juangriego
La Asunción
NUEVA ESPARTA
PN LAGUNA DE LA RESTINGA
Porlamar
PN CERRO EL COPEY
I. La Tortuga
I. Cubagua
I. Coche
Piedra Grande
PN MORROCOY
Tucacas
Maracaibo
Churuguara
Santa Cruz de Bucaral
Boca de Aroa
CAR.
Puerto Cabello
VENEZUELA
Maiquetía
D.F.
Caracas
Petare
Los Teques
C. Codera
Baragua
San Francisco
Pico El Cerrón 1,990 m
Siquisique
YARACUY
Cabimas
LARA
San Felipe
Morón
PN HENRI PITTIER
La Concepción
Lago de Maracaibo
Ciudad Ojeda
San Francisco
Barquisimeto
Valencia
Guacara
Turmero
La Victoria
Maracay
MIRANDA
Sabana de Uchire
Carora
Chivacoa
Tocuyito
Güigüe
ARAGUA
PN GUACHARO
Quíbor
Cabudare
Puerto La Cruz
Barcelona
Pozuelos
Puerto Píritu
ANZOÁTEGUI
Cumaná
PN MOCHIMA
SUCRE
El Pilar
Cariaco
Casanay
San Antonio del Golfo
PN EL GUACHARO
Caripito
San Antonio
MONAGAS
Quiriquire
PN PEN. DE PARIA
Irapa
Güiria
Golfo de Paria
Pedernales
Port-of-Spain
El Cerro del Aripo 940 m
Galera Pt.
TRINIDAD AND TOBAGO 5
Arima
Sangre Grande
Guaico
Chaguanas
Tabaquite
San Fernando
Rio Claro
Point Fortin
Siparia
Trinidad
Fullarton
106 103

72° D 68° Longitude West of Greenwich E 64° F 106 60° G

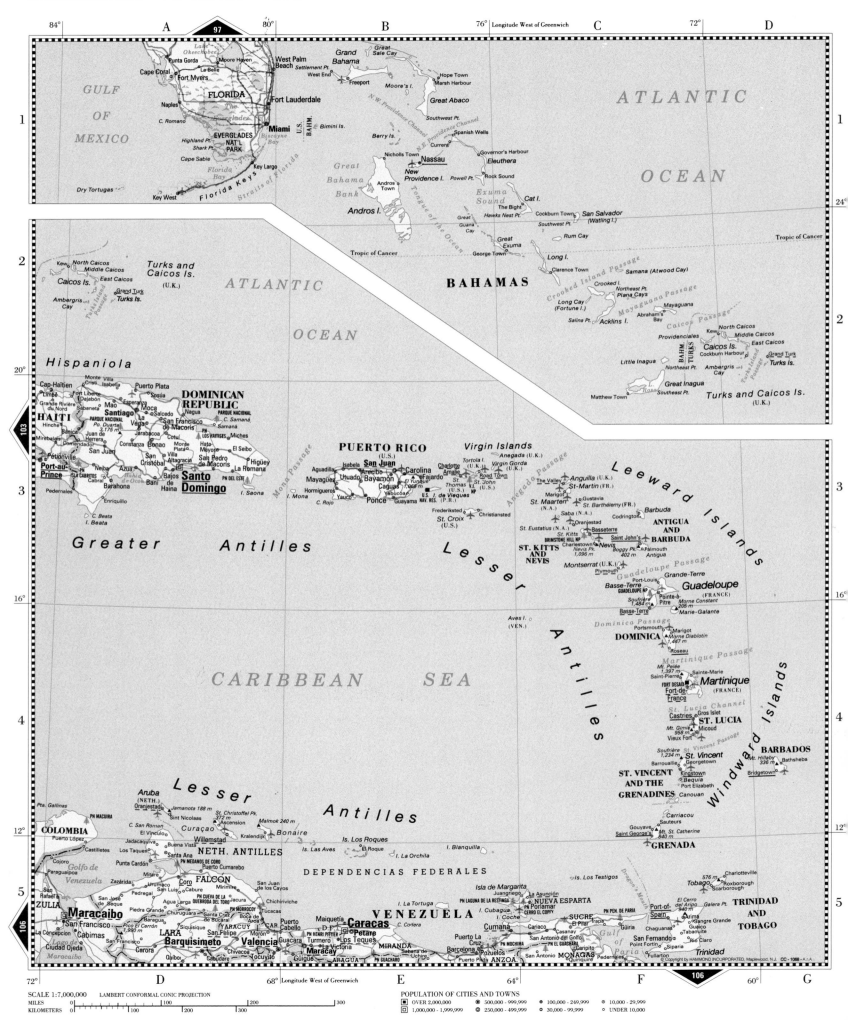

SCALE 1:7,000,000 LAMBERT CONFORMAL CONIC PROJECTION

MILES 0 100 200 300

KILOMETERS 0 100 200 300

POPULATION OF CITIES AND TOWNS

- OVER 2,000,000
- 1,000,000 - 1,999,999
- 500,000 - 999,999
- 250,000 - 499,999
- 100,000 - 249,999
- 30,000 - 99,999
- 10,000 - 29,999
- UNDER 10,000

South America

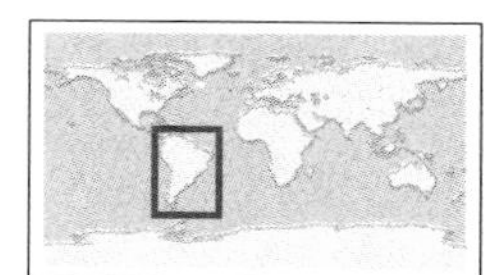

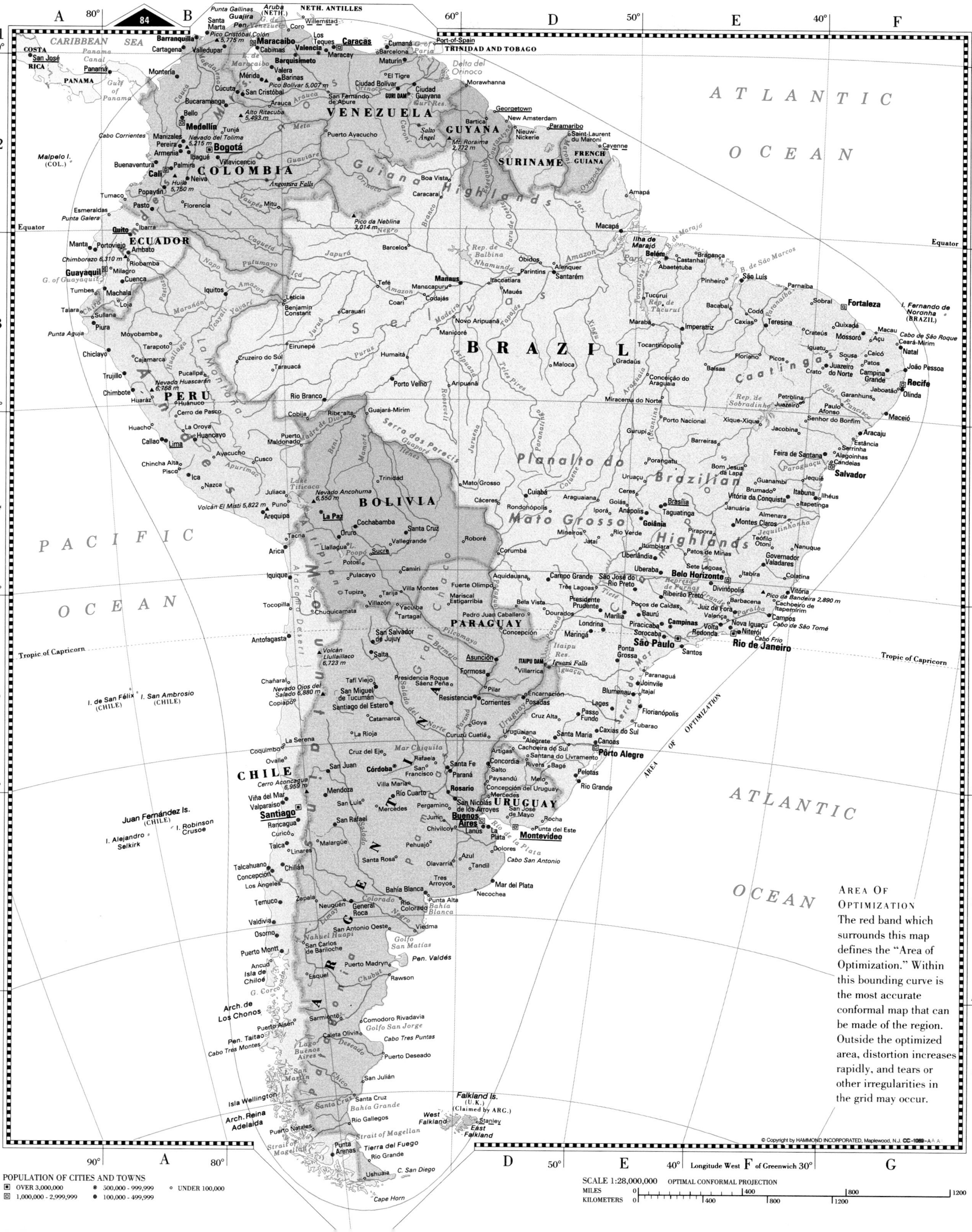

Area Of Optimization

The red band which surrounds this map defines the "Area of Optimization." Within this bounding curve is the most accurate conformal map that can be made of the region. Outside the optimized area, distortion increases rapidly, and tears or other irregularities in the grid may occur.

POPULATION OF CITIES AND TOWNS

- OVER 3,000,000
- 1,000,000 - 2,999,999
- 500,000 - 999,999
- 100,000 - 499,999
- UNDER 100,000

SCALE 1:28,000,000 OPTIMAL CONFORMAL PROJECTION

MILES 0 400 800 1200

KILOMETERS 0 400 800 1200

Longitude West of Greenwich

A
85°
103
B
80°
C
1
10°
2
5°
3
0°
4
5°
5
10°
6
15°
7
20°
8
A
85°
B
80°
Longitude
C
West of
75°
Greenwich
D
70°
E
65°
109
F
60°
CARIBBEAN SEA
NETH. ANTILLES
Aruba (NETH.)
Oranjestad
Willemstad
Curaçao
Kralendijk
Bonaire
El Roque
Islas Los Roques
I. Blanquilla
I. La Tortuga
SAINT VINCENT AND THE GRENADINES
Kingstown
Carriacou
Saint George's
GRENADA
Tobago
TRINIDAD AND TOBAGO
Port-of-Spain
Trinidad
Punta Gallinas
Pen. de la Guajira
Riohacha
Gulf of Venezuela
Pen. de Paraguaná
Coro
Barranquilla
Santa Marta
Ciénaga
Cartagena
Soledad
Pico Cristóbal Colón 5,775 m
PN SIERRA NEVADA DE STA. MARTA
Valledupar
Maracaibo
Cabimas
Ciudad Ojeda
Lake Maracaibo
Barquisimeto
Valencia
Caracas
Petare
Los Teques
Maracay
Puerto Cabello
San Felipe
Cumaná
Barcelona
Puerto La Cruz
Carúpano
I. de Margarita
Porlamar
Pen. de Paria
Güiria
Maturín
Delta del Orinoco
Ciudad Bolívar
Ciudad Guayana
San Fernando de Apure
Calabozo
Valera
Mérida
Pico Bolívar 5,007 m
Barinas
San Cristóbal
Cúcuta
Bucaramanga
PARQUE NACIONAL EL TAMA
VENEZUELA
Llanos
Puerto Carreño
Puerto Ayacucho
Cerro Yoví 2,441 m
Cerro Guaiquinima 2,100 m
Guiana Highlands
Salto Angel
PN CANAIMA
La Gran Sabana
Mt. Roraima 2,772 m
GUYANA
Georgetown
Kamaria Falls
Sierra Pacaraima
Boa Vista
Kanuku Mts.
Isla del Coco (COSTA RICA)
NICARAGUA
Liberia
Pen. de Nicoya
San José
COSTA RICA
Limón
Cartago
Isthmus of Panama
Colón
Panamá
PANAMA
Cerro Santiago 2,826 m
David
Santiago
Chitré
Pen. de Azuero
Punta Mariato
I. de Coiba
Punta Burica
G. de Chiriquí
G. of Panama
I. del Rey
PN DARIÉN
Punta Solano
Cabo Corrientes
Punta Charambirá
I. de Malpelo (COLOMBIA)
Buenaventura
Cali
Palmira
Tuluá
Armenia
Pereira
Manizales
Ibagué
Medellín
Bello
Itagüí
Montería
Sincelejo
Barrancabermeja
Bogotá
PARQUE NACIONAL CHINGAZA
Villavicencio
PARQUE NACIONAL SUMAPAZ
Tunja
Sogamoso
Cord. Occidental
Cord. Central
Cord. Oriental
COLOMBIA
Nevado del Huila 5,750 m
Neiva
Popayán
Volcán Puracé 4,646 m
PN PURACÉ
Pasto
Florencia
PN SIERRA DE LA MACARENA
PN CUEVA DE LOS GUACHAROS
San José del Guaviare
Mitú
Tumaco
Esmeraldas
Cabo Manglares
Santo Domingo de los Colorados
Quito
ECUADOR
Cayambe 5,790 m
PN YASUNÍ
Manta
Portoviejo
Chimborazo 6,310 m
Riobamba
Ambato
Latacunga
PARQUE NACIONAL MACHALILLA
Guayaquil
Milagro
PN SANGAY
Gulf of Guayaquil
Machala
Cuenca
Loja
Zamora
Cordillera Oriental
Cabo Blanco
Talara
Sullana
Piura
Bahía de Sechura
Desierto de Sechura
Chiclayo
Lambayeque
Cajamarca
Chachapoyas
Trujillo
CHAN CHAN
Chimbote
Nevado Huascarán 6,768 m
PN HUASCARÁN
Huaraz
Cordillera Blanca
Cordillera Central
PN RÍO ABISEO
Iquitos
Pucallpa
PERU
Huánuco
Cerro de Pasco
Cerro Yerupaja 6,634 m
Huancayo
Lima
Callao
PACHACAMAC
Ayacucho
Pisco
Ica
NAZCA LINES
Nazca
Cusco
MACHU PICCHU
Nevado Ausangate 6,384 m
PN MANÚ
Puerto Maldonado
La Montaña
Andes
Cordillera Occidental
Lake Titicaca
Puno
Juliaca
Arequipa
Volcán El Misti 5,822 m
Nevado Coropuna 6,425 m
Mollendo
Moquegua
Tacna
Arica
Volcán Tacora 5,980 m
PN LAUCA
Nevado Parinacota 6,342 m
Altiplano
Iquique
CHILE
Atacama Desert
Tocopilla
Punta Angamos
Volcán Ollagüe 5,869 m
Volcán San Pedro 6,159 m
Calama
Chuquicamata
Cerro Zapaleri 5,648 m
La Paz
Nevado Illimani 6,462 m
Nevado Ancohuma 6,550 m
TIAHUANCO
Cochabamba
Oruro
Sucre
Potosí
Cerro Huanchaca 5,950 m
BOLIVIA
Santa Cruz
Trinidad
PN ISIBORO SECURE
Riberalta
Cobija
Tarija
Villazón
ARGENTINA
Yacuiba
Gran Chaco
Chaco Boreal
PARAGUAY
Filadelfia
PN TENIENTE ENCISO
Tropic of Capricorn
PN DEFENSORES DEL CHACO
PACIFIC OCEAN
Equator
Amazon (Solimões)
Selvas
Manaus
Tefé
Coari
Tabatinga
Leticia
Benjamin Constant
PN AMACAYACU
Jutaí
Carauari
Eirunepé
Cruzeiro do Sul
Tarauacá
Rio Branco
Porto Velho
Guajará-Mirim
Humaitá
Lábrea
Manicoré
Novo Aripuanã
PN DO PICO DA NEBLINA
Pico da Neblina 3,014 m
PN SERRANÍA DE LA NEBLINA
Barcelos
PN DO RIO JAÚ
Represa da Balbina
Serra dos Pacaás Novos
Serra dos Parecis
Vilhena
Ariquemes
Ji-Paraná
B R

Northern South America

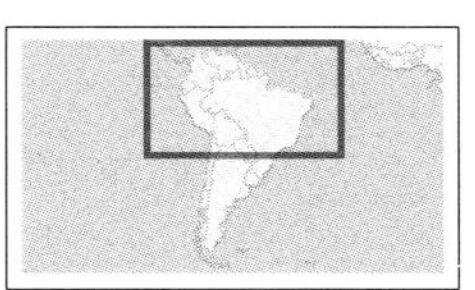

55° H 50° J 45° K 40° L 35° M 30° N

ATLANTIC OCEAN

SURINAME

FRENCH GUIANA

BRAZIL

Planalto do Mato Grosso

Planalto Central

Caatingas

Equator

St. Peter and St. Paul Rocks (BRAZIL)

Rocas

Fernando de Noronha (BRAZIL)

Trinidade (BRAZIL)

Martin Vaz (BRAZIL)

ATLANTIC OCEAN

Belém · São Luís · Fortaleza · Natal · João Pessoa · Recife · Maceió · Aracaju · Salvador · Vitória · Rio de Janeiro · São Paulo · Belo Horizonte · Brasília · Goiânia · Campo Grande · Cuiabá · Teresina · Macapá · Santarém

POPULATION OF CITIES AND TOWNS

- OVER 2,000,000
- 1,000,000 - 1,999,999
- 500,000 - 999,999
- 100,000 - 499,999
- 50,000 - 99,999
- UNDER 50,000

SCALE 1:15,000,000 LAMBERT CONFORMAL CONIC PROJECTION

MILES 0 100 200 400 600

KILOMETERS 0 200 400 600

Southeastern Brazil

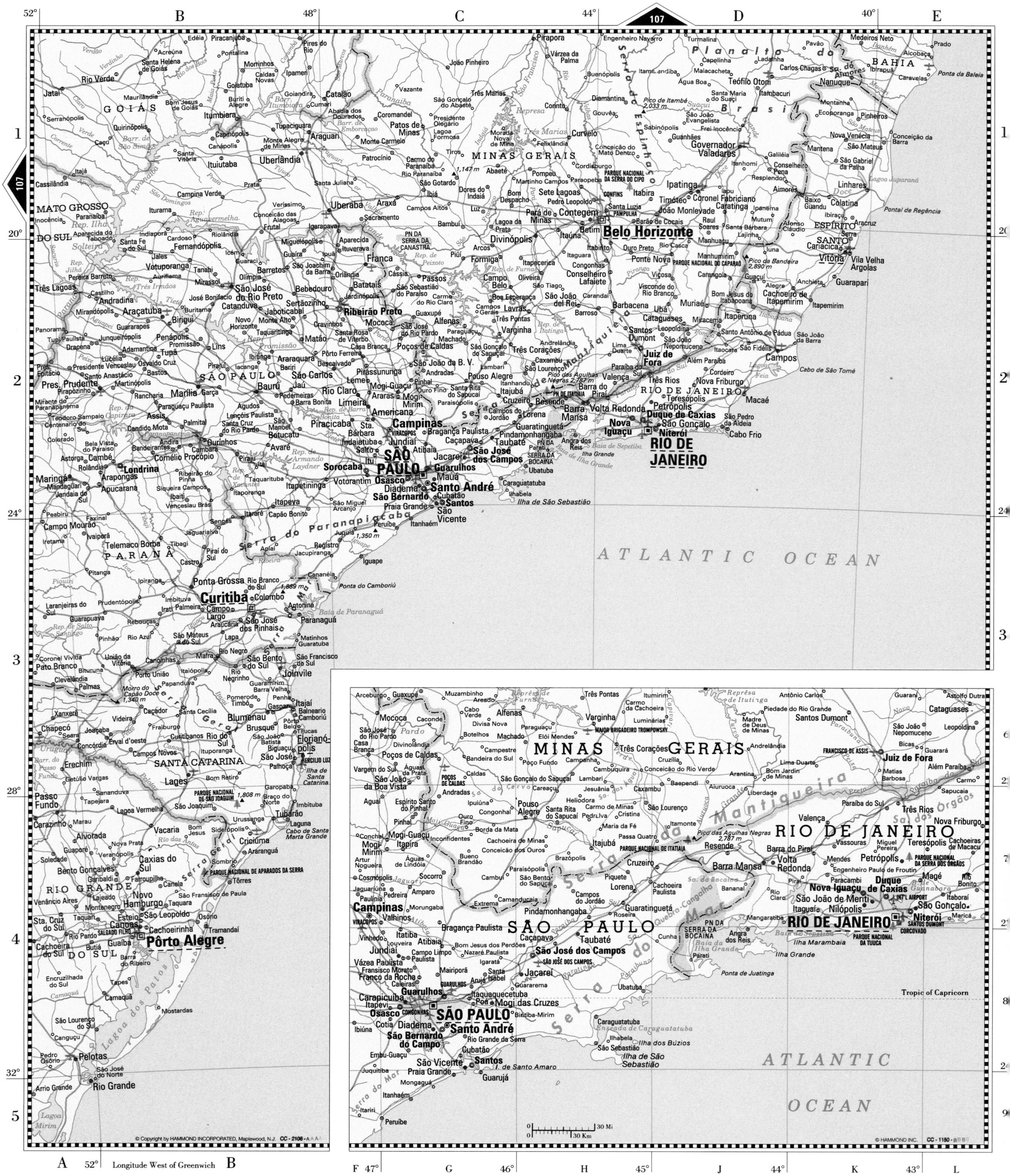

ATLANTIC OCEAN

Longitude West of Greenwich

POPULATION OF CITIES AND TOWNS

■ OVER 2,000,000	◉ 500,000 - 999,999	● 100,000 - 249,999	◎ 10,000 - 29,999
▣ 1,000,000 - 1,999,999	◎ 250,000 - 499,999	⊙ 30,000 - 99,999	○ UNDER 10,000

SCALE 1:7,000,000 LAMBERT CONFORMAL CONIC PROJECTION

MILES 0 100 200 300

KILOMETERS 0 100 200 300

Southern South America

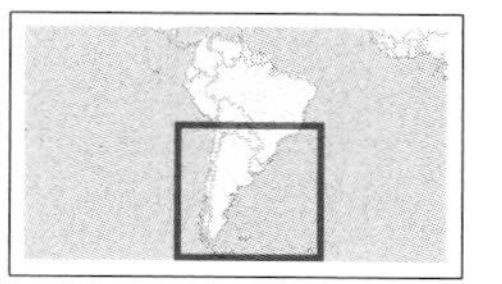

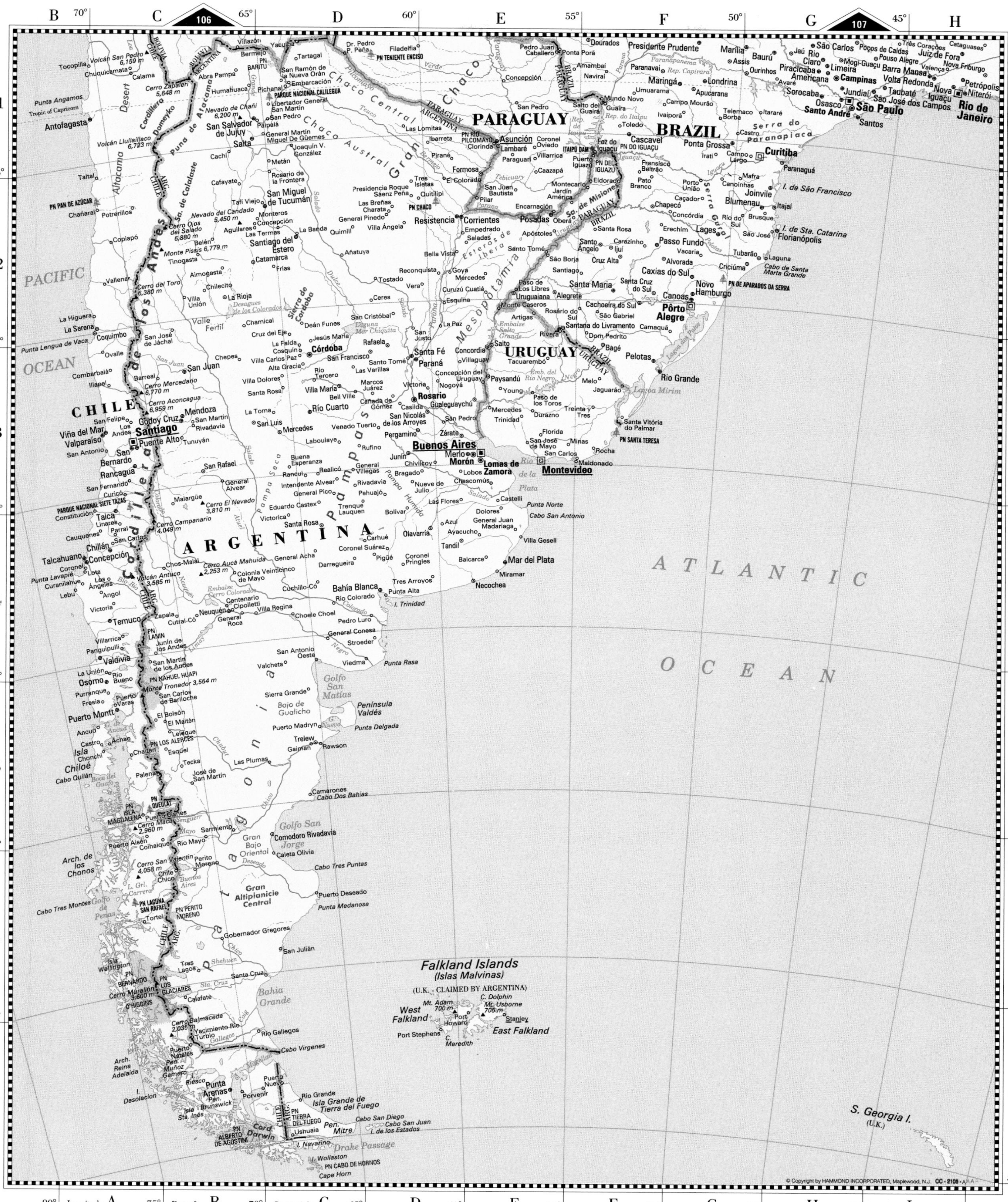

PACIFIC OCEAN

ATLANTIC OCEAN

CHILE

ARGENTINA

PARAGUAY

URUGUAY

BRAZIL

Falkland Islands (Islas Malvinas) (U.K. - CLAIMED BY ARGENTINA)

S. Georgia I. (U.K.)

POPULATION OF CITIES AND TOWNS

- OVER 2,000,000
- 1,000,000 - 1,999,999
- 500,000 - 999,999
- 100,000 - 499,999
- 50,000 - 99,999
- UNDER 50,000

SCALE 1:15,000,000 LAMBERT CONFORMAL CONIC PROJECTION

MILES 0 200 400 600

KILOMETERS 0 200 400 600

Longitude East of Greenwich

Index of the World

This index lists places and geographic features found in the atlas. Every name is followed by the country or area to which it belongs. Except for cities, towns, countries and cultural areas, all entries include a reference to feature type, such as province, river, island, peak, and so on. The page number and alpha-numeric code appear in blue to the left of each listing. The page number directs you to the largest scale map on which the name can be found. The code refers to the grid squares formed by the horizontal and vertical lines of latitude and longitude on each map. Following the letters from left to right, and the numbers from top to bottom, helps you to locate quickly the square containing the place or feature. Inset maps have their own alpha-numeric codes. Names that are accompanied by a point symbol are indexed to the symbol's location on the map. Other names are indexed to the initial letter of the name. The primary abbreviations used in this index are listed below.

Index Abbreviations

A	**A.F.B.**	Air Force Base
	Afghan.	Afghanistan
	Ala.	Alabama
	Alg.	Algeria
	Alta.	Alberta
	Ant. & Barb.	Antigua and Barbuda
	Antarc.	Antarctica
	arch.	archipelago
	Arg.	Argentina
	Ariz.	Arizona
	Ark.	Arkansas
	Austr.	Australia
	aut.	autonomous
B	**Bah.**	Bahamas
	Bang.	Bangladesh
	Belg.	Belgium
	Bol.	Bolivia
	Bosn.	Bosnia and Hercegovina
	Bots.	Botswana
	Braz.	Brazil
	Br., Brit.	British
	Br. Col.	British Columbia
	Bulg.	Bulgaria
	Burk. Faso	Burkina Faso
C	**Calif.**	California
	Camb.	Cambodia
	Can.	Canada
	cap.	capital
	Cent. Afr. Rep.	Central African Republic
	chan.	channel
	Chan. Is.	Channel Islands
	Col.	Colombia
	Colo.	Colorado
	Conn.	Connecticut
	C. Rica	Costa Rica
	Czech Rep.	Czech Republic
D	**DC**	District of Columbia
	Del.	Delaware
	Dem.	Democratic
	Den.	Denmark
	depr.	depression
	des.	desert
	dist.	district
	Dom. Rep.	Dominican Republic
E	**E.**	East, Eastern
	Ecua.	Ecuador
	El Sal.	El Salvador
	Eng.	England
	Equat. Guin.	Equatorial Guinea
	est.	estuary
	Eth.	Ethiopia
F	**Fed.**	Federal, Federated
	Fin.	Finland
	Fla.	Florida
	for.	forest
	Fr.	France, French
	Fr. Pol.	French Polynesia
	Ft.	Fort
G	**Ga.**	Georgia
	Ger.	Germany
	Greenl.	Greenland
	Gt.	Great
	Guad.	Guadeloupe
	Guat.	Guatemala
	Guy.	Guyana
H	**har., harb.**	harbor
	Hon.	Honduras
	Hun.	Hungary
I	**Ill.**	Illinois
	Ind.	Indiana
	Indon.	Indonesia
	Int'l	International
	Ire.	Ireland
	isl., isls.	isle, island, islands
	Isr.	Israel
	isth.	isthmus
	Iv. Coast	Ivory Coast
J	**Jam.**	Jamaica
K	**Kans.**	Kansas
	Ky.	Kentucky
L	**La.**	Louisiana
	Leb.	Lebanon
	Lux.	Luxembourg
M	**Madag.**	Madagascar
	Man.	Manitoba
	Mass.	Massachusetts
	Maur.	Mauritania
	Md.	Maryland
	Mex.	Mexico
	Mich.	Michigan
	Minn.	Minnesota
	Miss.	Mississippi
	Mo.	Missouri
	Mong.	Mongolia
	Mont.	Montana
	Mor.	Morocco
	Moz.	Mozambique
	mt.	mount
	mtn., mts.	mountain, mountains
N	**N., No.**	North, Northern
	N. Amer.	North America
	Nat'l Pk.	National Park
	N. Br.	New Brunswick
	N.C.	North Carolina
	N. Dak.	North Dakota
	Nebr.	Nebraska
	Neth.	Netherlands
	Neth. Ant.	Netherlands Antilles
	Nev.	Nevada
	Newf.	Newfoundland
	N.H.	New Hampshire
	Nic.	Nicaragua
	N. Ire.	Northern Ireland
	N.J.	New Jersey
	N. Korea	North Korea
	N. Mex.	New Mexico
	Nor.	Norway
	N.S.	Nova Scotia
	N.W.T.	Northwest Territories
	N.Y.	New York
	N.Z.	New Zealand
O	**Okla.**	Oklahoma
	Ont.	Ontario
	Oreg.	Oregon
P	**Pa.**	Pennsylvania
	Pak.	Pakistan
	Pan.	Panama
	Papua N.G.	Papua New Guinea
	Par.	Paraguay
	P.E.I.	Prince Edward Island
	pen.	peninsula
	Phil.	Philippines
	pk.	park
	plat.	plateau
	Pol.	Poland
	Port.	Portugal, Portuguese
	P. Rico	Puerto Rico
	prom.	promontory
	prov.	province, provincial
	pt., pte.	point, pointe
Q	**Que.**	Québec
R	**reg.**	region
	Rep.	Republic
	res.	reservoir
	R.I.	Rhode Island
	riv.	river
	Rom.	Romania
S	**S., So.**	South, Southern
	sa.	serra, sierra
	S. Africa	South Africa
	S. Amer.	South America
	São T. & Pr.	São Tomé and Príncipe
	Sask.	Saskatchewan
	S.C.	South Carolina
	Scot.	Scotland
	S. Dak.	South Dakota
	Sen.	Senegal
	Sing.	Singapore
	S. Korea	South Korea
	S. Leone	Sierra Leone
	Sol. Is.	Solomon Islands
	Sp.	Spain, Spanish
	St., Ste.	Saint, Sainte
	str.	strait
	St. Vinc. & Grens.	Saint Vincent and the Grenadines
	Switz.	Switzerland
T	**Tanz.**	Tanzania
	Tenn.	Tennessee
	Terr.	Territory
	Thai.	Thailand
	Trin. & Tob.	Trinidad and Tobago
	Tun.	Tunisia
U	**U. A. E.**	United Arab Emirates
	U. K.	United Kingdom
	Ukr.	Ukraine
	Urug.	Uruguay
	U. S.	United States
V	**Va.**	Virginia
	Ven., Venez.	Venezuela
	V.I. (Br.)	Virgin Islands (British)
	V.I. (U.S.)	Virgin Islands (U.S.)
	Viet.	Vietnam
	vol.	volcano
	Vt.	Vermont
W	**W.**	West, Western
	Wash.	Washington
	W. Indies	West Indies
	Wis.	Wisconsin
	W. Samoa	Western Samoa
	W. Va.	West Virginia
	Wyo.	Wyoming
Y	**Yugo.**	Yugoslavia
Z	**Zim.**	Zimbabwe

A

B

E

F

G

N

S

Venice – Zwolle

W

X

Y

Z